THE FUTURE OF EDUCATION FROM 14+

Policies, Politics and the Future of *Lifelong Learning*

Edited by
Ann Hodgson

POLICIES, POLITICS AND THE FUTURE OF LIFELONG LEARNING

Policies, Politics and the Future of Lifelong Learning

Edited by Ann Hodgson

KOGAN
PAGE

First published in 2000

Kogan Page Limited
120 Pentonville Road
London N1 9JN
UK

Stylus Publishing Inc.
22883 Quicksilver Drive
Sterling, VA 20166-2012
USA

© Individual contributors, 2000

British Library Cataloguing in Publication Data

A CIP record for this book is available from the British Library.

ISBN 0 7494 3202 0

Typeset by Kogan Page
Printed and bound in Great Britain by Clays Ltd, St Ives plc

Contents

Contents

Part 3 The policy focus under New Labour

Series editor's preface

It is becoming academically fashionable to knock the concept of lifelong learning and the Learning Society in reaction to the high policy rhetoric of the current Labour Government. However, while all the writers in this volume take a critical perspective, they think the concept of lifelong learning is a serious one, one that deserves closer analysis in order that everyone can gain from what it promises: personal, social and economic benefit.

Policies, Politics and the Future of Lifelong Learning is a comprehensive and, at the same time, a tightly argued collection of chapters. It takes the reader through the national and international context for lifelong learning policy, through the conceptual and policy challenges and into arguments for further change.

At the beginning of the book, Ann Hodgson comments on the 'peculiarly constrained definition' of lifelong learning in England as she traces its historical development. In the past, lifelong learning policy was concerned with the education of adults. In current policy, signalled by *The Learning Age*, it has become an umbrella term for post-compulsory education as a whole. This wider but, as we shall see, still constrained definition is the starting point for the book, as the writers attempt to dissect the different dimensions of current policies and politics. However, the book finishes by questioning both the parameters of current policy and its post-16 focus by arguing for a concept of lifelong learning based on 'all throughness'.

The first three chapters provide a historical, national and international framework for the analysis of different stages and models of lifelong learning policy. A prominent theme in these chapters is the analysis of market-oriented and regulatory policy approaches to lifelong learning. In Chapter 1, Ann Hodgson outlines an historical framework for the development of lifelong policy and argues that the current Government's 'Third Way' approach between markets and state regulation may not be strong enough to produce effective policy formation for lifelong learning.

Chapters 2 and 3 amplify further the international dimension of lifelong learning policy. Andy Green, using recent international comparative research, outlines different organizational approaches to the learning society and lifelong learning: state-led (France), social partnership-led (Germany) and market-led (UK). He signs off his chapter with an argument for a more 'scientific foundation' to lifelong learning policy based on the analysis of the effects of different policies in their national contexts. Marc Ant, drawing on his extensive experience of the development of vocational education policy in different European systems, outlines the utter complexity of EU policy as it tries to overarch national differences and to develop a supra-national policy framework.

The middle section of the book (Chapters 4–12) focuses on a range of policy themes. Three chapters in particular, those by Michael Young, Louise Morley and Greg Light, make fundamental conceptual challenges. Michael Young, in Chapter 7, argues that *The Learning Age* has little sense of a pedagogy or a curriculum for lifelong learning. He argues that it is important to 'bring knowledge back' and that learners should develop the capacities to contextualize, connect, criticize and apply the knowledge they acquire if they are to prepare for an uncertain economic future dependent on high skills. Louise Morley, in Chapter 6, criticizes the bureaucratization of a mass higher education system trying to introduce quality-related processes. She argues that policies aiming to improve the learning experience for students may actually inhibit the development of a higher education system that can genuinely cater for lifelong learning. In Chapter 12, Greg Light also focuses on higher education and the challenges confronting academic professionalism. He critiques the concept of professionalism underpinning the emerging Institute of Learning and Teaching and argues for the maintenance of a reflective professionalism that is both 'subversive' and 'liberating'.

In Chapter 4, Ann Hodgson focuses the issue of widening participation on the internal and external barriers to achieving this aim. She argues for the development of a comprehensive 'infrastructure for lifelong learning' if current policy is to move beyond its voluntarist and individualist approaches. This theme of developing a comprehensive infrastructure is taken up in a number of the middle chapters in the book. Gareth Williams, in Chapter 5, suggests that there is a need for the funding of individuals to take into consideration different phases of the life cycle, the spending power of individuals in their mid-life, their savings and pension plans. In Chapter 8, Ken Spours argues that the new National Qualifications Framework is not sufficiently inclusive and flexible to provide accreditation to motivate and support lifelong learners. He goes on to suggest that England follows the example set by its immediate neighbours, Scotland and Wales, in their recent lifelong learning policy documents which seek to connect the 16–19 and the adult phases.

Simon James and Norman Lucas take the argument for building an infrastructure for lifelong learning into that of further education institutions and regional organization. Norman Lucas, in Chapter 10, looks at the potential of further education colleges as institutions for social, economic and cultural regeneration. He argues that colleges will have to become much more focused on the needs of adult learners and specialized vocational education and training in order to become supportive lifelong learning institutions. By implication, this means the formation of tertiary institutions for 16–19 year olds, concentrating on a broad and more general education curriculum. Simon James, on the other hand, makes the case for a regional dimension to lifelong learning which, as a policy aim, has faded somewhat when New Labour's pre- and post-election stances are compared. He argues that Government will 'ignore the region and its dynamic at its peril' because regions could become the entity to organize a dynamic relationship between economic, educational, political and technological developments within a European rather than just a national context. In Chapter 11, Alison Fuller uses both statistical and qualitative research to suggest that the Government should give increased priority and resources to part-time higher education participants over 30 years old. Adults represent an area of major participation growth in recent years and part-time higher education provision can produce clear personal development and economic benefits.

Early on in the book, Ann Hodgson states that 'Lifelong learning is a concept that has not yet run its course'. This statement, while a perceptive policy observation, may not actually do justice to what the book is trying to achieve. The final chapter suggests that an 'all-through' notion of lifelong learning can be developed as an organizing concept. It suggests different dimensions of connection, linking the different phases of education, providing an additional rationale for the relationship between education and the workplace, and fully appreciating the dynamic between formal and informal learning. This inclusive interpretation of lifelong learning can also provide a means of relating relatively separate and fragmented education debates, so that those involved in early-years education can see themselves as much a part of the debate about developing lifelong learners as those in post-16 education and training already do.

This inclusive view has potential implications for a book series focusing on the future of education from 14+ because it marks a coming of age in which a debate that originated in post-compulsory education may now sweep across the education and training system as a whole.

Ken Spours (Series Editor)
Institute of Education
University of London

Notes on the contributors

Marc Ant

Marc Ant has worked for a number of years as both a trainer and project manager in a variety of European organizations. Currently, he lectures at the College of Europe, Bruges, and the Universität der Bundeswehr, Hamburg. Marc has published widely in the area of vocational education and training. His most recent book, written with J Kintzelé, A Van Haecht and R Walther, is entitled *Reporting Systems on Access, Quality and Volume of Continuing Vocational Training in Europe* and is published by Luchterhand Verlag, Germany. Marc is also a member of the Board of Editors of the journal *Grundlagen der Weiter-bildung*, also published by the Luchterhand.

Alison Fuller

Alison Fuller is a Senior Research Fellow at the Centre for Labour Market Studies at the University of Leicester, and a freelance researcher. She has published widely on vocational education and training, and in 1998 co-edited (with Lorna Unwin) a special issue of the *Journal of Vocational Education and Training* on the theme of contemporary apprenticeship. She founded (with Lorna Unwin and others) the Work and Learning Network. Alison has recently completed her doctoral thesis, entitled *Adults, Qualifications and Social Change* at the Institute of Education, University of London.

Andy Green

Andy Green is a Professor of Education at the Institute of Education, University of London. Previously he taught in further education colleges in south London. Current projects include 'Financing Vocational Education and Training' for CEDEFOP, and 'Education and Training Routes to High Skills Economies' (ESRC). Recent books include: *Education, Globalization and the Nation State*, 1997; *Convergences and Divergences in European Education and Training Systems,* 1999 (with Wolf and Leney); and *Further Education and Lifelong Learning: Realigning the sector for the 21st century* (edited with N Lucas), 1999. Andy is Co-director of the new DfEE Centre on the Wider Benefits of Learning.

Ann Hodgson

Ann Hodgson graduated from the University of London in 1975. Since then, she has worked as a teacher, lecturer, editor, civil servant and LEA advisor. Ann is currently a Senior Lecturer in Adult and Lifelong Education at the

University of London's Institute of Education. Recent publications include *New Labour's Educational Agenda: Issues and policies for education and training from 14+* (Kogan Page, 1999), co-authored with Ken Spours, and *Dearing and Beyond: 14–19 qualifications, frameworks and systems* (Kogan Page, 1997), co-edited with Ken Spours. Current research includes work on the funding of lifelong learning for the OECD and CEDEFOP as well as projects related to qualifications reform for the Nuffield Foundation and the Qualifications and Curriculum Authority.

Simon James
Formerly Head of Regional and Economic Development for the Further Education Development Agency (FEDA), Simon James is now FEDA's Regional Manager for the North based in Gateshead, having joined the organization from a senior post at Kent Training and Enterprise Council in 1996. Prior to this, he worked for the London Docklands Development Corporation and in the voluntary sector in London and the North East. He began his career with Scottish and Newcastle Breweries. Simon has a particular interest in the links between learning and economic development and the development of staff management and institutional capacity building.

Gregory Light
Gregory Light is a full-time lecturer in the Centre for Higher Education Studies (CHES) at the Institute of Education, University of London. He worked with the Institute from 1986 to 1996, teaching on the CHES programme of short courses for lecturers. He also worked in the Arts and Housing sector as a director, consultant and advisor on policy, management, communication and professional development issues. In 1996, he was a visiting scholar at Rice University, Texas. His primary interests are in the theory and practice of learning and teaching in higher education. His publications include articles on teaching, student learning and creative writing in higher education. He is currently completing a book on the professionalization of teaching in higher education.

Norman Lucas
Norman Lucas is Head of the Lifelong Learning Group at the Institute of Education, University of London. He was an elected member of the ILEA and a former FE teacher. Until recently, he chaired the University Council for the Education of Teachers Post-16 Committee (UCET). His research interests include initial teacher education and professional development, institutional management, FE incorporation and funding. He has recently published *FE and Lifelong Learning: Realigning the sector for the 21st century,* edited with Andy Green and published as a Bedford Way Paper, and *Learning to Live With it: The impact of FEFC funding,* co-authored with Jeremy McDonald and Dan Taubman and published by NATFHE.

Louise Morley
Louise Morley is a Senior Lecturer in Higher Education Studies and Assistant Dean of Professional Studies at the University of London's Institute of Education. She was previously at the University of Sussex, the University of Reading and the Inner London Education Authority. Her research and publication interests focus on equity, gender, power and empowerment in higher and professional education. Recent publications include *Organising Feminisms: The micropolitics of the academy* (1999), Macmillan; *School Effectiveness: Fracturing the discourse* (1999, co-authored with Naz Rassool) The Falmer Press; *Breaking Boundaries: Women in higher education*, (1996) and *Feminist Academics: Creative agents for change* (1995) both edited with Val Walsh and published by Taylor and Francis.

Ken Spours
Ken Spours is a Senior Lecturer in the Lifelong Learning Group at the Institute of Education, University of London. Ken specializes in research and development work on 14–19 qualifications. In 1997, Ken co-edited *Dearing and Beyond* with Ann Hodgson which was published by Kogan Page and in 1999 he co-authored a book with Ann on *New Labour's Educational Agenda: Issues and policies for education and training from 14+*. Recent research includes the ESRC 'Unified Learning Project', developing designs for an 'Overarching Certificate at Advanced Level' and work on the proposed 'Graduation Certificate at 19'. Ken is currently co-directing a national research project, funded by the Nuffield Foundation, to track institutional responses to the 'Qualifying for Success' reforms.

Gareth Williams
Gareth Williams, Professor of Educational Administration at the Institute of Education, is an economist by training who initially worked as an agricultural economist and an international civil servant at the OECD. He took an active part in the development of the economics of education at the LSE and Lancaster University. In recent years he has worked mainly on issues related to higher education policy, particularly finance, but also labour market issues and strategic management. Gareth writes extensively in the UK and beyond. His most recent books include *The Academic Labour Market* and *Changing Patterns of Finance in Higher Education*.

Michael Young
Michael Young studied natural sciences at Cambridge University and, after a year as a management trainee, became a secondary school science teacher. He went on to gain a BSc and MA in Sociology and in 1967 was appointed as a Lecturer (later Senior Lecturer) in Sociology of Education at the Institute of Education, University of London. In 1986, he became the first Head of the Post-16 Education Centre. He was awarded an Honorary Doctorate in Social Sciences by the University of Joensuu, Finland, and was appointed

Professor of Education in 1998. In 1971, Michael edited *Knowledge and Control: New directions for the sociology of education*. His most recent book *is The Curriculum of the Future* published by Falmer Press in 1998.

1

An international and historical context for recent policy approaches to lifelong learning in the UK

Ann Hodgson

Introduction

Where has the idea of lifelong learning come from, what does it signify and why has it become such an important aspect of international and national policy discourse? At the beginning of a new millennium, it is perhaps time to take stock and to look back at how the concept of lifelong learning developed towards the end of the 20th century and to assess its importance in current policy debates. This book suggests that despite its lengthy history, and the fickleness of policy makers, lifelong learning is a concept that does not yet appear to have run its course. Throughout the book, each of the various authors attempts to make sense of and to critique contemporary approaches to lifelong learning within Europe and, more specifically, the UK.

In this first chapter, I attempt to provide a general international and historical context for the other chapters in the book that deal with more specific aspects of lifelong learning policy. I begin by describing briefly how the concept of lifelong learning, which became a topic of international debate in the 1970s but was effectively put on hold during the 1980s, rose up the political agendas of many countries again over the past decade as a policy response to the type of economic, demographic, cultural and technological changes that became prevalent during that period. In the second part of the chapter, I focus in on the UK through a broad periodization of policy approaches to lifelong learning in this country over the past 30 years. This is followed by a discussion of the current UK Government's approach to lifelong learning. Here I identify the distinctive features of New Labour's 'Third Way' approach to policy in this area, which has aroused considerable interest internationally as well as nationally. I conclude by suggesting how each of the subsequent chapters in the book might contribute to the debate about the strengths and weaknesses of this approach to lifelong learning.

International trends in lifelong learning since the 1970s

Most of those who write about lifelong learning trace the origins of the concept back to the 1920s when the term 'lifelong education' first appeared in English translation linked to discussion of Nordic education systems (Hasan, 1996). The term 'lifelong learning' then appears to take its place in the 1970s alongside other terms such as 'recurrent education', 'popular education', 'continuing education', 'adult education' or simply 'post-initial education and training' in international policy documents of the time. The most often cited international policy document of this era, where the term lifelong learning is used, is the influential Faure Report, *Learning To Be* (Faure *et al*, 1972).

During the 1980s, according to Sutton (1996), the incidence of bibliographic references to the terms lifelong education and lifelong learning declined, while those to the term 'adult education' continued to remain at a constant level. He does not fully explain this phenomenon. It may be that the focus in many countries throughout the 1980s on combating the severe social and economic effects of recession and widespread unemployment by raising the literacy, qualifications and skills base of the adult population explains why a more specific term, such as 'adult education', proved more useful for policy makers. Using a more specific term might also have helped them to distinguish between the resource needs of younger and older learners in relation to the labour market in a time of economic constraint and limited state budgets for education and training.

During the 1990s, at international policy level, and in many individual countries at national level, lifelong learning became an umbrella term which subsumed part or all of what might earlier have been referred to as 'lifelong education', 'recurrent education', 'popular education', 'adult education' or simply 'post-initial education and training'. So we had, for example, the European Union 'Year for Lifelong Learning' in 1996, the OECD report *Lifelong Learning for All* in 1996 and the Taiwan 'Year of Lifelong Learning' in 1998, not to mention the stream of government policy documents from the UK and elsewhere which use the term 'lifelong learning' in their titles and liberally throughout their pages.

One could argue that the term 'lifelong learning' was seen as useful in the 1990s precisely because it is potentially so all encompassing, but in reality it can be tailored to the particular requirements of the country or organization from which the policy document originates. If you look beneath the surface of some of the different international and national documents on lifelong learning, it is possible to detect quite a wide difference between the scope and emphasis of many of them. Some, like the OECD report (1996), include all aspects of education and training from pre-school through to adult education and include learners of all ages within the concept of lifelong learning. Others, like the UK Government's first Green Paper on lifelong learning for England, *The Learning Age* (DfEE, 1998a), essentially see lifelong learning as beginning when initial compulsory schooling has been completed. In many cases, there is a focus on the education and training system to the exclusion of learning that takes place in other environments such as the workplace, the home or in the community. There is often too an emphasis on learning for work rather than learning for self-development, political awareness or community development.

In this sense, the term 'lifelong learning', as it was used in the 1990s, neither adequately replaced some of the terms that predated it, nor, in itself, described accurately any one concept or policy approach.

The term 'recurrent education', for example, which featured strongly in international policy documents in the late 1960s and early 1970s, and might be seen as a precursor of the more economic or vocational approach to lifelong learning so prevalent in many current national policy documents on lifelong learning, also contained within it a critique of 'front-loaded' initial education and training systems (Tuijnman, 1996). This element of critique was largely lost in the 1990s' use of the term 'lifelong learning'. Moreover, many of the policy implications that arose from the idea of recurrent education, such as spreading the entitlement to learning episodes throughout the life cycle, rather than focusing attention and resources on initial education systems, still only form part of lifelong policies in a minority of countries. In most countries, these types of policies would require the type of reallocation of state funding from initial to lifelong learning that most are not prepared to entertain (Green *et al*, 1998). The idea of the state funding paid educational leave or personal-learning accounts for those in work who want to study later in life, for example, is part of lifelong learning policy in Denmark (CEDEFOP, 1999), but is not viewed as affordable by any of the other countries that took part in a recent CEDEFOP study on vocational education and training (Green *et al*, 2000 forthcoming).

Similarly the term 'adult education', which lifelong learning is often assumed to include and even supersede, had a much broader definition in the report of the UNESCO General Conference in 1976 than was often accorded to lifelong learning in the 1990s:

> The term 'adult education' denotes the entire body of organised educational processes, whatever the content, level and method, whether formal or otherwise, or whether they prolong or replace initial education in schools, colleges, and universities, as well as an apprenticeship, whereby persons regarded as adult by the society to which they belong develop their abilities, enrich their knowledge, improve their technical or professional qualifications, or turn them in a new direction and bring about changes in their attitude or behaviour in the two-fold perspective of full personal development and participation in balanced and independent social, economic and cultural development.

If, in the 1990s, the term 'lifelong learning' became, in some senses, meaningless, because of its many and varied translations at the policy level, its existence as a concept or vision remained very powerful at the level of rhetoric. Lifelong learning was the 1990s' response to, or even defence against, a changing, frightening and unknown technological, economic, social and political environment – it became a concept as slippery and multifaceted as the environment in which it exists.

Context for and approach to lifelong learning in the 1990s

Much has been written about the context for the policy focus on lifelong learning in the 1990s. Some describe what they see as a wholly new context, part of the insecurity and flux of post-modernism or the influence of globalization. Others view the economic, technological, demographic, cultural and social trends prevalent in the 1990s as an intensification of a process that was present in earlier decades, but which grew in importance over the last quarter of the 20th century. Where there is agreement is that the speed of technological, particularly ICT, developments during the 1990s led to significant changes in employment trends, career patterns and skill demands (OECD, 1996). This, together with a widespread concern about the economic effects of increasingly ageing societies (OECD, 1998), encouraged national governments, and the international organizations to which they belonged, to consider which policy instruments might be used to meet these new demands. Education and training systems became an obvious policy focus because of their wide reach and potentially direct impact on human resource development. In a rapidly changing society, the argument for a move towards education and training systems that encourage learning beyond compulsory education and throughout the lifespan was compelling. Hence, the broad international policy focus on lifelong learning in the 1990s. The following extract from a report in 1994 by the Commission of the European Community is typical of policy documents of this period:

> All measures must therefore be necessarily based on the concept of developing, generalizing and systematizing lifelong learning and continuing training. This means that education and training systems must be reworked in order to take account of the need – which is already growing and is set to grow even more in the future – for the permanent recomposition and redevelopment of knowledge and know-how.
>
> (CEC, 1994: 136)

A recent CEDEFOP report on vocational education and training across a number of countries in the European Union suggests that it is also possible to identify some common broad policy approaches to the organization and financing of post-compulsory education and training that include:

1. increasing inter-departmental cooperation over vocational education and training at national government ministry level;
2. consolidating provision through legislative frameworks rather than through central government regulation in order to encourage more private inward investment and cooperation;
3. devolving power for allocating resources from central to regional, local or individual institutional level to increase provider responsiveness;
4. encouraging public/private partnership arrangements in relation to both capital and recurrent funding;
5. introducing the 'purchaser/provider' concept into the provision of many types of education and training and thus a limited element of competition between public and private providers;
6. careful targeting of government subsidies to all types of education and training providers, enterprises and individuals to stimulate private investment, to avoid 'deadweight' and to ensure equity;
7. introducing new types of funding mechanisms designed to encourage economic 'rationality' in providers and, in some cases, a focus on learner outcomes (Green *et al*, 2000 forthcoming).

However, as international comparative studies in lifelong learning suggest, within this broad overarching focus and common policy trends, individual national economic, social and political contexts and histories will strongly determine how different countries view the concept of lifelong learning, how much they are prepared to spend on it and the type of policy instruments they adopt (eg OECD 1998; Green *et al*, 1999, 2000 forthcoming).

One of the ways that the second of these reports has characterized different countries' approaches to their lifelong learning systems is to place them on a continuum between 'state-led regulated', 'social-partnership regulated' and 'demand-led regulated' and to indicate in which direction along this continuum they might be moving in the late 1990s. The use of a continuum of this sort recognizes the fact that an individual country's current policies for organizing and funding lifelong learning will, to a large extent, depend on the nature of the individual education and training system it has inherited and the relationship between the education and training system and the labour market in that particular country.

It is for this reason that I turn, in the next section, to a brief overview of the context for and historical approach to lifelong learning in the UK over the past 30 years, before discussing New Labour's policies in this area in the late 1990s and the beginning of the new millennium.

Lifelong learning in the UK from the 1970s to the 1990s

Although the term 'lifelong learning' was not extensively used in national policy documents in the UK before the late 1980s, education for adults has had a strong tradition in this country throughout the 20th century, promoted and supported primarily by non-governmental organizations, such as the Workers' Educational Association, trade unions, a number of influential universities, including Oxford and Cambridge, and the National Institute of Adult Education (later to become the National Institute of Adult and Continuing Education).

From the 1970s onwards, however, it could be argued that the profile of adult education both increased and changed as national governments gradually began to take greater control of its shape and function. Indeed, there are some, such as Fieldhouse (1996), who consider that this period marks the move away from an independent 'adult education movement' towards an era of lifelong learning, where adult education is simply considered as one part of the total education and training system.

From the late 1970s onwards, and increasingly during the Conservative years of the 1980s and early 1990s, there was a move by successive national governments to mould all parts of the education and training system more closely into a framework for lifelong learning to promote economic growth and to combat economic recession, increasing international competition and fluctuating employment trends. Adult education was thus forced to compete with other parts of the education and training system for national funding and for recognition of its own unique contribution and character within an increasingly vocational approach to adult learning. What had been separate, largely voluntary and privately funded up to the 1970s gradually became merged and increasingly dependent on public resources throughout the 1980s and beyond. By the 1990s, the discrete strands of adult education with their different histories and traditions – university adult education, LEA and community education (including adult basic education), and learning in the workplace (including trade union education and training) – were commonly seen as integral parts of lifelong learning provision.

1970s – lifelong learning as discrete experiences for different groups of learners

During the 1970s, it could be argued that education and training were experienced differently by different groups and ages of learners and that there was no sense of an all-through system of lifelong learning. Rather there were a number of strands of provision with their own purposes and trajectories. For a minority of young people, there was an academic route from O levels through A levels and on to higher education and the professions. For some young people (largely young men) there were apprenticeships with built-in off-the-job as well as on-the-job training. For the rest there were specialist, often short-term training programmes or jobs without training. Adult education and training provision consisted mainly of unaccredited on-the-job training, adult literacy courses and leisure or liberal education programmes run by local education authorities, non-governmental organizations and university extramural departments. Moreover, there were no obvious linkages between each of these discrete strands of education and training. 'Lifelong learning' provision in the 1970s was thus marked by three major divisions:

1.   A distinction between what was available to young people up to the age of 21 or so and what was available to those over this age.
2.   The type of provision that was open to those who did well in initial education and those who did not.
3.   The difference between full-time education, which was almost exclusively for young people pursuing academic programmes, and part-time education and training, which was predominantly for adults and those pursuing vocational education and training.

As a result of economic recession and rising levels of youth unemployment towards the end of the decade, governments of both political persuasions became preoccupied with full-time education for young people, issues related to the transition from school to work and programmes for the unemployed.

Nevertheless, during the early 1970s, adult education briefly rose up the political agenda in the UK with a review of non-vocational adult provision in both England and Scotland. The former led to the Russell Report (DES, 1973), which suggested that universities should focus on certain aspects of adult education only – liberal studies, continuing education, role education, industrial education, project research work and training for adult educators, with specific research on adult education as an academic discipline. The review in Scotland culminated in the Alexander Report (SED, 1975), which strongly promoted the idea of community education.

The Russell Report's recommendations were never fully put into practice because of the oil crisis and the amount of money already being given to the newly founded Open University (Fieldhouse, 1996). However, this report could be seen as leading to the setting up of the Advisory Council for Adult Continuing Education in 1977. This government-sponsored organization was given the task of developing policies for lifelong education and was influential in broadening the focus of adult education from an emphasis on liberal education to a vision of a more merged and inclusive system that encompassed all types of education and training for adults.

The recommendations of the Alexander Report, on the other hand, were taken up and several local education authorities in Scotland merged their separate adult and youth services into a new form of community provision.

The other important national policy development in relation to adult education during the 1970s was the setting up of the Adult Literacy Resource Agency in 1975 to support the 'Right to Read Campaign', which began as a grass-roots movement in the early 1970s and gradually grew in scope and importance throughout the decade.

1980s – the fight for access to lifelong learning and the move towards more vocationally focused provision

During the 1980s, there was a decline in LEA-organized non-vocational adult education and traditional liberal adult education provided by higher education institutions, but an increase in basic education, adult training and the number of mature students entering further education and 'mainstream' higher education programmes (Fieldhouse, 1996). This was the period where adult education of all types was moving away from its separate and different traditions and gradually becoming absorbed within the education and training system as a whole. It thus had to compete increasingly with other forms of education for central and local government funding and, with a greater dependence on these sources of funding, was subject to the drive towards 'vocationalisation' of the curriculum that characterized all aspects of the education and training system during the 1980s. What happened to the education and training of adults throughout this decade can be seen either as a necessary step towards the 'mainstreaming' and 'professionalization' of this type of provision in the move towards a system of lifelong learning, or as a loss of identity, purpose and focus.

What undoubtedly characterizes this era is the push by adults to gain access to all aspects of lifelong learning – work-related education and training, more formal and accredited further and higher education, as well as liberal and community education. Whether this push can be seen solely as a bottom-up drive by adult learners is debatable. What is clear is that central and local government policies and initiatives in education and training throughout the 1980s focused on getting adults into education and training in two major ways.

First, there was a drive to raise the status of adult learning by developing ways of measuring and accrediting it. The setting up of the Unit for the Development of Adult Continuing Education (UDACE) in 1984, for example, increased awareness of all aspects of adult education and training, with a particular focus on the accreditation of adult learning through its support of the Open College Network. Two years later, in 1986, the National Council for Vocational Qualifications was set up to develop a national system of vocational awards for both young people and adults, but with a specific stress on the latter.

Second, there was an emphasis on developing a range of educational and, more particularly, work-based programmes and courses designed to attract back into learning and employment those groups of adults who had traditionally not participated, for example, those with low qualification levels, ethnic minority groups and women.

The National Training Initiative, launched in 1981, concentrated throughout the 1980s on raising the basic skills levels of the adult workforce and attracting the unemployed back into work through innovative programmes such as those sponsored through REPLAN. These programmes, which were supervised by NIACE, concentrated initially on outreach work and collaboration between community education projects and agencies, but gradually became more vocationally oriented as they attempted to involve employers more actively in developing learning at work. The setting up of a network of Training and Enterprise Councils (TECs) in England and Wales and Local Enterprise Councils (LECs) in Scotland in 1988 was a further attempt to stimulate employer-led work-based training for adults, although at this period these organizations mainly found themselves administering government-sponsored programmes for the unemployed.

An example of the Government's drive to attract non-traditional groups of adults back into learning during this period is the Access initiative. This began in 1978 when the Department of Education and Science invited seven local authorities, including the pioneering Inner London Education Authority, to set up a pilot Access programme to increase opportunities for ethnic minorities to enter higher education and the professions. Six such courses were set up in 1979. The popularity of this type of Access provision, but with a broader student base, was so great that by 1985 there were 130 courses operating across the country, a figure that rose to 600 by 1990 (Fieldhouse, 1996).

These programmes allowed adult learners access to 'mainstream' higher education on a scale that had previously not been possible. The advent of these courses, in conjunction with changes to the higher education system itself – incorporation of polytechnics into the university sector in 1989 and a reduction in central government funding for liberal adult education courses – had a powerful effect on the provision of liberal adult education in higher education institutions. From the late 1980s onwards there was a move to 'mainstream' such courses and the amount of traditional liberal adult education was dramatically reduced (Fieldhouse, 1999). However, this was also the era of the 'University of the Third Age' movement, which could be seen as carrying forward the banner of adult liberal education, but without university oversight. By 1986, there were 115 groups of older adults with 7,000 members working and learning together in a self-directed manner across the UK as part of the 'University of the Third Age'.

1990s – market-led expansion of lifelong learning and the drive for economic competitiveness

As the section above suggests, the 1980s gradually witnessed a move away from discrete learning experiences for adults towards the development of more common education and training provision for learners of all ages, with a distinct focus on learning for work and skills development. However, as many of those writing at the end of the 1980s and beginning of the 1990s pointed out (eg Finegold and Soskise, 1988; CBI, 1989; Raffe, 1992), the numbers of young people and adults participating in education and training in this country still remained low in comparison with other European countries and we had fewer qualified young people, particularly in the area of vocational qualifications (Ryan, 1992). This was clearly a source of concern for a Conservative Government that saw an increase in participation in education and training and, more particularly, the development of a more highly skilled workforce as major ways of increasing national competitiveness in the global economy.

The Conservative Government's major education and training policy document at the beginning of the decade, *Education and Training for the 21st Century* (DfE/ED/WO, 1991), recognized the weaknesses of the current education and training system and introduced a set of proposals that set the tone for the 1990s. It attempted to create an infrastructure of independent post-16 providers that would compete for learners within a quasi-education market. Competition was not simply concentrated within each sector – higher, further, adult or school – it was also prevalent across sectors. Schools, further education colleges and sixth-form colleges could all offer 16–19 year olds full-time academic and general vocational learning; further education colleges and universities were both able to provide courses at level 4; private training providers, further education colleges and employers could all offer young people and adults work-related training.

It was felt that increasing competition between providers would make them both more efficient and also more responsive to learner demand. Since funding followed the learner, individual institutions would be encouraged to expand and to market their provision aggressively in the knowledge that other providers were able to offer learners similar programmes to their own.

Through the legislation that followed the White Paper, power was reduced at the local and regional tiers and was centred at both the national level – through the use of funding steers – and at the institutional level – through the autonomous use of resources. This process of deregulation, which had begun in 1988 with the Education Reform Act, was completed with the Further and Higher Education Act of 1992 and the era of largely unplanned market-led expansion of lifelong learning began.

The 1992 Act was also significant for adult learners in a different sense. It made a distinction between different types of adult provision. The first – 'Schedule 2 provision' – led to nationally recognized qualifications or vocational outcomes, which would be funded by the Further Education Funding Council (FEFC) and delivered primarily in further education colleges. The second – 'non-Schedule 2 provision' – consisted of non-accredited and 'non-vocational' provision that would be funded and largely delivered by LEAs. This aspect of the 1992 Act, which was hotly contested by a wide range of interested parties while the Bill was making its way through Parliament, immediately created an artificial divide between different types of adult learning and appeared to be moving in the opposite direction to the Government's stated aim of stimulating lifelong learning.

One could draw a parallel between the White Paper's introduction of divisions between different adult learners and different types of adult learning and its creation of a triple-track qualifications framework that created divisions between academic, broad vocational and occupationally specific types of learning outcomes. The problems that such a divided system creates for lifelong learning are discussed more fully in Chapter 8.

The deregulation of the education and training system was matched by a voluntarist approach to work-based learning. Employers were encouraged to take an active role in building the national skills base by serving on TEC boards and developing and promoting National Vocational Qualifications (NVQs). In addition, they were exhorted to increase the amount of training they provided with the encouragement of awards, such as the Investors in People standard, for those employers who demonstrated a commitment to human resource development. Since the Government did not encourage trade unions to play an active role in its strategy for national skills development, those adults who wished to gain access to work-based learning had to negotiate directly with their employers. It is hardly surprising, therefore, that towards the end of the 1990s, the gap between those adults who had access to training opportunities and those who did not remained significant, with those more highly qualified receiving more training than those with fewer qualifications, and those in larger companies having considerably more likelihood of receiving training than those in smaller or medium-sized enterprises (DfEE, 1998b).

This was the 'system' of lifelong learning that the New Labour administration inherited when it came to power in 1997.

New Labour's 'Third Way' approach to lifelong learning

As we have seen at the beginning of this chapter, it is possible to identify a general interest in many countries in the concept of lifelong learning and, despite different national histories and traditions, some broad common policy approaches to lifelong learning within the European Union and more widely. There is no doubt that the current New Labour Government in the UK shares this interest in the concept of lifelong learning and, as the quotation below from David Blunkett, the Secretary of State for Education and Employment, indicates, it views lifelong learning as a central strategy for ensuring the future prosperity of the UK, as well as building a more just and inclusive society.

Throughout the 20th century there was a continuing struggle to make the right to basic education a reality for all. The early part of the 21st century will be characterised by the transformation of the basis of economic success from fixed capital investment, to human capital. In a knowledge-driven economy, the continuous updating of skills and the development of lifelong learning will make the difference between success and failure and between competitiveness and decline... Lifelong learning is also essential to sustaining a civilised and cohesive society, in which people can develop as active citizens, where creativity is fostered and communities can be given practical support to overcome generations of disadvantage.

(Blunkett, 1999: 3)

In terms of its position on the continuum between a 'state-led regulated', 'social-partnership regulated' and 'demand-led regulated' approach to the organization and funding of lifelong learning, the UK at the beginning of the 21st century might be seen as situated quite strongly towards the 'demand-led regulated' end. This position reflects both the approach that New Labour inherited from the previous Conservative administration and, I would argue, its own approach during the first two to three years of office. There is no history of a strong social-partnership approach in this country and, as we have seen from the previous section of this chapter, there was a gradual move away from state-led regulation of education and training and a move towards a more 'marketized' education and training system during the 1990s.

However, if one wants to look in more detail at New Labour's approach to lifelong learning, and to distinguish this Government's approach from that of its predecessor, it is important to look beyond the three categories contained within this international comparative tool. What the continuum does not allow you to distinguish between is the different layers of state regulation – national, regional and local. This is a very important additional area to consider when analysing New Labour's policies in relation to lifelong learning, because it is in this area that it has introduced its most radical reforms. One of the major distinctions between this administration and the previous one, is that New Labour believes in planning at the local and regional levels and thus in a degree of market regulation which would have been unthinkable under the Conservatives.

New Labour's first policy document on lifelong learning, *The Learning Age* (DfEE, 1998a), signalled a desire to combat the perverse effects on learners of a market-led competitive education and training system and to rationalize local post-compulsory provision by introducing more local and regional planning. This was followed a year later by the *Learning to Succeed* (DfEE, 1999a) White Paper, which contained a range of proposals to create an entirely new national, regional and local infrastructure for planning, organizing and funding lifelong learning opportunities. *Learning to Succeed* sets in place a single national Learning and Skills Council which will have responsibility for funding all post-16 provision (with the exception of higher education) through 47 local Learning and Skills Councils. The national council, which will have strong employer representation on its board, will be advised by two committees – one for adults and one for 16–19 year olds. The quality of provision funded by the Learning and Skills Councils will be overseen by two inspectorates – OFSTED for all 16–19 provision and an adult inspection service for all provision for learners over the age of 19. Learning and Skills Councils will be expected to consult with and relate to a range of national, regional and local organizations, such as the Employment Service, Regional Development Agencies, local education authorities and local Lifelong Learning Partnerships which are intended to represent the interests of the local community and the needs of the learner.

This new infrastructure for planning, organizing and funding lifelong learning immediately creates an interesting balance or tension between national, regional and local tiers of government. There will be national funding steers and tariffs related to national skills needs, but with some element of local flexibility. There will be national learning targets, but with central government exhortation to develop targets and performance indicators at the local level that meet specific local labour market and skill needs. There is a national inspection framework but with a local improvement strategy. The relationship between local and national powers and responsibilities is thus potentially quite fluid and is likely to differ from locality to locality. Nevertheless, the relationship between these two layers of government is quite clear in comparison with the role of regional government in the new lifelong learning infrastructure. Regional Development Agencies, which are already in the process of being set up across the country following *The Learning Age* White Paper, do not figure highly in the *Learning to Succeed* White Paper and their role in lifelong learning and their relationship with the Learning and Skills Councils at national and local level still has to be clarified.

There are two other major ways in which New Labour's approach to lifelong learning differs from that of the Conservative administrations of the 1980s and 1990s.

New Labour stresses the importance of involving trade unions as well as employers in the debates about and initiatives designed to promote lifelong learning. It has, for example, raised the profile of schemes such as the 'Bargaining for Skills' initiative, which is designed to help trade unions negotiate with employers about improved training opportunities for their members; it has put into place incentives, such as the Trade Union Fund, to encourage trade unions to become more involved in employee skills development and it has ensured that there is trade union representation on the newly proposed Learning and Skills Councils. However, this in no way constitutes a real move towards a more European social partnership approach to lifelong learning. Unlike these types of systems, in the UK there is no requirement for either public or private enterprises to contribute a proportion of their salary costs to training funds for education and training administered by services representing the social partners. Nor are there the strong and transparent links between pay, recruitment, training and promotion that create a demand for training in social partnership systems such as those in Germany or Austria. What New Labour's approach does indicate is its commitment to the idea of a tripartite partnership approach to lifelong learning in which those who share the benefits of learning are also expected to share the responsibility and costs for it. This is what has been referred to elsewhere as a 'weak framework' approach to social partnership (Hodgson and Spours, 1999).

Finally, New Labour's focus on lifelong learning as a mechanism for tackling the problems of social exclusion is something that marks it out from the Conservative approach to this area. The current Government has used a range of policy instruments to widen participation in lifelong learning in order to ensure that those who have traditionally been excluded from education, training and qualifications acquisition in this country, such as those from lower socio-economic groups, the unemployed, women, ethnic minorities and part-time workers, are encouraged to take up the opportunity to learn and to gain accreditation for their learning. Strategies for widening participation have included targeted funding to further education colleges and universities to recruit and support specific groups of learners, media campaigns designed to attract more people into learning, significant funding for basic skills initiatives, the provision of Individual Learning Accounts and the setting up of the University for Industry (see Chapters 5 and 10 for further details of these initiatives).

These three new strands of policy, together with a continued focus on stimulating individual demand for learning, focusing on the needs of the learner rather than those of the provider and continued support for devolved budgets and a learning market at the provider level to ensure efficiency and responsiveness to the learner, but within a stronger framework of planning, partnership and collaboration, constitute what could be described as New Labour's Third Way approach to lifelong learning. From an historical UK perspective, the concept of the Third Way could be seen as lying between Conservative free-market ideologies and Old Labour state ownership and regulation. This approach to lifelong learning thus remains largely voluntarist and gives considerable power to the market, but it is a market modified by local and national (and in the future possibly regional) planning and organizational steers.

At the moment much of New Labour's policy in this area rests on exhortation, increased learning opportunities and a range of incentives to stimulate a demand for lifelong learning at all levels and in all contexts. There are clear national learning targets to aim for and there is a potentially strong framework of organization, funding and quality assurance arrangements for lifelong learning that will be established over the next few years through the *Learning to Succeed* proposals.[1] Beyond the provision of a minimum wage, however, there is no attempt to regulate the labour market or to create a tighter legislative framework around social partnership arrangements in relation to lifelong learning. Some of the frameworks that a lifelong learning system arguably demands, such as a lifelong learning qualifications system, are not in place and we have a number of deep-seated historical problems to overcome in this country. We have, as indicated earlier, poor rates of full-time post-16 participation and achievement in education and low levels of literacy and numeracy in comparison with many other European countries. We have, too, a history of low employer involvement in training and a weak vocational education and training route (Senker *et al*, 1999). There is still much to be done in this country to create an attractive, accessible and credible lifelong learning system and there is still a question mark over whether New Labour's current Third Way approach is strong enough to tackle some of the major challenges we face at the beginning of a new millennium.

The chapters that follow either provide a more detailed context for this 'Third Way' approach, lay out the challenges for lifelong learning policy in this country, or analyse and assess aspects of it in more detail. Chapter 2 examines the political context for lifelong learning in the European Union, while Chapter 3 describes different models of organizing lifelong learning in Europe and identifies where the UK stands in relation to these models. Chapters 4 to 7 raise a number of significant challenges for lifelong learning in the UK and beyond in relation to widening participation, funding, quality and curriculum. Chapters 8 to 12 critically explore some of New Labour's key policies for lifelong learning – qualifications reform, local and regional organization, Individual Learning Accounts, the University for Industry, further education provision, the Institute of Learning and Teaching in Higher Education and the development of relevant work-related learning opportunities. The final chapter of the book attempts to appraise to what extent the UK's current overall approach to lifelong learning meets the challenges of the 21st century and what still needs to be done.

Note

1. The National Learning Targets for England for 2002 are: 80 per cent of 11-year olds reaching the expected standard for their age in literacy and 75 per cent reaching the standard in numeracy; 50 per cent of 16-year olds getting 5 higher grade GCSEs and 95 per cent getting at least 1 GCSE; 85 per cent of 19-year olds with a Level 2 qualification; 60 per cent of 21-year olds with a Level 3 qualification; 50 per cent of adults with a Level 3 qualification; 28 per cent with a Level 4 qualification; a 7 per cent reduction in non-learners; 45 per cent of medium-sized or large organizations recognized as Investors in People and 10,000 small organizations recognized as Investors in People.

References

Blunkett, Rt Hon D (1999) Foreword, in DfEE (1999b)

CEDEFOP (1999) *Financing Vocational Education and Training in Denmark*, CEDEFOP, Brussels

Commission of the European Community (CEC) (1994) *Growth, Competitiveness, Employment: The challenges and ways forward into the 21st century*, Office for Official Publications, CEC, Luxembourg

Confederation of British Industry (CBI) (1989) *Towards a Skills Revolution*, CBI, London

Department for Education/Employment Department/Welsh Office (1991) *Education and Training for the 21ˢᵗ Century*, HMSO, London

Department for Education and Employment (DfEE) (1998a) *The Learning Age: A renaissance for a new Britain*, DfEE, London

Department of Education and Science (DES) (1973) *Adult Education: A plan for development* (The Russell Report), HMSO, London

DfEE (1998b) *Labour Force Survey*, reported in Labour Market Quarterly Report, SEN 336, DfEE, Sheffield

DfEE (1999a) *Learning to Succeed: A new framework for post-16 learning*, DfEE, London

DfEE (1999b) *The Learning and Skills Council Prospectus: Learning to succeed*, DfEE, London

Faure, E et al (1972) *Learning to Be: The world of education today and tomorrow*, UNESCO/Harrap, Paris

Fieldhouse, R (1996) An Overview of British Adult Education in the Twentieth Century, in *A History of Modern British Adult Education*, ed R Fieldhouse and associates, NIACE, Leicester

Fieldhouse, R (1999) University Liberal Adult Education: the historical background, in *Liberal Adult Education: Towards a contemporary paradigm*, UACE Occasional Paper No 25, Universities Association for Continuing Education (UACE)

Finegold, D and Soskise, D (1988) The Failure of Training in Britain: analysis and prescription, *Oxford Review of Economic Policy*, **4** (3), Oxford University Press, Oxford

Green, A, Hodgson, A and Williams, G (1998) *Synthesis of Country Reports on Alternative Approaches to Financing Lifelong Learning*, OECD, Paris

Green, A, Wolf, A and Leney, T (1999) *Convergence and Divergence in European Education and Training Systems*, Bedford Way Papers, Institute of Education, University of London, London

Green, A et al (2000 forthcoming) *Financing Vocational Education and Training in Europe*, CEDEFOP, Brussels

Hasan, A (1996) Lifelong Learning, in *International Encyclopaedia of Adult Education and Training*, ed A Tuijnman, 2nd edn, Elsevier Science, Oxford

Hodgson, A and Spours, K (1999) *New Labour's Educational Agenda: Issues and policies for education and training from 14+*, Kogan Page, London

Organization for Economic Co-operation and Development (OECD) (1996) *Lifelong Learning for All*, OECD, Paris

OECD (1998) *Maintaining Prosperity in an Ageing Society*, OECD, Paris

Raffe, D (1992) *Participation of 16–18 Year Olds in Education and Training*, NCE Briefing Paper No 3, National Commission on Education, London

Ryan, P (1992) *International Comparisons of Vocational Education and Training for Intermediate Skills*, Falmer Press, London

Scottish Education Department (SED) (1975) *Adult Education: The challenge of change* (The Alexander Report), HMSO, Edinburgh

Senker, P *et al* (1999) Working to Learn: an holistic approach to young people's education and training, in *Apprenticeship: Towards a new paradigm of learning*, ed P Ainley and H Rainbird, Kogan Page, London

Sutton, P (1996) Lifelong and Continuing Education, in *International Encyclopaedia of Adult Education and Training*, ed A Tuijnman, 2nd edn, Elsevier Science, Oxford

Tuijnman. A (1996) Recurrent Education, in *International Encyclopaedia of Adult Education and Training*, ed A Tuijnman, 2nd edn, Elsevier Science, Oxford

UNESCO (1976) General Conference, Nairobi, 19th Session Report, UNESCO, Paris

Part 1

The European context

2

The vocational training policy of the European Commission and its discourse on lifelong learning

Marc Ant

Vocational training in the treaties of the European Community/Union

Although the European Community was originally conceived as a purely economic entity, it nevertheless became clear from the outset that other policy fields were also to be included. According to the Monnet doctrine (Olivi, 1998), the European Union could only be achieved through successive sectoral integration during which the member states would progressively transfer political power to the new European institutions. Therefore, the European founding founders concentrated their efforts on a limited number of fields of political and economic interest, but included enough references to other political fields to be able to expand their scope of action in the future. Looking back at events of the past 30 years, it must be acknowledged that this approach has been quite successful, since the European context is now influencing more and more people on more and more issues.

This strategy was also applied to vocational training. Although present since the beginning, this domain only began to acquire importance in the second half of the 1980s. The original Article 56 of the Treaty of the European Coal and Steel Community in 1951 was only a timid attempt to create the bases for a wider training programme for coal and steel workers needing retraining due to structural changes in this sector. Therefore, several programmes were set up to provide the steel and coal industry with the necessary funds to ensure professional readaptation of their workers (Baudin, 1997).

Similarly, the concept of vocational training was also included in the Treaty of Rome of 1957, establishing the European Economic Union. Article 128 enabled the European Council to establish general principles for the implementation of a common policy in the field of vocational training. Unfortunately, this article produced little effect, as the European member states were not able to agree upon any of these common principles. Several years of discussions and negotiations were necessary before the publication of the European Council Decision of 2 April 1963 laying down the general principles for implementing a common vocational training policy. These principles turned out to be rather vague, making it impossible in practice to construct a policy based upon them. Furthermore, in the 1950s and the 1960s, unlike today, education and training were not a major preoccupation: they were treated only as second- or even third-rank issues in comparison with economic and financial matters.

Only in the first half of the 1970s, under the leadership of Commissioner Ralph Dahrendorf, was a new attempt made to implement a common European education and vocational training policy. But the time was not yet ripe and the conception produced by Commissioner Dahrendorf was felt to be too progressive by many countries. The proposal put forward by Dahrendorf was excessively oriented towards harmonization and did not sufficiently respect the principle of subsidiarity. Therefore, the policy report that represented the elaboration of this new education and vocational training policy (Janne, 1973) was finally rejected by the Council of Ministers of Education, or rather by the Ministers of Education meeting within the European Council (European Council, 1974).

From that moment on, for quite a few years, no major breakthrough was reported, apart from the creation of CEDEFOP (European Council, 1975) in Berlin in 1975 and a European Council Resolution of 6 June 1974 on the mutual recognition of diplomas, certificates and other evidence of formal qualifications.[1] Only in the late 1980s did the situation start to change as the European Commission introduced action programmes to enhance and develop vocational training in Europe. The difference of this approach from that advocated by Dahrendorf was clear. Since the European Commission had to acknowledge the fact that the member states were reluctant to adopt a proper European policy, the most promising solution appeared to be to organize programmes that would finance projects following specific principles agreed on a common basis between the Commission and the member states.

Hence, the European Commission created transnational programmes, such as COMETT, ERASMUS, EUROTECNET and FORCE, which functioned on a common agreement between the Commission and the member states and followed individual and very specific objectives. The member states had no reason to fear an attempt to weaken their national education and vocational training systems, as these programmes did not foresee any structural changes on a national basis, and the Commission finally had the opportunity to take the lead while running the action programmes under its own responsibility. However, these programmes stood on weak legal ground, as the European treaties did not refer to them in explicit terms and the matter had to be referred to the European Court of Justice to clarify the situation. In the 'Erasmus case', the Court ruled on 30 May 1989 that Article 128 was an adequate legal basis for the European programmes (Decision of the European Court of Justice No 1425/1989).

But it was the Treaty of Maastricht adopted in 1992 that established for the first time education as a policy field of the European Union (Article 126) and placed vocational training on a broader basis through Article 127. This article states that *'the Community shall implement a vocational training policy, which shall support and supplement the action of the Member States, while fully respecting the responsibility of the Member States for the content and organisation of vocational training'*. We note that a strong reference is made to the responsibility of the member states: the Commission is obliged to cooperate with them in order to attain its priorities for action.[2]

In 1997, the Treaty of Amsterdam made no major changes to the general orientations of Article 127, which then became Article 150, apart from the fact that Article 251 now took effect. This meant that both the Economic and Social Committee and the Committee of the Regions had to be consulted, thus to some extent shifting power from the Commission and the member states to the European Parliament and the Committees. Also, for the first time, a preamble of a European Treaty refers to education and vocational training '... *determined to promote the development of the highest possible level of knowledge for their peoples through a wide access to education and through its continuous updating'*.

It is therefore only since 1992 that the European programmes have been based on clearly identifiable articles, leaving no room for discussion about their legitimacy. At the same time, the first and the second generation of the previous European programmes (until 1995, COMETT, EUROTECNET, FORCE, LINGUA, PETRA), as well as the first and the second generation of the Leonardo da Vinci and the Socrates programmes (1995–1999 and 2000–2006), have become the European Commission's effective instruments for implementation of a European policy on education and vocational training, in full compliance with the legal dispositions of the different member states, as Article 150 prohibits even the slightest attempt to harmonize the systems.

Since the first common principles of 1963, in all the European Commission and the European Council have produced more than 100 major official regulations or policy documents (directives, regulations, decisions, recommendations, opinions) concerning vocational training in Europe (Ant, 1998). Field (1998: 25–26) describes the evolution of the vocational training policy of the European Commission as follows:

> In the period between 1957 and 1973 education and training were relatively minor interests. From 1974 to 1985 the Union showed some interest in education, but its major concern was with vocational training. From 1986 to 1992, education and training became significant areas of policy, with a

stream of action programmes contributing to the steady achievement of the single market. From the ratification of the Treaty of the European Union, the EU has adopted a more radical approach seeking to promote the concept and practice of the learning society.

It is unquestionable that the real development of the European vocational training policy only came into effect in the second half of the 1980s through the implementation of the transnational funded specific action programmes. The conclusion must be that all other attempts to establish a purely European policy in the field of vocational training were and still are bound to fail, since the different member states still fear that a common approach could have too much of an impact upon their own training and, more particularly, education systems. Interestingly enough, while the European member states did not have any fundamental objection to abandoning their national currencies, things were very different when it came to education and training. Education (and to some extent training) is too closely bound up with national cultures and identities to let the system be ruled by some distant administration in faraway Brussels. And this situation is unlikely to change in the near future. European vocational training policy can therefore be no more than an appendage of national training policies.

The policy-making process of the European Commission in vocational training

Thus, the legal situation of vocational training in Europe has become more clearly defined since 1992. This process has been accompanied by the creation of a series of vocational training programmes by the European Commission to permit the implementation of a European vocational training policy and to ensure its financing. And as Baudin (1997) reminds us, in order to implement a policy, the development of an action requires three elements: a legal basis, political determination and financial means.

As we have already mentioned, the legal basis for a European vocational training policy was given by Article 127 of the Treaty of Maastricht, and Article 150 of the Treaty of Amsterdam. The financial means, ie 620 million Euros for the first phase of the Leonardo da Vinci programme (European Council, 1994), then found their way into the budget of the European Community.

The political determination of the Commission was expressed mainly in the Cresson White Paper (European Commission, 1995). This defines the common principles upon which this policy is based. The rules for the implementation of this policy are defined by the Leonardo da Vinci programme and various supplementary actions, such as the European Year of Lifelong Learning.

The Cresson White Paper, which starts with an analysis of the complex changes taking place in our European society, refers to three major factors of upheaval that apparently determine the evolution of our societies: the information society, internationalization and the scientific and technical world. It proposes as an answer – the promotion of a broad-based knowledge society and suggests five guidelines for action:[3]

1. Encourage the acquisition of new knowledge, ie raise the general level of knowledge.
2. Bring schools and the business sector closer together, while developing all forms of apprenticeship in Europe.
3. Combat exclusion.
4. Promote proficiency in three Community languages.
5. Treat material investment and investment in training on an equal basis. (EEC Council Meeting, 1995: 52)

The practical implementation of these principles is ensured by the Leonardo da Vinci programmes I (1995–1999) and II (2000–2006), which represent the action programmes of the European Commission. The first Leonardo da Vinci programme was granted a budget of 620 million Euros and functioned on the basis of an annual call for tenders to which all kinds of institutions could respond. Of course, successful application was linked to respect for a certain number of formal and qualitative criteria derived mainly from the Cresson White Paper, but, in the end, numerous training activities are being financed all over Europe through this programme.

In general, the European policy process in the field of vocational training takes place on several different interacting levels:

- the *macro-level*, which refers to the existence of a legal basis legitimizing the action to be undertaken (Article 150 of the Treaty of Amsterdam; the Cresson White Paper);
- the *meso-level*, which represents the intermediary level of the action programmes;
- the *exo-level*, which is occupied by the different political actors, like the member states' representatives, the representatives of the social partners, of the regions, lobbyists, general interest groups, and so on;
- the *micro-level*, which is the level of companies, para-public institutions, universities, networks and practical players that develop and realize concrete transnational training projects.

This process could be characterized as a 'top-down–bottom-up' event. First, in a top-down manner, leading from theory to action, the European Commission refers on the macro-level to a certain economic and social context and promotes vocational training through its 'mediatized' discourse as the solution for the identified problems. Second, this discourse becomes on the meso-level the legal basis and the justification for the action programmes that enable the Commission, despite many constraints from the member states, to take the lead. Since the Commission plays the lead role in the organization and administration of the action programmes, it has a rather strong position: it is not only responsible for the political aspects of the programmes, but also for their operational running. Third, the Commission is not the sole player in the action. On the exo-level, it has to take into account the external opinions and positions of the member states and of different interest groups that go beyond its own scope of action. It must also comply with the constraint of social consensus, as its decisions can not be opposed to public opinion or to its political competitors, like the Parliament. Fourth, all these factors determine to a very large extent the degrees of freedom for a candidate who is looking for financing within the framework of the Leonardo da Vinci programme. In any case, in order to have the slightest chance of applying successfully for funding, the European promoters must not only follow the general guidelines set out in the Cresson White Paper or the specific parameters of the Leonardo da Vinci programme, but also respect the administrative procedures imposed by the European Commission (Ant, 1997).

In practice, the implementation of the Leonardo da Vinci programme is accompanied by an elaborate discourse, in which the Commission regularly presents, analyses and interprets the results of the projects. Of course, these interpretations have to be seen in the light of the original policy definition and it is therefore hardly surprising that the analyses of the results of the programmes (European Council, 1997) necessarily reflect the principles set out originally in the policy guidelines.

These documents represent the success stories of the programmes, as they attempt to prove that the projects financed are in line with the economic and social setting originally described by the Commission in documents like the White Paper. The conclusion is that the programmes represent a major contribution to the attempt to solve the problems of Europe. Naturally, these conclusions are not really a surprise: first of all, they represent political documents and it is hardly likely that the Commission would admit its own failure or insufficiencies.[5] Second, the results are the logical effect of the application and selection procedure of projects, as the application forms necessarily have to comply with the guidelines for action or priorities defined within each programme in order to have the slightest chance of being considered. Therefore, as a matter of course, the projects prove the principles or guidelines set up originally to be correct: all other projects that might have proved something else are excluded from the start.

This interpretation is delivered by documents like the *Interim Report on the Implementation of the Leonardo da Vinci programme*[4] (European Commission, 1997a), describing the present state of achievement, or more prospective documents, such as *Towards a Europe of knowledge* (European Commission, 1997b). This document is meant to justify the Commission's future action in the framework of the training programmes, while defining the guidelines for Community action in the areas of education, training and youth for the period 2000–2006. As the introduction mentions, it is intended to pave the way for the legal instruments to be proposed in the spring of 1998, with the relevant decisions to follow in 1999 and implementation on 1 January 2000 of the next generation of European education and vocational training programmes.

Thus, we have reached the bottom of the process, which is now reversed as all these conclusions serve to justify the choices taken within the framework of the new Council decision for the second phase of the Leonardo da Vinci programme (European Council, 1999). As the conclusions published about the programme are consistent with the political discourse defined in the first place, they can legitimately be used as a motivation for the second phase of the programme. Here, the process goes up again – 'bottom-up', from action back to theory – so that in the end, one can indeed conclude that the legal principles have produced the expected outcomes and that these outcomes are used to stimulate the continuation of action as they reappear in the legal definition of the new steps to be undertaken. The end of the chain is to integrate the political principles into new legal dispositions, which are bound to ensure a further revision of the European treaties.[6] At this point, the circle closes again and the European Commission has achieved its original goal: to implement its own political objectives and to maintain a high degree of power over their implementation.

So, instead of making political proposals that are judged inappropriate by the different member states, as Dahrendorf tried to do in the 1970s, the introduction of action programmes in vocational training and other fields has enabled the Commission to play a subtle game. It implements its policy orientations not against, but with the help of the member states and the social partners, since they have willingly accepted their validation role and are more than happy to participate in the distribution of the budget. Unlike Dahrendorf, the Commission has reversed the game by first paying attention to action and only second including these principles within the legal dispositions. This process can be seen as the 'Pygmalion effect' (Rosenthal and Jacobson, 1968) of the vocational training policy in Europe.

Obstacles to successful implementation of the process

Of course, the European Commission, in this case the former Directorate General XXII, responsible for vocational training, has not been able to implement this 'top-down–bottom-up' process fully and to take full advantage of it. The main reasons for this are its own administrative weaknesses and organizational problems, which contributed to the events of February and March 1999 in Brussels and have been sufficiently commented on in the European press.[7] They have shown that, despite its political ambition to enhance a new dimension in vocational training in Europe, the major preoccupation of the European Commission is not primarily the promotion of innovative ideas and projects, but the respect (or non-respect) for fortuitous procedures and regulations.

However, the successful implementation of a vocational training policy must be accompanied by an efficient management and here, in my opinion, the European Commission has completely failed to play its part. In general, problems in the Commission are not solved but merely reported in audit reports. Each action must be audited to determine whether it has been performed consistently with existing regulations, procedures and practices. Here again, the problem is that the technical organization of European action programmes is so complex that it becomes rather difficult, after the event, to retrace what has been done before in a context of insufficient regulations, time and financial constraints, as well as political pressure. In order to avoid the kind of conflicts that appeared at the beginning of 1999, two major issues must be clarified: first, the rules of the game must be defined beforehand, and, second, one must decide whether these institutions are subject to European public regulations or to the private law of the State of Belgium. A middle position leaves too much room for interpretation and may have destructive effects.

Lifelong learning as a major part of the European vocational training discourse

The lifelong learning concept is a good example of an attempt to implement a specific aspect of the European vocational training policy. Already the Delors White Paper underlined its importance, when it stated that '*All measures must therefore be based on the concept of developing, generalizing and systematizing lifelong learning and continuing training*' (European Commission, 1994: 136).

Following this line of debate, the Cresson White Paper (European Commission, 1995) took over and set in train at different levels its version of the lifelong learning concept. For instance, it refers to a report from the Round Table of European Industrialists stressing the need for flexible training with a broad knowledge base, advocating a *learning to learn approach* throughout life (p 27). It defines lifelong learning as a continuing process of skill acquisition (p 33) and requests that access to training should be guaranteed throughout life. The White Paper also states that it was meant to launch the European Year of Lifelong Learning (p 50) and concludes that: '*There is too much inflexibility, too much compartmentalization of education and training systems and not enough bridges, or enough possibilities to let in new patterns of lifelong learning*' (p 74).

The first concrete result of the Cresson White Paper was the creation of the Leonardo da Vinci programme in 1994 and the launch of the Year of Lifelong Learning in 1996. With regard to the Leonardo da Vinci programme

(European Council, 1994), the concept of lifelong learning was introduced at several levels. The Decision of the Council states that lifelong learning means lateral cooperation between different types of training as well as measures concerning the continuity of training throughout life. Its objective was the promotion of lifelong training to encourage ongoing skills development to meet the needs of employees and enterprises and to contribute to the reduction of unemployment and facilitation of personal development. It also states that the acquisition of core skills is to be considered as the basis of lifelong training. In general, the first phase of the Leonardo da Vinci programme was subdivided into three different domains, eg initial vocational training, continuing vocational training and lifelong learning.[8]

The Council Decision concerning the second phase of the Leonardo da Vinci programme (European Council, 1999) continues to refer substantially to the concept of lifelong learning, by which it means *'the education and vocational training opportunities offered to individuals throughout their lives to enable them continually to acquire, update and adapt their knowledge, skills and competences'* (p33). The Decision supported the concept of lifelong learning by referring to the extraordinary European Council on Employment held in Luxembourg on 20 and 21 November 1997, which *'recognized that life-long education and vocational training can make an important contribution to member states' employment policies in order to enhance employability, adaptability and entrepreneurship and to promote equal opportunities'*. It also mentions that *'life-long learning should be provided for persons of all ages and all occupational categories, not only because of technological change but also as a result of the reduction in the number of persons in active employment in the age pyramid'* (p33). However, despite all these good intentions, it still remains difficult to identify explicit national lifelong learning policies, except perhaps in two or three member states.

Although all projects submitted and accepted under the Leonardo da Vinci programme were required to refer to one of these domains, the attribution of the projects to one of these three by the promoters was more than haphazard. For most applicants, the concept of lifelong learning was not clear and was used as a catch-all for those projects that could not clearly be identified as belonging to initial or continuing vocational training. In this sense, the concept of lifelong learning cannot be considered as a major breakthrough in the debate about European vocational training policy. It was used as a keyword for a discourse that used concepts that were rather ill defined and not based on any thorough or scientific considerations. Therefore, the impact of the Leonardo da Vinci programme, in terms of the lifelong learning concept, must finally be considered as extremely limited, despite the many publications and conferences on the subject.

Another attempt of the European Commission to promote lifelong learning as one of its key concepts was the declaration of the European Year of Lifelong Learning in 1996 (European Council, 1995). Although the Commission, especially its Directorate-General XXII, invested a lot of effort in the promotion of this concept during 1996, it is still difficult to discover exactly what impact this year has had on European public opinion, European vocational training systems or practices. As on so many other occasions, the European Year of Lifelong Learning was based upon the same basic discourse, for example, the importance of change, the need for adaptation, for new patterns of learning and new work organizations, the risk of inequality and exclusion, and of course education and training as major contributors to solutions to tackle unemployment. Against this background, the Year was intended to stress the importance of lifelong learning, to encourage personal development, to familiarize people with new knowledge, to give an added boost to EU education and training programmes, and to provide a framework for discussions in the context of the above-mentioned White Papers.

Again, who would be likely to contradict these intentions, and who would refuse resources for events, seminars, conferences, competitions, dissemination activities of good practices, publications and so on related to the Year of Lifelong Learning? Considering the number of activities organized throughout Europe and the number of brochures handed out, obviously, one is forced to conclude that the European Year was a major success, as is confirmed by its final report (European Commission, 1999). However, here again, we encounter the 'self-fulfilling prophecy' in European vocational training referred to earlier: the same discourse (White paper) is used to motivate a distinct range of actions (European Year), and the results are declared more than satisfactory (final report), so that the original concept can be used to justify further action (Leonardo da Vinci II).

But no serious quantitative and qualitative analysis of the outcomes and results is being made, the impact of all actions is not studied, no questioning of the appropriateness of the actions and their justification is undertaken, and certainly no debates about the subject have taken or are taking place. Despite the considerable amount of effort and money that are put into all these activities, the return on investment remains unclear, as no scientific measures have been set up to evaluate it.

Conclusions

Thus, from an analysis of the existing literature but also from the viewpoint of a former actor within the European Commission, I have tried to paint a clearer picture of this utterly complex and complicated process called European policy making. This statement normally applies to all kinds of European policy areas and as matters become more and more complex everyday, policy making increasingly lacks transparency.

We are in the presence of a process in which a very large number of stakeholders are involved and in which each one, individually or collectively, wishes to wield as much influence as possible. Above, it is a process of negotiations, and below, of intrigues. The process is unidentifiable for an external observer and is presented as a major achievement to the outside world through an elaborate and omnipresent discourse. This discourse is used by the European Commission in a very subtle way and serves its cause: the Commission can play the leading role without offending the member states.

This discourse is based on the assumption that vocational training should serve an economic purpose in order to increase the competitiveness of enterprises and the adaptability of employees. It is used, in the sense of a 'self-fulfilling prophecy', to motivate theory and action in two directions: from top to bottom (ie from the basic assumptions in the treaties via the elaborate description in the White Papers and the action programmes to the level of the European promoters of training projects) and from bottom up (ie from the analysis of the results of the projects up to the justification of the new action programmes and perhaps new articles in the forthcoming treaties).

But, as can be seen with the practical example of the Leonardo da Vinci programme (1995–1999) and the Year of Lifelong Learning in 1996, despite the considerable financial resources involved, it remains unclear what impact the projects or measures have had, especially on national training systems or European training practices.

However, for many reasons, questions like 'What are the effects? What is the return on investment?' or 'What are the real outcomes?' are becoming increasingly important, and the European Commission has not even begun to come up with any kind of answer to them.

The problem, in my opinion, is that if we continue to hold an elaborate discourse about the positive effects of vocational training on competitiveness, employability and combating social exclusion, without, at the same time, providing the means to evaluate the effectiveness of the investment, in economical, social and pedagogical terms, then it will be more than likely that in the future vocational training will no longer be considered as an investment, but as a cost, both by enterprises and individuals.

We cannot continue, like Woody Allen, to pretend that although we don't know the problem, we know that training is the solution. We must turn our attention much more to the effects side and consider training as one element in a long chain of instruments and measures. Training can have little effect on individuals, companies or the social system, unless it is embedded in a larger context of structural, systematic and global measures. Training also has little effect if it is considered as an instrument of mass production, while forgetting that it has a value in its own right. The purpose of vocational training should not only be to improve the results of a company or make the individual eligible for a new job; training can and should take place for personal reasons, the result of good and appropriate training being that the company becomes more productive and the individual gets a better job – and not the opposite.

Notes

1. Out of this resolution emerged two directives: Council Directive 85/384/EEC of 10 June 1985 and Directive 1999/42/EC of the European Parliament and of the Council of 7 June 1999. Considering the time that has elapsed between the two, one cannot really speak about a matter of priority in this field of European policy-making.
2. These are to facilitate adaptation to industrial changes, to improve initial and continuing vocational training in order to facilitate vocational integration and reintegration into the labour market, to facilitate access to vocational training and encourage mobility, to stimulate cooperation on training between educational or training establishments and firms, and to develop exchanges of information and experience on issues common to the training systems of the member states.
3. It is not the subject of this contribution to analyse critically the Cresson White Paper. However, despite the fact that the European Commission has proclaimed on many occasions that a discussion on the White Paper has been going on, it was impossible to find more than a few publications that critically analyse the contents of the White Paper. I can't help reaching the conclusion that most of the competent authors who could have contributed to the debate on a more critical basis all depend, in one way or another, upon European finance and probably fear losing an important part of their financial resources by criticizing the Commission. As a result, between 1995 and 1999 the European Commission has financed on average 750 projects every year within the framework of this Programme, implicating as many transnational partnerships from the European member states and the associated countries from central and Eastern Europe.
4. Let us also note that the problem here is that the existing treaties have not been completely replaced by the new ones, but that the different regulations were either added, changed or completely cancelled. The difficulty is that two different kinds of treaties exist: those including the alterations (which are indeed the originals) and those in which the changes have been incorporated (consolidated versions). Second, one has to mention that the numbering of the different articles has also been changed so that it has become difficult to follow the evolution of the different dispositions for the field of vocational training, for example.
5. The 20-page Interim Report of 1997 represents a compilation of a larger study on the practical and structural implementation of the programme and reports from member states.
6. Let us note here that documents like White Papers have no legal value as such. However, they serve as political orientation guidelines that define action.
7. But it still amazes the author of this contribution how uncritically the European press has swallowed information about the presumed

dysfunction in the framework of the Leonardo da Vinci programme without the slightest attempt to question its validity. A few interviews and some obscure self-created documents of self-proclaimed justiciaries were enough to disgrace and disqualify institutions and persons. In this context, the European press did not play its role as the fourth power of the State, but it became the *adlatus* of the players of a morbid political game where elections had to be prepared and revenge to be taken.

8. At this point, it is important to comment on the translation of terms from one language to another. In the French and German versions of the Decision for example, the third element of the three domains is designated as *continuum*, a term that the UK delegation refused to accept during the preparatory negotiations in the Council. However, just as it is difficult to justify the translation of the French *société cognitive* to the English *learning society*, the translation of the original French *continuum* does not correspond to the broader *lifelong learning* concept. The concept of *continuum* refers to a structural integration of the different levels of the education and training system, whereas the *lifelong learning* concept refers to the formal and informal learning of individuals beyond the initial school system.

References

Ant, M (1997) Informationen für den Leonardo da Vinci Antragsteller – Struktur und Aufbau des Berufsbildungsprogramms Leonardo da Vinci der Europäischen Kommission, *Grundlagen der Weiterbildung Zeitschrift*, 1 (8), 24–28

Ant, M (1998) Die primären und sekundären Rechtsbestimmungen zur europäischen Berufsbildungspolitik, in *Europahandbuch Weiterbildung*, ed A Kaiser *et al*, Loseblatt-Sammlung, Neuwied, Kriftel, Luchterhand, Berlin

Baudin, P (1997) Le contenu social des politiques communautaires, in *Une Europe sociale. Pourquoi… Jusqu'où?*, Institut Universitaire International Luxembourg, p 173, Nomos, Baden Baden

European Commission (1994) *Growth, Competitiveness, Employment. The challenges and ways forward into the 21st century*, Office for Official Publications of the European Communities, Luxembourg

European Commission (1995) *Teaching and Learning: Towards the learning society*, Office for Official Publications of the European Communities, Luxembourg

European Commission (1997a) *Interim Report on the Implementation of the Leonardo da Vinci programme*, COM(97) 399 final, Office for Official Publications of the European Communities, Luxembourg

European Commission (1997b) *Towards a Europe of knowledge*, Communication from the Commission, COM(97) 563 final, Office for Official Publications of the European Communities, Luxembourg

European Commission (1999) Report from the Commission to the Council, the European Parliament, the Economic and Social Committee and the Committee of the Regions on the implementation, results and overall assessment of the European Year of Lifelong Learning (1996), submitted in accordance with Article 8 of the

European Parliament and Council, Decision No 2493/95/EC, COM/99/0447 final, Office for Official Publications of the European Communities, Luxembourg

European Council (1974) Resolution of the Ministers of Education, meeting within the Council, of 6 June 1974 on cooperation in the field of education, OJ C 098, 20.08.74, p 2

European Council (1975) Regulation No 337/75 of the Council of 10 February 1975 establishing a European Centre for the Development of Vocational Training

European Council (1994) Council Decision of 6 December 1994 establishing an action programme for the implementation of a European Community vocational training policy, 94/819/EC: OJ L 340, 29.12.94, p 8

European Council (1995) Decision No 2493/95/EC of the European Parliament and of the Council of 23 October 1995 establishing 1996 as the 'European year of lifelong learning', 95/431/EC: OJ L 256, 26.10.95, p 45

European Council (1997) Council Conclusions of 22 September 1997 on the communication concerning the White Paper 'Teaching and learning towards the learning society', OJ C 303, 04.10.97, p 8

European Council (1999) Council Decision of 26 April 1999 establishing the second phase of the Community vocational training action programme 'Leonardo da Vinci', 1999/382/EC: OJ L 146, 11.06.99, p 33

Field, J (1998) *European Dimensions: Education, training and the European Union*, Kingsley, London

Janne, H (1973) Für eine gemeinschaftliche Bildungspolitik, in *Bulletin der EG*, Beilage 10/3, Forschung, Wissenschaft und Bildung: Wissenschaftliche und technische information, R Dahrendorf, Brüssel

Olivi, B (1998) *L'Europe Difficile. Histoire politique de la Communauté européenne*, *folio*, pp 17–18, Paris

Rosenthal, R and Jacobson, L F (1968) *Pygmalion in the Classroom: Teachers' expectations and pupils' intellectual development*, Holt, Rhinehart & Winston, New York

3

Lifelong learning and the learning society: different European models of organization

Andy Green

Lifelong learning implies the distribution of learning opportunities throughout the lifetime; the learning society implies that these opportunities should be available to all and occur in all areas of society, from the school and college, to the home, the community and the workplace. These notions have become fashionable for good reasons. Rapid changes in technology and work organization mean that more people will be required to have higher levels of skill and to undertake retraining continuously throughout their working lives. Increased leisure time for adults, won through shorter working hours or enforced through unemployment, allows new opportunities for formal learning and creates demand for education at different phases of the life cycle. Longer life expectancy, and the ageing of populations, means that more active retirees are seeking stimulation through new forms of learning. These greater demands for learning opportunities cannot be met entirely by the existing institutions for formal learning, nor need they be. Information technology makes possible a variety of new modes and sites for learning (OECD, 1996).

So much is common in the new rhetoric shared by policy makers across the developed world. However, beyond this there is little agreement. Visions of lifelong learning and the learning society differ markedly in both ends and means. In some versions the main objective is individual development and improved quality of life; in others it is the promotion of social equality and social cohesion; most commonly, perhaps, it is enhanced productivity and national economic competitiveness. There is equal divergence in the models for achieving the learning society. Some stress the role of the market and the responsibility of the individual; some advocate multiple stakeholding and social partnership; others, although increasingly rarely, advocate the central role of the state in orchestrating and managing the learning society. The outcomes of these different models would, of course, be highly divergent – as varied, in fact, as are the current systems of education and training across the developed countries.

The purpose of this chapter is to examine the implications of some different ways of organizing lifelong learning and the learning society. This can be done in two ways. Firstly, we can construct some hypothetical models – abstracting from the core elements of different policy positions – and examine, deductively, what kind of learning society they might be expected to generate. Secondly, we can examine a number of different country systems that may be deemed to belong to different types, and assess what kind of lifelong learning arrangements they are tending towards. This chapter will adopt both strategies in a provisional attempt to sketch out some of the alternatives facing policy makers who wish to translate the rhetoric into reality. Three hypothetical models will be examined, characterized respectively as market-led, state-led and social partner-led. Three European systems will be examined which, respectively, tend in these ideal-typical directions: those of the UK, France and Germany. To contain the analysis within manageable proportions, only the post-compulsory phases of lifelong learning will be considered and, within those, principally the areas of upper secondary education and initial vocational training, and continuing education and training: less will be said about higher education and training for the unemployed.

Different models of the learning society

General policy documents and commentaries on lifelong learning and the learning society rarely fall into neat and distinctive categories. More often they display, overtly or covertly, different emphases that might, when implemented as specific policies in particular contexts, yield substantially different results. It is easy enough to identify, say, the OECD's *Lifelong Learning for All* (1996) as a text that gives substantial emphasis to economic competitiveness and the role of markets in lifelong learning provision. Equally one could cite from the same year the UNESCO report, *Learning – the treasure within* (UNESCO, 1996), as one that gives pride of place to considerations of life quality, social cohesion and equity and that sees lifelong learning as above all a matter of public responsibility. However, clearly both pay tribute to the multiple goals and means normally associated with the rhetoric of lifelong learning. For the purposes of analysis, however, it is useful to construct some ideal-typical models, even if they do not correspond precisely to any particular policy position. These models, differentiated according to their core organizational principals, represent positions along a continuum.

At one extreme, there is the market-led model that conceives of the learning society as a grass roots, demand-led efflorescence of new opportunities, networks and partnerships, facilitated by new technologies and driven by the market. In this model, the individual takes primary responsibility for his or her own learning and governments limit their roles largely to advocacy and 'steering'. Organizations recognize their interest in developing learning environments, and invest in them to a degree that is commensurate with the benefits they deliver for them. At the other extreme is the state-led model that gives the key role to the state as the organizer and principal source of funds for lifelong learning. This model rejects the market approach as leading to under-investment and inequality. Instead of leaving the market to make the key decisions about how much should be invested in what, it accords public authorities with key roles in planning and regulation in the interests of the overall public good. In between there is another possible model, based on social partnership, which recognizes the importance of individual responsibility and also advocates multiple agency, diverse stakeholding and maximal use of new learning technologies. However, it differs from the first in placing greater stress on the limitations of the market and the importance of regulation.

Each of these models has to deal with key problems that arise in modern polities seeking to achieve the learning society. They have to establish means for identifying current and future learning and skills needs for individuals, firms and the national economy. They have to respond to the diverse demands of different key stakeholders: employers seeking to meet their perceived skills needs at affordable costs, individuals looking for affordable learning opportunities which further their personal and career development, and providers looking to maintain the viability of their institutions and jobs. Meeting these demands generally involves diversifying provision and extending certification, but this must be done whilst maintaining transparency of standards and the value of qualifications. It also means a constantly increasing rate of participation in education and training, and perhaps the greatest dilemma for policy makers currently is how this can be funded. No government any longer believes that the state can meet the entire costs of lifelong learning provision, if indeed they ever did (Green *et al*, 1999). The key question, therefore, becomes how to spread the cost of lifelong learning equitably between the various beneficiaries – individuals, employers and the state – and how to do this without reducing access or promoting inequalities.

A number of strategies are possible for encouraging individuals and employers to invest more in lifelong learning (Green, Hodgson and Williams, 1998). Raising the quality, appropriateness and accessibility of learning opportunities attracts individuals to participate. Making provision more efficient reduces costs and also encourages individuals and employers to invest. Above all, the benefits of learning need to be evident to both the individual and the employer. This means that qualifications need to be transparent, clearly and reliably indicating the skills and aptitudes possessed by their holders. Individuals and employers need reliable information on the benefits of qualifications and skills in terms of improved employability and productivity. Employers need to understand how to utilize available skills and to reward individuals who possess them (Green and Steedman, 1996).

One of the major problems with achieving a learning society is that both individuals and employers tend to under-invest in skills and learning. Individuals may be reluctant to invest because they cannot gain access to resources, because they are unsure of their own abilities to benefit from learning opportunities, or because they are uncertain of the future benefits and, in particular, whether future economic returns will justify the costs and forgone opportunities. Employers tend to under-invest in training because they are uncertain about whether their investment will show a return – that is whether the additional skills will actually improve productivity of the employee they have paid to train and whether that employee will remain in their employment long enough to repay the costs. Where labour markets are only lightly regulated a common problem for employers is that other employers may poach the employee whom they have trained, thus causing them to loose their investment. In the language of human capital theory, unregulated training markets suffer the perennial problem of 'externalities'. Neither the individual nor the employer can be certain of capturing all the benefits from their learning investment and both are reluctant to pay for the benefit that accrues to another party (Carnoy, 1993).

Different models of lifelong learning deal with these problems in different ways and according to different rationales. In the market-led model, policy makers believe that individuals and employers are best placed to the make decisions about what skills and learning experiences are worthwhile. Modern economies are too complex and unpredictable, so the argument goes, for the state to forecast future skill demands accurately and planning an industrial strategy that creates the future demand is deemed undesirable, both because it inhibits the individual freedom of entrepreneurs and job-seekers and because it is less efficient than market-led development. Planning through concerted social partner negotiations is also considered inherently problematic since interest group domination is more likely to result than stakeholder consensus. The result of the market-based approach is, therefore, that education and training supply is predominantly market driven. This can lead to rapid, if uncoordinated, development, a diversity of learning opportunities, flexible modes of provision, and general responsiveness to immediate demand. It may also generate strong efficiency incentives, as multiple providers compete to meet demands for learning opportunities.

The potential disadvantages of the market-driven approach are several. Firstly, it may lead to the satisfaction of immediate learning demands but fail to satisfy the longer terms needs of individuals, firms or the national economy. Secondly, it may lead to sharp inequalities in the uptake of learning opportunities, because of the unequal dispersal of resources and information amongst learners and because of discrimination by employers or providers. Thirdly, it may tend to undermine the quality and transparency of learning and qualifications. In a market-driven system, competitive pressures on providers may encourage cost-efficiency at the expense of quality and the lowering of standards to meet the qualification aspirations of consumers. Alternatively, it may simply lead to such diversification in the supply of courses and qualifications that the system loses transparency – that is to say that no one can tell any longer quite what learning opportunities are available, what the learning product or outcome is and what it is worth. Lastly, market-led systems are subject to the problem of under-investment described above (Ranson, 1994).

Market-led systems do, of course, have ways of mitigating some of the problems above. Good quality information and guidance are used to help individuals and employers make appropriate decisions about investments in learning; government-guaranteed loans can be supplied to give individuals opportunities to invest, and tax concessions and other incentives can be offered to both individuals and employers to encourage them to invest. State-organized standard setting and quality control can be used to maintain standards and other rationalizing interventions can be used to encourage coherence of provision. Less can be done to mitigate inequalities, without 'distorting' the market, but exhortation and maximum availability of information can be used to encourage everyone to take up learning opportunities.

State-led systems will adopt different approaches to these problems. State planning, informed by stakeholder views, will determine the broad outlines of provision in order to meet the longer-term needs of the economy and society and to reconcile the demands of different interest groups. This may take the form of manpower forecasting, where this, for all its susceptibilities, is deemed a useful corrective to the 'short-termism' of the market and the limited rationality of individual decision-making. It may go further and involve industrial policy that can best predict future manpower needs by creating them. Provision is likely to be tightly regulated to maximize equity, coherence, transparency, and consistency of standards. Investment is encouraged through an array of statutory regulations, for example through licence-to-practice laws, training taxes or obligations on firms or rights to training leave. Since the market is thought to under-invest in education and training, the state will lever investment, either by spending taxpayers' money and directly funding the majority of provision, or by obliging employers to invest. The advantages of such an approach may be more concerted and long-term decision-making, greater consistency and coherence in provision, transparency and reliability in qualifications, and more equitable opportunities for individuals, if this is an explicit part of state policy. The disadvantages may be a slow pace of change, less diversity and responsiveness to particular needs, misjudged plans, and bureaucratic inefficiency (Green, 1995; OECD, 1996).

The social partner approach borrows from both the above approaches and seeks to provide checks and balances to their respective excesses. The state plays a key role in setting the frameworks for the rights and responsibilities of the different partners, but works with the partners at different levels in concerting action. Planning and coordination are not from the top but through the concerted action of the different interest group bodies at national, regional, local and workplace levels. Coherence, consistency and transparency in provision and qualifications remain primary goals but these are sought through negotiating procedures that ensure maximal flows of information and equitable representation of legitimate interest groups (Green, 1995). Investment by individuals and employers may be encouraged by the use of similar instruments to those employed in the state-led model, but these are more often established through social partner negotiations at national, sectoral or local levels. The social partner approach promises the same advantages of planning and 'concertation' as with the state-led approach, but through wider participation in decisions and on the basis of a wider platform of information. However, it is subject to some of the same problems in terms of relative inflexibility and inertia, which can become more acute if consensus is hard to reach (Streeck, 1987 and 1997).

European post-compulsory education and training systems typically borrow from all these approaches and no one country fits a particular model precisely. They are also dynamic systems, moving over time from one place on the models' continuum to another. The dominant model of post-compulsory education and training in the European Union used to be the centralist, state-led model. At around 1980, this was the category into which one would have put most of the Nordic states, excepting perhaps Denmark, France and most of the Mediterranean states, many of whose systems have historically been influenced by France. Various hallmarks of the centralist model would have been identifiable, including strong central control over post-compulsory curricula and qualifications, state employment and deployment of teachers, strong institutional framing by government, bureaucratic regulatory control through inspection and licensing, low levels of local state and institutional autonomy, and the use of statutory measures to level employer investment in training. Secondary schooling was mainly in public comprehensive schools, teaching a broad curriculum, and the dominant institutional form of post-compulsory education was the school-based academic and vocational school (Green, Wolf and Leney, 1999).

Social partner-led systems were confined to a few countries that were German-speaking or geographically proximate to Germany – ie Germany, Austria, Switzerland and Denmark. These countries generally had in common high levels of unionization, strong traditions of craft and professional organization, heavily regulated labour markets and relatively high levels of social cohesion (Green, Wolf and Leney, 1999). The dominant political economy of these states in the post-Second World War period was influenced by the Erhardtian principles of the social market in Germany with neo-corporatist forms of concerted interest group bargaining based on legally empowered and encompassing employer and employee organizations at national, sectoral, local and workplace levels (Marquand, 1988; Streeck, 1997). Secondary schooling in these countries was mainly in public but selective schools and the dominant model of post-compulsory provision was the social partner based apprenticeship.

Market-led systems, based on regulation by contract and financial incentives and competitive quasi-market measures, had not yet been created at this time.

During the past fifteen to twenty years there have been some distinctive changes. The Nordic states have shifted substantially towards decentralized local and institutional control. Spain and Belgium have moved towards regional/linguistic community control. Centralist systems within the European Union are now largely confined to France, Greece, Luxembourg and Portugal. Quasi-market models, on the other hand, have grown in strength, representing the dominant form in the UK and the Netherlands, but also having considerable influence, particularly within northern and central Europe. Typical hallmarks of this model are school choice, local school management, institutional competition, performance-related funding, regulation by contract, funding regime and market relations, flexible and loosely regulated labour markets, and voluntarist training regimes (Green, Wolf and Leney, 1999). Only the social-partner based, regionalized systems have remained largely stable, but even here there are signs of change (Bynner and Silbereisen, 2000).

It is not easy to predict how far these shifts will continue in the future, but it is reasonably clear that different models will continue to coexist with the European Union. Lifelong learning systems are likely to remain stubbornly national despite the centripetal forces generated by globalization and supranational political organization. Education systems tend to be highly path dependent, partly because of the strong influence exercised by national cultures and political traditions and partly because they are embedded, particularly at the post-compulsory level, in networks of relations with labour markets and industrial structures, and these have not yet converged within the European Union (Caillods, 1994; Ashton and Green, 1996; Kelleher and Scott, 1996). We can, therefore, still identify different models and it is useful to assess some of the implications of different forms of governance and regulation for adult continuing training, by looking at the examples of France, Germany and the UK.

France – the state-led model of lifelong learning

Continuing vocational training (CVT) in France is characterized by a state-led system of social partnership regulation (Green *et al*, 1999). CVT regulation is based on a framework of statutory instruments (dating back to 1971) which lays out the roles, obligations and rights of the various partners in training, combined with a mesh of voluntary sectoral agreements between the social partners which tie parties to various actions and practices. These impose obligations on employers to contribute to collective training funds and to consult with Works Councils on training matters and entitlements for employees over training leave. They also involve a multiplicity of sectoral agreements linking recruitment and pay with qualification levels. The framework has been designed to promote equitable distribution of training costs between firms and to achieve a balance between meeting the skills needs of individuals, enterprises, sectors and regional economies.

Various state initiatives target support in specific areas. A 1984 Law for participation in the development of vocational training (EDDF) subsidized groups of small employers successfully submitting plans to enhance training efforts (initially for up to 40 per cent of training costs – now below 30 per cent). A training related tax credit was initiated in 1989 for firms undertaking intensified training programmes over a three-year period. The main lever of investment both from the state and from employers, however, is still the training levy. Currently enterprises of 10 or more employees must contribute a levy equivalent to 1.5 per cent of their payroll and smaller enterprises a levy equivalent to 0.15 per cent. Of the 1.5 per cent levy for larger enterprises, 0.9 per cent goes towards reimbursing employers for the costs of authorized forms of internal or external training (by approved suppliers) specified in their training plans, 0.4 per cent goes towards alternance training for new recruits, and 0.2 per cent towards individual training leave costs. Levies are collected by social partner mutual organizations (OPACIFs). Forty-six of these are at the sector level and 20 at the regional inter-professional level, thus providing a framework for encouraging both sector-specific and general professional skills (Greenhalgh, 1999). Employer investment in training is now, on average, well above the required level and, from the limited comparative data we have, it would appear that French enterprises organize more training hours than employers in many other European countries. A significant proportion of this training is likely to be general and non-specific to particular firms. By the mid-1980s, 10 per cent of all annual training hours were based on statutory paid leave (Greenhalgh, 1999).

The major benefit of this type of system is that it seeks to address perennial problems of market failure in training that lead both individuals and enterprises to under-invest. France tries to overcome externalities in training through public subsidy for training investment and by forming clubs of providers that distribute the costs of training and collectively decide on training priorities. Equitable sharing of costs prevents 'free-riding' by non-training employers and, in theory, encourages greater investment in training by employers. Other benefits are also claimed for this kind of social partner system. First, there are strong and transparent links between recruitment, promotion, pay and training which stimulate demand for training. Second, 'mutualization' of the levy and the forming of a common pool for CVT theoretically mean that training opportunities can be more equally distributed even in times of recession or downturn in certain sectors. Third, this type of system also allows for forward planning in relation to CVT. The social partners are able to set their overall objectives for the allocation of funds, as well as for enterprises setting out their own training plans. In

France, the Government keeps a careful watch on how levy money is spent – if it does not follow predetermined training plans, then the company may be asked to repay a proportion or all of the money claimed. There is thus a strong link between planning and social partnership arrangements.

Levies have strong detractors, particularly amongst business leaders. The compulsory levy was abandoned in the UK in most sectors in the early 1970s after repeated lobbying from employers and complaints that it was bureaucratic, prejudicial to small employers and not conducive to high-quality training (Sheldrake and Vickerstaff, 1987). The French system has also not been without its critics. It is often perceived as overly complex, and bureaucratic and there are concerns that the training market is being driven more by the financial concerns of the mutual organizations than by the skills needs of individuals and enterprises (Drake and Germe, 1994). However, it has been associated with increased investment in France. Expenditure by French firms on training as a proportion of wages more than doubled in the 17 years after the introduction of the levy (Greenhalgh, 1999), reaching an estimated average of 3.1 per cent of payroll by 1990. Most large firms admittedly invest much more than they are obliged to and would probably do so without the levy; but small-firm investment does appear to have been forced up by the levy.

Germany – the social partnership model

Germany provides the pre-eminent example of the social partnership model of lifelong learning. The apprenticeship system is jointly controlled by the state and the social partners, with the federal state setting the legal frame-work that determines the roles, rights and responsibilities of the different partners. An elaborate system of social partnership involves representatives of employers, employees, and educators, alongside the federal and regional state officials, at all tiers of the system, from the Federal to Lander and to shop-floor levels. The bodies that represent these groups at the different levels are variously responsible for determining the regulations and content of the different branches of the apprenticeship system at the federal level (BIBB), for administering and monitoring the delivery system at the local levels (Kammern and shop-floor and works council), and for the assessment and certification of the apprentices themselves (Kammern for training and Lander training committees for vocational education) (CEDEFOP, 1987).

The system has become comprehensive in scope, to a degree unmatched in other countries, through the delicate balancing and concerting of the interests and responsibilities of the different parties concerned. Employers generally support the Dual System because it provides a pool of skilled, occupationally socialized and relatively flexible labour at acceptable costs. Legal incentives play a part since Land laws frequently require firms employing young people in classified occupations to provide training according to the regulations. However, the major incentives for firms are internal. They want the skills that the system delivers and the costs of training have been generally acceptable since they are offset by savings accrued through trainee productivity, enhanced flexibility in labour deployment and the reduction of costs for future employee selection, induction and training (Wagner, 2000). Sectoral agreements reduce the risks of 'poaching' and reinforce company predispositions to regard training investment as both in their self-interest and a collective good worthy of support. Young people are motivated to train because the apprentice qualification gives access to a range of skilled jobs from which they would otherwise be excluded: federal law requires skilled qualifications for the practice of a wide range of occupations and sectoral agreements also tend to 'credentialize' access to jobs. Legal compulsion also plays a part in that young school leavers in many Lander are obliged to undertake continuing part-time education anyway. However, the incentives are, again, primarily non-coercive. Apprenticeships involve relatively low wages for several years, but the long-term benefits of the generally good quality training apprentices receive make this a worthwhile sacrifice.

The Dual System has been successful not only because of its broad coverage of most sectors of employment, but also because of its generally high quality. This is ensured by the tight specification of national standards through the tripartite BIBB and through the close monitoring of the process by chambers of commerce at the local level and by works councils at the firm level. Even the assessment system rests on joint social partner action, with training committees and teams of apprenticeship jurors at the Kammern representing different interests. Ubiquity and quality in the Dual System result in over 65 per cent of young people qualifying as skilled workers, with sound vocational skills and a solid foundation of general education. Having undergone a broad occupational training, apprentices have the technical skills and knowledge and the general professional socialization that will equip them to work in their chosen Beruf or in an allied occupation. They also have an educational foundation that prepares them for further training. Indeed, some 20 per cent of apprentices go on later to qualify as Meisters (Wagner, 2000). The Dual System as a whole thus not only serves the immediate skills needs of employers; it also acts to drive up levels of skills by converting most jobs into skilled occupations and creating a surplus of skills available for companies upgrading their work processes.

Continuing vocational training in Germany is also largely the responsibility of the social partners. Meister training typically occurs in state-run vocational institutions, but most of the training of employees occurs in firms. This is not compelled by statutory regulation, as in the case of the apprentice training, but it takes place against a background of legally entrenched social partner negotiation. At the company level, co-determination laws (Mitbestimmungen) give employee representatives rights alongside managers, shareholders and other stakeholders. According to the European Commission's Continuing Training in Enterprise Survey, all firms employing over five people must have works councils that must approve all hirings, dismissals, transfers, work allocations and alterations in the scale and speed of production. Furthermore, legislation in 1976 gave workers equal representation on supervisory boards of all companies with over 2,000 workers, with the shareholder's chairperson exercising the casting vote (Perkin, 1996). Company training decisions are thus the product of negotiation at company and shop-floor level. Investment in employee training is high both because of the mutually agreed commitment to high skills production and because sectoral agreements on pay bands for levels of work reduce the degree to which firms can poach employees trained by another company through enhanced pay offers.

The German social partnership system has certain drawbacks. Access to apprenticeship training is determined in the labour market and this provides a hierarchy of learning opportunities where women and children of immigrant families tend to be concentrated in less prestigious training occupations. There have, in the past, also been problems with the relative rigidity of the training system and with long gestation periods for the creation of new training specifications, although this problem is now being addressed. There are also concerns as to whether the high skills culture of firms in Germany will survive global economic pressures. Some firms are opting out of sectoral agreements, co-determination practices are beginning to weaken in some sectors and banks are beginning to rethink their customary role of providing the long-term patient capital to firms which underwrites the expensive traditional high-skills, high-wage culture. Most crucially, large German firms are becoming increasingly internationalized financially, with higher rates of foreign capitalization and more investment in operations based outside Germany, and all this could undermine the training culture.

Nevertheless, the German social partnership system has, to date, delivered high levels of post-compulsory participation in training. Two-thirds of German youth go through apprenticeship, and rates of adult in-company training are also high. According to the European Union Continuing Training in Enterprises Survey (EC, 1999), German firms in the sample organized 9.9 hours of training per 1,000 worked. Despite a sample biased against the high training sectors in Germany, this worked out almost as high as the French firms (11.1 hours) and higher than the Danish (8.1 hours) and UK (8.7 hours) firms. The result is a highly qualified labour force. Labour force survey statistics for 1997 show that 72.1 per cent of the population aged 16 to 64 in Germany had a qualification at craft level or higher, compared with only 37 per cent in the UK.

The UK market-led approach

Relative to the French and German examples, the UK approach to lifelong learning is still relatively market-driven, notwithstanding New Labour's increased emphasis on collaboration rather than competition amongst providers, and the renewed interest in regional planning (through the Regional Development Agencies and the proposed local Learning and Skills Councils) and partnerships (DfEE, 1998, 1999).

Initial and continuing training in the UK remains within a largely voluntarist model. There is no national training levy on firms, firms are not obliged to train employees (although there are now weakly enforced entitlements to paid training leave for young employees without level 2 qualifications), and adults have no statutory entitlements to training. Licence to practise laws are less extensive in the UK than in France and Germany and sectoral agreements concerning qualifications and pay for different occupations are both less wide-ranging and less enforced. Membership of employer organizations is not compulsory and encompassing, as in Germany, and neither employee not employer organizations have binding powers over their members. Given the relatively weak regulation of labour markets and high rates of labour mobility, combined with the lack of statutory instruments for company training, there are relatively weak incentives for employers to train or for individuals to invest in training.

Governments have adopted a number of measures to encourage individuals and employers to invest in training. The development of a national qualification system is designed to increase the portability and transparency of qualifications, making it easier for individuals to gain recognition of their skills and for employers to judge their value. Employers are encouraged to invest in training through exhortation, through their involvement in Training and Enterprise Councils, through tax rebates on training costs and through measures like 'Investors in People' which seek to disseminate good human resource development practice (although by 1997 only 26 per cent of larger (200+) firms had taken this up and only 13 per cent of firms with less than 50 employees). Individuals are encouraged to invest through tax exemptions on training expenditure, and through the availability of grants, loans and guidance. The take-up to date of Career Development Loans has been slight (only 0.5 per cent of the eligible workforce) and signs are that the Individual Learning Accounts, which involve government grants of £150, may suffer the same fate. However, it is certainly the case that more, and better quality, information and guidance are becoming available to school leavers and adults. Recent initiatives include the University for Industry (now termed Learning Direct), which will substantially increase both online and person-to-person sources of information on learning opportunities, and a restructuring of the advice and guidance systems.

The UK's market-led system of lifelong learning relies to a large extent on voluntary individual initiative and willingness to invest. Not only does the voluntary system eschew statutory embedding of rights and obligations; it also maintains low levels of public investment. Public spending on training for adults was a mere 0.1 per cent of GDP in the mid-1990s compared with 0.38 per cent in France. Recent policy trends seem unlikely to alter this pattern substantially. The 1998 White Paper measures include a wide array of new public investments, but for comparatively small sums. Instead, the strategy rests heavily on the wide dissemination of high-quality information in the hope that individuals and employers will exercise rational choice to invest in the longer term. Rising participation in higher education suggests that this form of education constitutes a safe bet for a proportion of the public. However, the very uneven take-up of work-related training amongst adults and the continuing exclusion of substantial parts of the adult population from further learning suggest that these assumptions may be overly optimistic in relation to more excluded groups. The market-led approach may well deliver learning efficiently to certain sections of the population. However, it would seem less likely than the other models to lead to an inclusive learning society.

Current trends in the European Union member states suggest there will continue to be substantial national diversity in approaches to lifelong learning. There are some pressures towards convergence. European Commission programmes in the area of higher education and vocational education and training encourage policy borrowing and harmonization between states to a limited degree. Common contexts, such as economic globalization, regionalism and demographic change encourage national policy makers to focus on similar issues. Most significantly, budgetary restraints in all countries force common thinking on efficiency and accountability. However, different approaches to lifelong learning will remain so as long as there are national differences in cultural traditions, political structure and, in particular, labour market structures and regulations. Such diversity presents opportunities as well as difficulties within Europe. Not least among the opportunities are the possibilities for rational investigation of the effects of the different policies and systems. Lifelong learning is a powerful mobilizing rhetoric, but it badly needs a more scientific foundation. Comparative analysis of the effects of different policies in different contexts is one way to address this.

References

Ashton, D and Green, F (1996) *Education, Training and the Global Economy*, Elgar, London

Bynner, J and Silbereisen, R (2000) *Adversity and Challenge in Life in the New Germany and England*, Macmillan, Basingstoke

Caillods, F (1994) Converging Trends amidst Diversity in Vocational Training Systems, *International Labour Review*, **133** (2), pp 241–57

Carnoy, M (1993) School Improvement: is privatization the answer?, in *Decentralization and School Improvement*, ed J Hannaway and M Carnoy, Jossey-Bass, San Francisco

CEDEFOP (1987) *The Role of Social partners in Vocational Training and Further Training in the Federal Republic of Germany*, CEDEFOP, Berlin

DfEE (1998) *The Learning Age: A renaissance for a new Britain*, DfEE, London

DfEE (1999) *Learning to Succeed: A new framework for post-16 learning*, DfEE, London

Drake, K and Germe, J-F (1994) *Financing Continuing Training: What are the lessons from international comparison? Synthesis Report*, CEDEFOP, Berlin

European Commission (EC) (1999) *Continuing Training in Enterprises: Facts and figures. European Training Youth*, EC, Brussels

Green, A (1995) The Role of the State and the Social Partners in VET Systems, in *Youth, Education and Work: World Yearbook of Education 1995*, ed L Bash and A Green, Kogan Page, London

Green, A and Steedman, H (1996) *Widening Participation in Further Education: Research and literature review*, Report to the Further Education Funding Council, Centre for Economic Performance, LSE, London

Green, A, Hodgson, A and Williams, G (1998) *Alternative Approaches to Funding Lifelong Learning*, OECD, Paris

Green, A, Wolf, A and Leney, T (1999) *Convergence and Divergence in European Education and Training Systems*, Institute of Education, University of London, London

Green, A *et al* (1999) *Financing VET*, Interim Report to CEDEFOP, CEDEFOP, Thessaloniki

Greenhalgh, C (1999) Adult vocational training and Government policy in France and Britain, *Oxford Review of Economic Policy*, **15** (1), pp 99–113

Kelleher, M and Scott, P (1996) Convergence and Fragmentation? Vocational Training within the European Union, *European Journal of Education*, **31** (4), pp 436–83

Marquand, D (1988) *The Unprincipled Society: New demands and old politics*, Cape, London

OECD (1996) *Lifelong Learning for All*, OECD, Paris

Perkin, H (1996) *The Third Revolution*, Routledge, London

Ranson, S (1994) *Towards the Learning Society*, Cassell, London

Sheldrake, J and Vickerstaff, S (1987) *The History of Industrial Training in Britain*, Avebury, Aldershot

Streeck, W (1987) Skills and the limits of neo-liberalism: the enterprise of the future as a place of learning, *Work, Employment and Society*, **3** (1), pp 89–104

Streeck, W (1997) German capitalism: Does it exist? Can it survive? *New Political Economy*, **2** (2), 1997

UNESCO (1996) *Learning – the treasure within*, Report of the International Commission on Education for the 21st Century, UNESCO, Paris

Wagner, K (2000 forthcoming) The German apprenticeship system under strain, in *The German Skills Machine*, ed P Culpepper and D Finegold, Berghahn Books

Part 2
Challenges in the UK context

4

The challenge of widening participation in lifelong learning

Ann Hodgson

Introduction

The large number of recent national and international policy documents that advocate increasing participation in post-compulsory education and training testifies to the fact that this is a major policy focus for many countries in Europe and beyond (eg OECD, 1985, 1996; European Commission 1995, 1997; DfEE, 1996, 1998;). The allied but slightly different imperative to widen participation in lifelong learning is a more recent arrival on the national policy agendas of many countries, including the UK, although it has formed part of the debate in adult and community education circles in this country and beyond for many years as part of a broad social justice and access agenda (Tuijnman, 1996).

Policies that are designed to widen as well as to increase participation clearly bring with them a new set of challenges for policy makers and practitioners involved in post-compulsory education. So too does the emphasis on lifelong learning, which might be seen as a series of connected formal and informal learning experiences or episodes, as opposed to a focus simply on formal education and training provision organized and delivered by specialist providers. This chapter seeks to explore what these challenges might mean for policy makers and practitioners within the UK context. The chapter will consist of five sections and will draw on a series of interviews with post-16 education providers in the UK to illustrate some of the practical challenges both practitioners and policy makers face in this area. The first section of the chapter will examine some of the national and international debates about widening participation in lifelong learning. Section two will look at the current position in relation to widening participation in this country. The chapter will then go on, in section three, to lay out some of the major barriers to widening participation in lifelong learning, dividing these into 'internal' barriers which pertain to the education and training system itself and 'external' barriers which lie beyond that system. Here I will make particular reference to the views of post-16 providers, since they clearly play a major role in the realization of lifelong learning in this country. Section four looks at the effects that some of the UK Government's policies in the area of widening participation, discussed briefly in Chapter 1 of this book, are having on post-compulsory education and training providers in the UK. The chapter concludes by identifying ten major challenges for the UK's education and training system as a whole if the Government's goal of widening participation in lifelong learning is to be achieved.

The debates about widening participation in lifelong learning

The case for increasing participation in post-compulsory education and training has been argued eloquently elsewhere (OECD, 1996; Green, Wolf and Leney, 1999). It has also been used by national governments in many countries to lobby for more resources for post-compulsory education and training (OECD, 1998; Green *et al*, 1999). What I wish to focus on here is the way in which over the past couple of years national policy debates in this country, as in others within the European Union, have moved slightly beyond this position towards an interest in *widening participation* in lifelong learning to those who have traditionally not participated in education and training. This new set of debates still forms part of the older international human capital debate which uses evidence of broad-ranging economic, demographic, cultural and social change to argue for increasing participation in post-compulsory education and training as a way of increasing the skills base of the working population. However, there is now some evidence in more recent policy documents in the UK of a greater emphasis on how lifelong learning might be seen as a policy instrument for promoting greater social justice, equity and inclusion (Fryer 1997; Kennedy, 1997; DfEE, 1998; Welsh Office, 1998). The issue of how to widen access to lifelong learning opportunities, as later sections of this chapter illustrate, thus also becomes of particular interest.

However, it could be argued that within this new set of debates about widening participation in lifelong learning, the focus at national government policy level is still narrow in comparison with earlier debates about lifelong learning in adult and community education.[1] Five dimensions of narrowness can be identified.

First, the current debates tend to revolve largely around policies designed to boost post-compulsory education and training. For this reason, they are often locked into the logic of remediation, rather than taking a longitudinal approach to lifelong learning that builds upwards from nursery education and attempts to look at what each phase of education has to contribute to the overall goal of lifelong learning.

Second, there is a preoccupation with economic rather than social outcomes from lifelong learning that leads to an emphasis on rates of return to, rather than on the wider social benefits of, learning. The concept of lifelong learning has thus often been quite narrowly defined and portrayed in national and international literature with a major focus on securing economic competitiveness, although some countries (eg Sweden, Norway) have seen it as an all-age concept and have also stressed the importance of personal development and democracy (OECD, 1998).

Third, in national policy documents learning is often equated with what takes place within the formal education and training system rather than with a broader definition of learning that also includes those experiences and activities that occur outside educational institutions and at the interface between education, work and the wider community. The latter definition begins to challenge the somewhat arbitrary boundaries between educational institutions, as well as raising issues of what the concepts of learning and participation actually mean for policy makers and providers of lifelong learning.

Fourth, much of the discussion about, as well as the policies on, lifelong learning relates to the individual rather than to social groups or to society as a whole. Although there have been wider debates about how lifelong learning can help to transform societies, debates about and policies for widening participation in lifelong learning have largely revolved around the role of the individual in relation to educational opportunities. This again has meant that discussions on rates of return to education and training have dominated the debate, opening up issues surrounding the rights and responsibilities of the individual in funding her/his own education and training (eg NCIHE, 1997; DfEE, 1998; OECD, 1998). Alongside these policy debates, some of the wider debates about learning for democracy and for critical engagement with political processes, which form the backdrop to much of the liberal adult education literature, have been reduced to discussions about issues of self-fulfilment, employability, confidence building and active citizenship.

Finally, and related to the last point, the present policy focus on widening access to lifelong learning has been criticized by many academics for uncritically accepting some of the contentious assumptions that underlie the debate itself – the drive for economic growth, the need for flexibility and the existence of 'choice' for all individuals (eg Edwards, 1997; Williamson, 1998). They argue that because lifelong learning has been seen by many national governments, including our own, as a possible and useful policy response to the type of economic and societal change forced on them by international trends such as globalization, the need for flexibility and constant change has been seen as a given rather than as something that is open to question or challenge. It could be argued, therefore, that because lifelong learning has become so universally accepted in policy debate as a concept and as a goal for governments, this, in itself, has brought about the move towards a focus on who is not participating in education and training and what can be done to remove barriers to their participation. On the one hand, this move could be viewed as a benevolent step towards greater equity and inclusion, with an emphasis on policies that promote equality of opportunity in relation to education, employment and the material goods that accompany them. On the other hand, because the current debates on widening participation have tended, as suggested earlier, to revolve around the rights and responsibilities of the individual, these same policies might also be seen as a way of creating a no excuses or 'zero tolerance' attitude towards those individuals who do not want to participate in this way. The one option that is not allowed, it seems, is to opt out of the concept and goal of lifelong learning: even challenging the supremacy and legitimacy of the aim of widening participation in lifelong learning might therefore be considered subversive. The danger of this approach is that it opens up the potential for placing the blame for social exclusion and poverty on the non-participating individual, rather than looking to broader societal trends and issues.

The current policy debates about widening participation in lifelong learning might thus be seen as having an instrumental side – everyone has to participate in order to benefit society as a whole (particularly in terms of wealth creation) – and a more altruistic side – there are those who have consistently missed out and involvement in learning is the major way to redress the balance. The problem with this latter view is that there are other factors – class, race, gender (and their effects on the economic status of the individual or family group), the role of the labour market and the economy – that also need to be tackled and which lifelong learning policies alone will not be able to address (Coffield, 1997; Macrae, Maguire and Ball, 1997).

Opening up the possibilities for participation in education and training on its own will, therefore, be unlikely to bring about the type of economic and social changes that many governments, including our own, appear to expect. There will need to be structural changes that go beyond the reach of education and training policy, as well as realistic incentives to participate in lifelong learning and the creation of better access to learning opportunities. As we shall see from later parts of this chapter, in many countries, including the UK, it is the second and third of these, rather than the first, that are currently being addressed through lifelong learning policy initiatives.

Widening participation in lifelong learning in the UK – some key statistics

Research into participation in education and training in the UK, often reflecting the approach taken by international studies, has tended to be rather fragmented, with different researchers and government agencies focusing on discrete phases or types of education – initial post-compulsory education (particularly 16–25 year olds), further education, higher education or adult education. This has tended to obscure the 'big picture' in relation to participation in lifelong learning and has often meant that policies have been based on a snapshot taken from a particular angle. Moreover, because many of the statistics have been collected from the viewpoint of a particular sector of the education and training system, what we have, for the most part, is a picture of participation in formal education and training, rather than a picture of participation in lifelong learning. Studies undertaken by those involved in the field of adult education have attempted to look more broadly at lifelong learning rather than simply education and training (eg Sargant, 1991; Sargant *et al*, 1997; La Valle and Finch, 1999), but they have also often run into difficulties about what counts as learning rather than, say, leisure.

Arguably, one of the key changes that will be needed to accompany a policy focus on widening participation in lifelong learning will be a more unified research effort into patterns of participation over the whole lifespan. In the absence of this type of research base, however, here I will look briefly at a sample of key statistics from different parts of the education and training system in the UK which taken singly and together tend to suggest that there are still deep divisions between those who participate in education and training and those who do not and, more worryingly, between those who are likely to participate in the future and those who are not. Moreover, if participation is seen not only as gaining access to education and training opportunities, but also as the possibility of achieving a qualification or other learning outcome that makes a difference to future economic and social life chances, then, as we will see, the divide between those who participate and those who do not might be seen as even greater.

Initial post-compulsory education and training

Statistics on participation and attainment for 16–19 year olds suggest that the post-compulsory education and training system has, over the past five years, moved into a distinctive new phase which has been described elsewhere as 'system slowdown' (Hodgson and Spours, 2000). This term is used to denote a situation in which there is little or no growth in virtually all the major indicators of participation and achievement for the 16–19 year old age group. This period started in 1994 with the peaking of full-time participation rates at 16 following several years of strong growth. In the years since, the plateauing trend has moved to full-time participation at the ages of 17 and 18, to higher education participation rates and to attainment rates in 16–19 qualifications. Most recently, there are signs that the number of young people entering Modern Apprenticeships may also be peaking (DfEE, 1999a). It must also, of course, remain a source of concern that approximately 9 per cent of 16–18 year olds are neither in employment nor in education and training, with a further 17 per cent in a job that offers no formal education or training (SEU, 1999). Moreover, participation in full-time education for 16–19 year olds is low in comparison with the majority of OECD countries (OECD, 1996) and, perhaps more importantly for the discussion here, is still strongly related to socio-economic group. In 1997, for example, participation rates for young people with parents in higher level occupations (professional/managerial) were over 20 percentage points higher than those for young people whose parents were employed in semi-skilled or unskilled occupations (Payne, 1998).

There are those who challenge the prolongation of initial post-compulsory education (Schuller, 1998). However, I would argue that while *the length of initial education continues to be the best single predictor of participation in adult learning'* (Sargant *et al*, 1997: vii), increasing, and particularly widening, participation in initial post-compulsory education should remain a focus of government policy in the UK.

Further education colleges

Another set of interesting and illuminative statistics was collected by the Further Education Funding Council in 1997 (FEFC, 1997) as part of its focus on widening participation. What the FEFC study demonstrates is that the type of broad categories that have often been used for monitoring equal opportunities (gender, race and so on) need to be more sensitively broken down to paint a more textured picture of patterns of participation on which widening participation policies or strategies can be developed. The study found not only that certain groups were less likely to participate in further education:

- people without qualifications;
- the unemployed;
- women from low-income groups, and those who are lone parents;
- certain groups of men, including white men in low-income groups;
- some minority ethnic groups, including refugees;
- those over 50;
- people with literacy and/or numeracy difficulties;
- people with learning difficulties and/or disabilities from minority ethnic groups;
- people with profound and multiple learning difficulties and/or disabilities;
- adults with mental illness;
- young people with emotional and behavioural difficulties;
- ex-offenders;
- part-time and temporary workers;
- unskilled manual workers (FEFC, 1997);

but that there were also disturbing trends in relation to the way that certain students progressed or achieved even once they had taken the step of entering a further education college. Adults on full-time or part-time courses who receive some kind of benefit, for example, have significantly higher than average withdrawal rates and lower than average achievement rates and withdrawal rates are higher than average for students from some minority ethnic groups, such as black male Caribbean students and full-time students of Pakistani origin, than they are for others.

Higher education

The idea that widening participation might require more than simply putting into place policies that increase access to educational opportunities is also borne out by statistics that were gathered for the National Committee of Enquiry into Higher Education (NCIHE, 1997). Reports 5 and 6 (Coffield and Vignoles, 1997; Robertson and Hillman, 1997) suggest that although the numbers of young people entering higher education has grown significantly over the past couple of decades, with approximately one in three young people progressing into higher education from school or college, there is still a predominance of learners from higher socio-economic groups entering higher education and successfully gaining qualifications. Furthermore, there is a marked difference in the type of universities and courses that are being accessed by learners from different socio-economic backgrounds, as well as the rates of return to higher education for certain groups. So, for example, there are now equal proportions of men and women in higher education, but women are under-represented on postgraduate courses and at all levels in academic staffing. Ethnic minority students (with notable exceptions for certain groups, such as Bangladeshis, Black-Caribbean and Black-other) are better represented in higher education, in terms of their proportion of the whole population than are white students, but they are largely to be found in post-1992 universities and also appear to gain less economically from their higher education qualifications.

Lifelong learning

As mentioned earlier, the majority of participation studies tend to relate to a particular phase or type of education and to analyse statistics related to participation in formal educational provision. Three recent studies (RSA, 1996; Beinart and Smith, 1998; La Valle and Finch, 1999; Tuckett and Sargant, 1999) take a slightly different approach by collecting and analysing data on participation in all types of learning in both formal and informal contexts and by attempting to gain a picture of future intentions about learning, as well as patterns of current engagement with learning.

What the most recent of these surveys shows is that only 25 per cent of the total population in the UK is currently engaged in learning: a figure that, according to Tuckett and Sargant, represents no change since a similar survey was carried out in 1996 (Sargant et al, 1997). There are similar findings too in relation to the nature of those who participate in learning and those who do not, so that despite national government policies designed to widen participation, the conclusion of the earlier survey also still rings true in 1999:

> Whilst the UK may aspire to transform itself into a learning society in which all participate, the experience on the ground is that the learning divide is as marked today as it has ever been. Age, class, previous educational experience and where you live all affect access to learning, and the confidence to join in.
>
> (Tuckett, 1997: v)

Nor do the survey findings about learners' intentions to undertake some form of study in the future give great cause for optimism. While nearly three-quarters of those currently learning wish to continue doing so, fewer than 10 per cent of those who have done no learning since school say they are likely to engage in any form of learning in the future.

It could be argued that these figures, together with those cited earlier in this section of the chapter, point to the existence of considerable and seemingly intractable barriers to widening participation, promoting progression and raising levels of achievement in lifelong learning in the UK. What the following section of this chapter attempts to do is to use the views of 12 post-16 providers from adult, further and higher education institutions in different parts of England, gathered through telephone interviews undertaken during the summer term 1999, to examine some of these barriers in more depth.

Barriers to widening participation in lifelong learning – the post-16 provider's perspective

Despite what has been said earlier about the importance of seeing lifelong learning as more than what takes place in educational institutions, a recent survey of adult learning pathways (La Valle and Finch, 1999) indicates that many of the obstacles to learning that adults themselves identify relate to a lack of confidence in their ability to learn which often stems from damaging experiences of formal education or lack of qualifications. Ensuring that learning environments are positive, stimulating and supportive is thus of paramount importance in promoting wider participation in lifelong learning.

The post-16 providers I interviewed from all three sectors – adult, further and higher education – were prepared to admit that their practices (or at least the practices within their institutions) might be seen as partially responsible for some of the barriers to widening participation and particularly to successful progression and achievement. In the discussion below I will refer to these as *internal* issues. However, interviewees also highlighted a number of other issues they felt constituted significant barriers to widening participation that relate more to the context in which educational institutions find themselves and over which they felt they had little if any control. These I will refer to as *external* issues. In addition, there are, as we shall see, areas where internal and external barriers overlap and reinforce one another, thus increasing the overall challenge of widening participation in lifelong learning.

Internal issues

Many of the issues that immediately sprang to interviewees' minds when they were responding to my questions about what they saw as the barriers to widening participation were of a very practical kind, such as the strait-jacket of timetables, term times and, in some cases, staff contracts, which continue to prevent many institutions from organizing more flexible provision. In the higher education institutions (and some further education colleges) practitioners felt that managers often did not appreciate the need for ongoing specialist guidance and counselling for new learners, as well as more straightforward information giving. There is also a real issue about providing the type of intensive ongoing support that many learners require (AUCC, 1999). For adult and further education providers the type of accommodation that is available to them is often seen as a barrier, particularly for many of the more 'fragile participants' who have been turned off by school and need to be able to study in a non-school environment. There are also, of course, particular problems in relation to accommodation and transport for providers of all types in rural communities. A slightly less cited barrier, although one that the managers I interviewed in the traditional further and higher education institutions all eventually stressed, was the lack of innovative, inspirational staff who would be open to using new approaches to learning and teaching in order to motivate the different types of students who might be attracted by strategies for widening participation.

However difficult some of these practical issues may be to address, they pale into insignificance when compared with some of the more fundamental cultural issues that interviewees gradually began to mention as they reflected more deeply on the barriers to widening participation in their institution.

One of the most frequently cited of these cultural issues, which relates mainly to higher education institutions, but which can also exist in some further education institutions, such as traditional sixth-form colleges, is that these institutions are continuing to pursue their traditional selective missions which often directly conflict with the concept or practice of widening participation. They are prepared to forgo national government financial incentives to widen participation both because they can afford to, since they are often over-subscribed, and because this is where their expertise lies. In such institutions, according to my respondents, lip service is often paid to the concept of widening participation – for example it is mentioned in the mission statement or responsibility for operationalizing it is hived off to certain individuals or programme areas – but the reality is 'business as usual'.

This issue is most prevalent in areas where there is still intense competition between providers for learners (particularly those learners who are most likely to stay on their course and to achieve a successful outcome), despite government exhortation and incentives to collaborate in the interests of life-long learning.

Another deep-rooted cultural issue, which interviewees from higher education institutions raised, is the existence of a strongly male-dominated and white, middle-class environment in higher education. This is perceived not only as a barrier to widening participation for women and ethnic-minority groups in higher education institutions themselves, but also as a deterrent to the progression and achievement of women and ethnic-minority students and academics more broadly. When one considers some of the statistics in this area – for example that only 9 per cent of UK professors are women and that women are about three times less likely to be professors than men when age and publication rate are taken into account (Park, 1992), the extent of this particular cultural barrier is self-evident.

External issues

The most immediate set of externally determined barriers to widening participation that interviewees mentioned was, not surprisingly, related to lack of money for making the necessary changes required. All the post-16 providers I interviewed felt that they had suffered a reduction in real terms in their capital and recurrent budgets as a result of the period of rapid expansion and 'marketization' of further and higher education that began in the early 1990s. Although they appreciated that the current administration was beginning to address this issue by providing more resources for further and higher education, there was still a feeling that money was tight. In addition, further education providers clearly articulated a strong sense of unfairness in terms of the lower levels of funding they were receiving both for 16–19 years olds (in comparison with the amounts being allocated to school sixth forms) and for students on higher education courses (in comparison with the units of funding allocated to higher education providers). All those I interviewed, but particularly practitioners from adult or further education institutions, stressed how expensive and long-term reaching out to non-traditional learners is and complained that many of the widening participation 'pots of money' were both small-scale and short-term. They therefore argued that they did not have the spare capacity to create the kind of flexibility, provision and infrastructure that a successful widening participation agenda would require.

Moreover, poverty still remains a major barrier to participation, progression and successful completion for both 16–19 year olds and, more particularly, for those returning to learning as mature students (Callender, 1999).

A less obvious but equally powerful set of issues that post-16 providers identified as barriers to widening participation relates to what has been described elsewhere as the 'Conservative legacy' (Hodgson and Spours, 1999). The unplanned nature of expansion in further and higher education during the early 1990s left many providers with different types of skewed student cohorts, making it more difficult for them to change direction in terms of their student intake. Some of the providers from further and higher education institutions claimed they already had a significant majority of 'widening participation students', for example, while others had next to none. This polarization tends to exacerbate the inertia within the education and training system as a whole and allows institutions at the elite end of the scale to remain selective rather than addressing the demands of the Government's widening participation drive. The position is not helped by the way that national league tables are constructed and used as a way of judging education providers and increasing competition between them.[2] New Labour may claim that it wishes to move from a national culture of selection to one of inclusion in post-compulsory education and training, but the measures that it has employed to 'uphold standards' and improve quality are, arguably, directly working against widening participation (Chapter 8 contains a more detailed discussion of this issue).

Finally, many of the post-16 providers with whom I spoke felt that the current qualifications system often proved a barrier rather than a facilitator of access and progression for many learners. Its sheer complexity, the disjuncture between the qualifications framework for higher education and the rest of the education system, the inaccessibility and size of many of the qualifications and the system's division into three distinct tracks – general (academic), general vocational and vocational – with a different status accorded to each track, do little to support the concept or reality of lifelong learning. Moreover, the relationship between the qualifications system (particularly vocational qualifications) and the labour market still remains a highly problematical one in terms of both rates of return to learning and the role of employers in skills development (Keep and Mayhew, 1997; Rees, 1997).

Effects at provider level of national policies for widening participation

Despite this somewhat formidable set of internal and external barriers that post-16 providers saw as standing in the way of the Government's expressed desire to widen participation in lifelong learning, they did, in all cases, express some optimism that change was beginning to happen as a result of New Labour's policies in this area.

As Chapter 1 has indicated, widening participation in lifelong learning has been one of New Labour's major policy thrusts in the area of post-compulsory education and training. Extra money has been made available to providers of adult, further and higher education for this purpose and has come in the form of grants for specific projects, but also through changes to the per capita amount for students from certain postcode areas alongside an increase in the amount of support for individual students through Access Funds, Educational Maintenance Allowances and Individual Learning Accounts (although these initiatives should be seen in the light of the introduction of fees and loss of maintenance grants for undergraduate courses in higher education). In addition, the cap on the number of students entering higher education has been lifted with a resumption in the growth of sub-degree level courses.

The majority of the providers I interviewed said that it was too early to judge what effects these national policies for widening participation were having on their institution. In all cases, however, they felt there were indications of change, if only in the type of the debates that were now taking place inside their organizations. The nature of the change taking place varied very much according to the sector, but also related to the historical mission of the particular provider. The adult education providers interviewed, for example, felt that many of the practices they had been pursuing for a number of years were now being recognized, valued and extended and that this sector had specific expertise to offer other post-16 providers. Indeed, one adult-education provider expressed a fear that her institution might now be in competition with others for funding for this area of work. On the whole, further and higher education providers had begun to widen participation in certain curriculum areas and not in others. Most interviewees, particularly those from higher education, felt that there was still a long way to go and both felt that their funding regimes had often been driving them in the opposite direction for some time. There was a degree of cynicism among these providers as to how much the new type of funding levers designed to widen participation would stimulate real change. As one said, *'money does talk, but it depends on the amount of money and its proportion of the whole budget'*.

Nevertheless, there were a number of ways in which providers felt that they could perceive changes happening as a result of national policies on widening participation. These fall broadly into four areas: awareness raising and debate; collaboration and partnership; needs analysis, outreach and access; and changes to provision, delivery and learner support.

Awareness raising and debate

Several providers observed that their institutional mission statements and strategy documents now reflected the national focus on widening participation and that institutional targets were being used to increase the recruitment of certain groups of learners. In addition, some institutions were beginning to realize the need for management information systems that could track students against their entry qualifications in order to see progression and achievement patterns for different types of learners. However, this is still very new practice in most institutions, particularly higher education providers.

What is more prevalent in higher education institutions is that those that have traditionally used their Schools of Continuing Education as their 'outreach arm' are now looking to spread this type of provision and practice more widely throughout their organization.

Most of the providers interviewed commented that the Government's focus on widening participation and its policies in this area had stimulated debates about widening participation. A spin-off from this has been greater credibility and status for those involved in widening participation work as well as for the students with whom they work. One further education provider spoke about a *'level of seriousness'* about outreach and access work: what had previously been seen as *'grotty'* was now considered *'sexy and appropriate'* and she felt that she was *'planning a future which I want to be part of'*.

Collaboration and partnerships

Part of New Labour's avowed strategy for widening participation in lifelong learning is to create a seamless web of educational opportunities for learners. Collaboration and partnership have been seen as key mechanisms for achieving this aim (DfEE, 1998, 1999b). Several providers gave examples of how this was working in practice both through Lifelong Learning Partnerships and through more ad hoc consortia or federations of adult, further and higher education providers in a particular geographical area. This type of partnership allows for complementarity rather than competition, with each institution playing a particular role in relation to the others in the federation. The benefit for the learner is that progression routes and possibilities, which are often complex and unintelligible to the non-professional, are made more explicit.

These types of organizational arrangements and partnerships indicate the beginnings of a genuine desire to collaborate rather than to compete, but they are often bureaucratic and time consuming and driven by financial imperatives or sweeteners. Moreover, the competitive ethos that held sway under the Conservative administration is, according to several of the practitioners I interviewed, still very much alive and well.

Needs analysis, outreach and access

Not surprisingly, several of the post-16 providers I spoke to mentioned that there was an increasing emphasis on needs analysis, outreach work and access within their institutions as a result of Government policies for widening participation. In higher education, the focus has been largely on researching issues related to widening participation, identifying the needs of under-represented groups, considering quotas for admissions in certain curriculum areas, exploring the possibilities of accreditation of prior experience and/or learning and organizing staff development for admissions officers. In adult and further education the emphasis has been more on the expansion of outreach work, with more attention to marketing and publicity in relation to targeted groups of learners.

Changes to provision, delivery and learner support

From my conversations with post-16 providers, it would appear that changes to provision and delivery to support widening participation are taking place, but again these are less evident in the more traditional universities or departments of universities. Typical developments include: the expansion of provision that is tied into credit accumulation and transfer systems (CATs systems); an increase in part-time, evening and weekend provision; the introduction of key-skills programmes in some higher and many further education institutions; designing learning programmes with integral study support; and the development of Entry Level provision in some FE colleges for those learners who would not have traditionally been able to gain accreditation for their learning. In general, it seems that more money is being spent on facilities such as Open Learning Centres, advice and guidance systems, learning support provision and programmes using information and communications technology (ICT) in order to encourage learners to study at home and in the community as well as in educational institutions. According to a couple of the practitioners I interviewed, this desire to widen participation to part-time learners by increasing institutional flexibility is also finally focusing institutions' attention onto the needs and wants of part-time staff who often play a key role in this area.

Taken on its own, each of these four areas of change may not appear particularly significant, but as a whole they could be seen as constituting the beginnings of a real strategy for widening participation. However, none of the institutions in my small sample was making changes in all areas and I suspect these institutions are not untypical of other post-16 providers. What is emerging as a result of New Labour's focus on widening participation in lifelong learning, therefore, is the development of a set of practices that is unevenly spread both across and within different post-16 provider institutions, but which nevertheless represents a small movement towards a commonly understood and, in many cases, desired goal. If, as has been argued elsewhere (McGivney, 1992), education providers themselves often represent one of the barriers to widening participation in lifelong learning, then this small movement should be greeted with some optimism. However, as has been suggested earlier in this chapter, the major problem still remains to tackle some of the wider social, cultural and economic barriers to widening participation that do not lie within the control of education providers.

Ten potential challenges for the education and training system as a whole

From what has been said above, it is clear that widening participation in life-long learning cannot be seen simply as a task for education and training providers or policy makers. Nevertheless, I would argue that there are at least 10 key challenges that those concerned with the education and training system will have to tackle if the Government's aim of widening participation in lifelong learning is to succeed:

1. ensuring that the new local and regional infrastructures outlined in *Learning to Succeed* (DfEE, 1999b) work in practice and address the challenge of developing new and different contexts for learning as well as the interfaces between these and traditional sites of learning (see Chapter 9 for further discussion of this issue);
2. developing a qualifications system to support lifelong learning (see Chapter 8 for details of what this might involve);
3. providing adequate financial support for all those who wish to participate (see Chapter 5 for a fuller discussion of this issue);
4. building an effective infrastructure of post-16 providers with sufficient resources, accommodation and staffing to meet the needs of an increasing number and diversity of lifelong learners;
5. finding the right balance between meeting the needs and wants of individual learners while retaining a strong infrastructure of providers in all areas;
6. debating the missions of different types of providers in order to increase complementarity and reduce competition;
7. training lecturers, support workers, managers and administrators in post-16 institutions in the new skills required to support lifelong learning;
8. coping with the additional learner support issues thrown up by widening participation;
9. understanding the potential and limitations of ICT for widening participation in lifelong learning;
10. supporting a research programme to track participation in lifelong learning over the whole lifespan and to examine the social as well as the economic effects of widening participation in lifelong learning.

The chapters that follow will begin to explore to what extent New Labour's policies are addressing these areas.

Notes

1. The term lifelong learning has not always been used in these debates (Sutton, 1996). Earlier terms, such as 'recurrent education' and 'lifelong education', also regularly occur and although not entirely synonymous with lifelong education are similar enough to be considered as part of a general debate in this area.

2. League tables for schools and colleges, for example, stress key indicators that relate to pupil performance in national examinations, such as GCSEs, A Levels and GNVQs. Clearly it is easier (and cheaper) for schools and colleges to demonstrate success in these terms with pupils who enter their establishments with higher levels of attainment in national tests. League tables for higher education institutions make use of different types of indicators that relate to their performance in research as well as teaching. Although these indicators are changing to take widening participation goals, among others, into consideration, there is still little incentive for institutions that are oversubscribed in terms of student applications and have a high research rating to make changes to their admissions policies or internal practices.

References

Association for University and College Counselling (AUCC) (1999) *Degrees of Disturbance: The new agenda – the impact of increasing levels of psychological disturbance amongst students in higher education*, British Association for Counselling, Rugby

Beinart, S and Smith, P (1998) *National Adult Learning Survey 1997*, Research Report 49, DfEE, London

Callender, C (1999) *The Hardship of Learning: Students' income and expenditure and their impact on participation in further education*, FEFC, Coventry

Coffield, F (1997) *Can the UK Become a Learning Society?*, King's College lecture

Coffield, F and Vignoles, A (1997) Widening participation in higher education by ethnic minorities, women and alternative students: Report 5 in National Committee of Inquiry into Higher Education (1997), *Higher Education in the Learning Society*, NCIHE, London

DfEE (1996) *Lifetime Learning: A policy framework*, DfEE, London

DfEE (1998) *The Learning Age: A renaissance for a new Britain*, Cm 3790, DfEE, London

DfEE (1999a) *Statistical First Release 46/99 – TEC delivered government supported training: Work-based training for young people and for adults in England and Wales*, DfEE, London

DfEE (1999b) *Learning to Succeed: A new framework for post-16 learning*, DfEE, London

Edwards, R (1997) *Changing Places? Flexibility, lifelong learning and the learning society*, Routledge, London

European Commission (1995) *Teaching and Learning – Towards the learning society*, European Commission, Brussels

European Commission (1997) *Learning in the Information Society: Action plan for a European initiative*, European Commission, Brussels

FEFC (1997) *How to Widen Participation: A guide to good practice*, FEFC, Coventry

Fryer, B (1997) *Learning for the 21st Century: First Report of the National Advisory Group for Continuing Education and Lifelong Learning*, NAGfCELL, London

Green, A, Wolf, A and Leney, T (1999) *Convergence and Divergence in European Education and Training Systems*, Institute of Education, University of London, London

Green, A *et al* (1999) *The Financing of Vocational Education and Training*, CEDEFOP, Thessaloniki

Hodgson, A and Spours, K (1999) *New Labour's Educational Agenda: Issues and policies for education and training from 14+*, Kogan Page, London

Hodgson, A and Spours K (2000) Expanding higher education in the UK: from 'system slowdown' to 'system acceleration', *Higher Education Quarterly*, **54** (4)

Keep, E and Mayhew, K (1997) Vocational education and training and economic performance, in *Britain's Economic Performance*, ed T Buxton, T Chapman and P Temple, Routledge, London

Kennedy, H (1997) *Learning Works: Widening participation in further education*, FEFC, Coventry

La Valle, I and Finch, S (1999) *Pathways in Adult Learning*, Research Report RR 137, DfEE, London

Macrae, S, Maguire, M and Ball, S (1997) Whose 'learning' society? A tentative deconstruction, *Journal of Education Policy*, **12** (6), pp 499–509

McGivney, V (1992) *Tracking Adult Learning Routes*, NIACE, Leicester

National Committee of Inquiry into Higher Education (NCIHE) (1997) *Higher Education in the Learning Society*, NCIHE, London

Organisation for Economic Co-operation and Development (OECD) (1985) *Education and Training Beyond Basic Schooling*, OECD, Paris

OECD (1996) *Lifelong Learning for All*, OECD, Paris

OECD (1998) *Alternative Approaches to Financing Lifelong Learning*, OECD, Paris

Park, A (1992) Women, Men and the Academic Hierarchy: Exploring the relationship between rank and sex, *Oxford Review of Education*, **18** (3), pp 227–39

Payne, J (1998) *Routes At Sixteen: Trends and choices in the nineties: An analysis of data from the England and Wales Youth Cohort Study*, DfEE Research Report RR55, DfEE, London

Rees, G (1997) Vocational education and training and regional development: an analytical framework, *Journal of Education and Work*, **50** (2), pp 141–149

Robertson, D and Hillman, J (1997) Widening participation in higher education for students from lower socio-economic groups and students with disabilities, Report 6 in National Committee of Inquiry into Higher Education, *Higher Education in the Learning Society*, NCIHE, London

Royal Society of Arts (RSA) (1996) *Attitudes to Learning – MORI state of the nation poll: summary report*, RSA Campaign for Learning, London

Sargant, N (1991) *Learning and Leisure*, NIACE, Leicester

Sargant, N *et al* (1997) *The Learning Divide: A study of participation in adult learning in the UK*, NIACE, Leicester

Schuller, T (1998) Three steps towards a learning society, *Studies in the Education of Adults*, **30** (1), pp 11–20

Social Exclusion Unit (SEU) (1999) *Bridging the Gap: New opportunities for 16–18-year olds not in education, employment or training*, SEU, London

Sutton, P (1996) Lifelong and continuing education, in *International Encyclopaedia of Adult Education and Training*, ed A Tuijnman, 2nd edn, Pergamon, Oxford

Tuckett, A (1997) Foreword, in *The Learning Divide: A study of participation in adult learning in the UK*, ed N Sargant *et al*, NIACE, Leicester

Tuckett, A and Sargant, N (1999) *Marking Time: The NIACE survey on adult participation in learning 1999*, NIACE, Leicester

Tuijnman, A (1996) *International Encyclopaedia of Adult Education and Training*, 2nd edn, Pergamon, Oxford

Welsh Office (1998) *Learning is for Everyone*, HMSO, London

Williamson, B (1998) *Lifeworlds and Learning: Essays in the theory, philosophy and practice of lifelong learning*, NIACE, Leicester

5

Paying for lifelong learning: problems and possibilities

Gareth Williams

The problem of recognizing lifelong learning

Lifelong learning is a concept. This creates some difficulties in any discussion of how to pay for it. Money and the resources it represents are provided and used by people and institutions, not concepts. To make matters worse, lifelong learning is a fuzzy concept. Money, especially public money, must be spent with specific purposes in mind and accounted for in some detail. Which persons are recognized as lifelong learners in any particular context and which agencies are recognized as providing it?

In this context, it is instructive to look at the most reliable policy statement on education that the Government publishes each year, the Department for Education and Employment *Annual Departmental Report* (DfEE, 1999a) which now doubles as the official public statement of the Government's expenditure plans for education. The main body of the text contains several references to lifelong learning, including a long chapter entitled 'Lifelong learning and employability'. This is linked to the department's major Policy Objective 2, '*developing in everyone a commitment to lifelong learning, so as to enhance their lives, improve their employability in a changing labour market and create the skills that our economy and employers need*' (p 97). Objective 2 also includes further and higher education. These verbal texts are converted into numbers representing cash in Annex A, though to attempt to trace the process by which the words become numbers is to feel rather like poor Sisyphus trying to push his rock up the hill. The Objective 2 heading in Annex A accounts for nearly three-quarters of the total departmental expenditure in 1999/2000. Annex B converts the figures into cash for recognizable spending agencies like the Higher Education Funding Council (HEFC) and the Further Education Funding Council (FEFC), student loans, access funds and work-based training for young people. The 1999 Departmental Report is the first time that the links between Annex A, which lists expenditure by programme objectives, and Annex B, which shows who will be spending the money, has been reasonably transparent. In earlier years, understanding how Annex A – in effect the policy statements – was converted into Annex B – the policy instruments – was impossible for an outsider. It is still easier to believe that the number in Annex A is actually arrived at by adding up the items in Annex B and calling them Policy Objective 2. But that is how concepts work.

Successive expenditure plans also show how in public policy terms, the concept of lifelong learning developed in the late 1990s. In the 1997 DfEE annual report (DfEE, 1997: 8) the planned expenditure for the objective '*To encourage lifetime learning so that people can use their skills and knowledge to compete effectively in a changing labour market*' proposed expenditure under this heading of £20 million in 1999–2000. In March 1998, the objective had changed by a few words '*To encourage people to continue throughout their lives to develop their knowledge, skills and understanding and improve their employability in a changing labour market*' (p 10). This change in terminology raised the proposed spend from £20 million to about £9.4 billion. Then, by 1999, the objective had become that set out in the previous paragraph and the proposed expenditure increased to £11.3 billion.

The purpose of this illustration is not to criticize the DfEE or the Government. A huge amount of work goes into the annual departmental report and it had, by 1999, become an informative and useful document for anyone with a serious interest in the implementation of national policy. The intention is to help make the point that there is a distinct difference between writing text about lifelong learning as a concept and converting this into meaningful statements about paying for it. Concepts are almost infinitely elastic. Public funds, unfortunately, are not.

To increase the resource base for lifelong learning there are four main policy alternatives: to redefine the concept, to reallocate resources into lifelong learning from other parts of education without changing the concept of what it is, to reorganize it so that more learning is provided for any given input of resources or to raise additional funds – redefinition, reallocation, reorganization, raising resources.

Redefinition

As is apparent from the introduction to this chapter, the concept of lifelong learning has been undergoing a process of rapid redefinition. Few authors take the term literally, to mean a concern with all learning from 'womb to tomb'. Yet, for some purposes at least, it is helpful to do so. If the concept of lifetime learning really underpinned education and education policy, it would have implications for pre-school education and the whole of compulsory education. Learning also takes place in a wide variety of settings outside the formal schooling system – on the parent's knee, on the job, on the sports field, in front of the television set, in the pub, off the Internet, as well as in the school and college. Some learning is productive in that it helps individuals to develop personally, socially and economically. Some may be counterproductive, such as acquiring the ability to make terrorist bombs or more effective narcotic drugs. All these issues are philosophically debatable. Who says terrorist bombs for freedom fighters in a tyrannical regime are unproductive? But once public money is a central concern, it ceases to be a parlour game and precision becomes necessary over where the boundaries are being drawn, even if this means some degree of arbitrariness.

The practical questions for this chapter are how formal learning episodes need to be before they count and where lifelong learning begins. The answer to both questions must be pragmatic. Lifelong learning for purposes of public policy debate includes all learning activities that, in some circumstances at least, are eligible for public funding. This includes a wide range of learning in education and training establishments, but excludes many activities carried out by organizations such as the Women's Institute, churches, public house quiz teams and the sales and customer care activities of pharmaceutical and computer companies. Even this common-sense approach is not watertight, especially if international comparisons are involved. In Japan, where public funding plays a much smaller part in the finance of education and training generally than in European countries, a recent report on lifelong learning *conceptualises it in part as a lifestyle commodity encompassing attendance at conferences and a wide variety of recreational activities. One corollary of this is that the Japanese report is the most likely to consider a wide variety of private expenditures as forming part of the resources available for lifelong learning'* (OECD, 2000: para 16).

In public policy terms, this Japanese approach raises the question of whether there should be any interest in how grown-up people spend their own money. It seems unrealistic in the current British context to try to include all lifestyle activities that include any learning, though it may be desirable as a long-term objective.

However, it should also be noted that in the United States, although private funding is almost as prevalent as it is in Japan, many activities like conferences and activity holidays may be eligible for tax relief. Thus, although such recreational diversions do not qualify directly for public funding, they do so indirectly. Unquestionably, tax relief, both for employers and for households, is one of the possible instruments for encouraging private investment in continuing learning in the UK. However, advocates of lifelong learning will need to convince the financial sceptics that tax concessions do increase the overall spend on lifelong learning and not simply result in public funds relieving private individuals and organizations of some of the costs of what they would do anyway. Another disadvantage for some commentators is that tax relief helps only those who pay taxes: it does little to open lifelong learning opportunities for the socially excluded.

The more difficult boundary problem is at what age the funding of lifelong learning starts. Common sense decrees that the funding of compulsory education raises an entirely different set of issues from education and training beyond that level, which must be, in a strict sense, voluntary. In practice, the question is whether lifelong learning can be deemed to start at the end of compulsory education, at the age of 18 (still the legal age of majority for many purposes) or after initial further or higher education. More bluntly, is higher education a part of 'lifelong learning'? In many ways, the post-initial education option makes most sense in that it emphasizes the idea of lifelong learning as something supplementary to initial 'front end' education that takes place already. The concept then means something more than being merely a different way of organizing existing expenditure on education and training.

However, that solution is not entirely satisfactory for two reasons. The first is that a very large amount of initial higher education now takes place when people are considerably older than traditional higher education students.[1] Thus, what is initial education for some people is continuing education, or professional development for others. It may be that if this approach to lifelong learning were more widespread, many more people would choose to blur the distinction between initial education, work and continuing education.

Conversely, there is a case for claiming that the break should be made at 16, which is a point at which compulsory education ends in the UK and when young people are considered to be adults for some legal purposes. This is, in part, the approach being used in the emerging British Government policy in which education and training of 16 to 19 year-olds outside school sixth forms will be deemed to come under the lifelong learning umbrella (DfEE, 1999b). It remains to be seen whether there will be practical difficulties in effectively treating the education or training of some young people as being clearly part of their initial education, while for others it will be more closely linked to a lifelong learning system.

I believe that there is a fundamental difference between initial education of young people below the age of 18, for which it can reasonably be argued that the state should be prepared to take full responsibility, and the education and training of older people, where a substantial amount of personal choice must be allowed. One aspect of that choice should be the right for all individuals to delay all or part of their 'initial education' until later in life. One component of the concept of lifelong learning is, after all, that individuals should have a realistic chance of educating themselves further, or training to acquire new skills at any stage in their lives.

This chapter argues, therefore, that, as a funding issue, lifelong learning can most usefully be treated as all organized education and training for people above the age of 18 that is at least partly eligible for public funding. This has been accepted in large part by the Government in establishing the Learning and Skills Council (DfEE, 1999b), which will have a very wide range of responsibilities in funding learning outside higher education. The case to bring universities and degree-level education within the overall framework is the only one that remains to be argued.

However, one problem with broadening the definition of lifelong learning is that funding problems are not the same across the whole spectrum of lifelong learning. The issues in the funding of full-time university students are very different from those that need to be considered in providing retraining for those who become structurally unemployed in mid-career as a result of new technology. The broader the definition, the more ambiguities in any funding strategy.

As far as can be inferred from the DfEE annual report cited earlier in this chapter (DfEE, 1999a), public expenditure on 'lifetime learning' in practice consists of the expenditure of the HEFC, the FEFC and the Teacher Training Agency (TTA), government expenditure on student loans and a selection of much smaller expenditure heads of which the largest are concerned with youth training.

The new National Learning and Skills Council (NLSC), announced in the June 1999 White Paper (DfEE, 1999b) and which comes into operation in April 2001, along with 47 local learning and skills councils, is intended to be responsible for the distribution of all public funds for post-16 education and training with the exception of sixth forms in schools (at this point), and higher education (that is formal learning beyond NVQ Level 3 supported by the HEFCE). The NLSC will be responsible for the £5.2 billion that is disbursed currently by the Training and Enterprise Councils (TECs) (£0.8 billion), the FEFC (£3.3 billion) and £1.1 billion that is still currently routed through local authorities. This compares with about £4 billion disbursed annually by the HEFCE. In broad terms, the NLSC will be responsible for all of the programmes under DfEE Policy Objective 2, apart from the activities funded by the HEFCE.

The funding methodology of the new NLSC will need to take account of the needs of a very wide range of post-16 learners studying full time and part time for national and other qualifications and registered in public and private establishments and, in some circumstances, at home or in the workplace. There will also be scope for local variations to meet local skills shortages or particular groups of socially excluded people. The rapid development of various kinds of distance-learning packages that can be accessed through the Internet will complicate still further an intrinsically difficult problem.

It is inevitable that any new funding methodology will need to be driven primarily by demand for specific cost-effective learning from students and employers, moderated by regulations to ensure the quality of the learning programmes made available. However, although a necessary part of the methodology must be student demand driven funding, this will not be sufficient to ensure that the new framework meets all its objectives. Almost by definition special incentives will be necessary to enable and encourage people from socially excluded groups to take advantage of the opportunities available to them. An intrinsic difficulty in devising any publicly funded life-long learning system is that it is most likely to lead to those who have already derived most benefit from their initial education most eagerly seizing the opportunities to upgrade and update their skills (eg Coffield and Williamson, 1997). The gaps between the high-skill haves and the low-skill have-nots will tend to widen rather than narrow.

From an economic policy viewpoint, this dilemma is a more acute version of a problem that dogs all education beyond basic levels. How should the competing claims of equity and efficiency be balanced? From the standpoint of national efficiency, public funds spent on continuing education and training should ensure that there is the highest possible return on every pound spent. There can be little doubt that many of the highest returns to lifelong learning will come from enabling people at the leading edges of technology, or other professional and management practices, to keep abreast of global leaders. Information technology, medicine, law, accountancy, biotechnology and many other areas of professional work can make powerful claims for priority in resources for updating and upgrading. Unless clear political priorities are established, it is relatively easy to demonstrate that the returns to further training of highly skilled professionals are greater than the provision of more basic skills to those who never acquired high skills in the first place.

Learning to Succeed (DfEE, 1999b) emphasizes the desirability of enhancing both the skills levels of the workforce and the employability of young people and adults. It focuses on the need for partnership between the government, individuals, employers, providers and communities. It might be argued that employers and individuals will readily pay for the professional development of those who are already highly skilled and that the Government's efforts need to be more explicitly focused on those for whom the private returns are not so obvious.

To some extent, the first part of this strategy happens already. Even casual observation shows that large employers, at least, are more than willing to invest in the professional development of their senior managers and leading professionals. The difficulty is, and is likely to continue to be, with the smaller enterprises and the employees with lower levels of skills.

Reallocation

It is misleading to start any discussion of the finance of lifelong learning in the UK from the premise that it will be inordinately expensive, because learning by adults is a minority activity at present. There are currently nearly two million students in higher education, over four million in further education colleges and over one million registered for courses in adult education institutions. The probability that an 18-year-old school leaver will enter a qualification-related course in higher education at some time in his or her life is well over 50 per cent (Smithers and Robinson, 1996). The 1997 National Adult Learning Survey (Beinart and Smith, 1998) found that three-quarters of the 16–19 year-olds and over two-thirds of adults not in full-time education had been involved in a learning episode within the previous three years. This is a substantial majority and, even allowing for the preponderance of students in the younger age groups, provides some reason to believe that a comprehensive policy of lifelong learning need not be prohibitively expensive. This needs to be borne in mind when evaluating the reasons why people have difficulty in sustaining their learning and in considering where public funding can most usefully be directed.

Rapid technological and social change makes it desirable that most people experience some formal skill updating at several points in their lives. This is for their own benefit at least as much as for the national economy. The main cause for concern is not the number of people who engage in learning but its distribution. Just as there is a substantial minority of young people who do not do any initial post-compulsory education, there remain significant numbers who never do any formal learning as adults. For the most part they are the same people. Unemployment and low-skill employment are correlates of both.

There is also an issue of the relative value of different kinds of learning. *Learning to Succeed* has, in effect, made the value judgement that information technology skills are of more social value than other kinds of learning. In the embryonic scheme of individualized learning accounts (see below), for example, recognized courses for adults in IT attract an 80 per cent subsidy, while other subjects are subsidized up to 20 per cent of the costs. To give another example, there is more public subsidy for full-time courses in higher education than in most items of further education. Until October 1998, the subsidy for full-time European Union students on first-degree courses was 100 per cent. Now, the Government decision to have a standard fee for all students means that, while this subsidy is about 80 per cent on average, it varies between subjects from about 90 per cent in medicine to about 60 per cent in the humanities and law. Even this is a considerably higher subsidy than students receive in most other constituents of post-school learning.

One policy starting point for funding must be that voters and taxpayers appear to be unwilling to finance any significant increase in the aggregate public expenditure on lifetime learning. A government with a large parliamentary majority can do slightly more than shift resources within the lifetime learning budget heading as now defined, but not very much more. It is reasonable to hope for some annual increase in the public resources available, but unrealistic to expect big increases from public funds. Any increase is likely to be carefully targeted on specific national priorities. These are likely to continue to be leading edge technology and the encouragement of participation by socially excluded groups.

Interests outside higher education have some tendency to see it as the rich partner, which might be squeezed to help support some of the less favoured constituents of the post-16 sector. It was rumoured that the Kennedy Report into further education funding (Kennedy, 1997) intended to propose a shift of resources away from higher education into further education, but the Committee was dissuaded from doing so. The continued separation of the Higher Education Funding Councils from the Learning and Skills Councils will ensure that for the immediate future this particular decision will continue to be made at the top political level. From the viewpoint of the optimization of public funding for lifelong learning as a whole, it is an open question whether this should continue to be the case indefinitely.

Apart from such broad political debates, if it is accepted that the overall total of public expenditure for lifelong learning is constrained, the main resource reallocation conflicts that will persist are: continuing professional development at the top levels versus broad-based skills updating lower down; an emphasis on economy-related skills versus broader personal and social development; flexible off-site learning versus structured courses; and public subsidy to support private initiatives versus public money concentrated in areas where private money is hard to secure. None of these are black and white issues, none is entirely a matter of value and none can be solved entirely empirically. Certainly value for money estimates of different ways of spending additional funding, however rough, are necessary, but the 'value' obtained is largely a matter of political judgement.

An important policy issue for government is whether to continue to allow most such decisions to be made on a quasi-market basis, or whether to take more active measures to orientate spending in accordance with agreed national priorities. Media advertising of higher education courses has now reached commercial proportions. To the extent that this involves the use of HEFC money, there must be a question as to whether this represents a proper use of public funds. At a minimum, there needs to be some serious research to assess the extent to which such advertising results in more students, or students being more satisfied with the courses they choose. The evidence of rising course non-completion rates is not encouraging in this respect. It could be argued that once the Quality Assurance Agency has verified the quality of all courses, there is very little net gain from persuading students to attend one institution rather than another.

Reorganization

The main issue under this heading is whether the various agencies and institutions offering lifelong learning can be organized more efficiently. At one level the answer is that, after 20 years of reductions in expenditure per student in both further and higher education, the opportunities for further incremental efficiency gains without severe effects on quality must be limited.

In my view, the main hope for significant efficiency gains and broader participation must continue to come from the growth of good-quality flexible learning packages using new technology. As is well known, the growth of almost infinitely flexible learning opportunities through the World Wide Web has been phenomenal during the later 1990s. Even an hour of amateur net surfing can produce limitless learning materials in almost any subject. In addition to such freely available information, there are deep layers of password-protected material available to those who subscribe to particular 'virtual' colleges and universities. These are certain to continue to grow very rapidly. The benefits of this form of information gathering for part-time adult students are obvious. Students can use the material at times and in places that are individually convenient to them and, for the most part, the economies of scale mean that even organized subscription learning activities are much less costly than traditional learning methods.

A major task for policy makers and educators is to find realistic and acceptable ways of filtering the material for students to ensure its quality, to guarantee that Internet-based learning is genuinely accessible to all and to prevent this particular form of course delivery from driving out other components of worthwhile learning, such as social interaction, practice and the assessment of the internalization of learning by individual students. Well-designed courses and training programmes of the future will be able to reduce costs by making generous use of materials from the Internet, as libraries and paperback books have reduced the real costs of learning over the previous four centuries, but they make their most useful contribution when linked to well-planned reading lists compiled by experienced teachers and trainers.

In the long run, the market for learning will ensure that the Internet assumes its proper place. The levels of customer satisfaction with any particular offering will become apparent much more clearly and much more quickly on a course that is trying to sell itself globally than in a large number of what are, in effect, local monopoly providers of learning whose clients have little contact with one another. Yet the numbers of potential students and the possible dangers of propaganda posing as education make it impossible for legitimate universities and colleges to ignore the power of the Internet as a learning medium. Just as librarians, academic referees and teachers help students to evaluate printed materials before they are knowledgeable enough to do so for themselves, so it is important for the material Web to be subjected to analogous evaluation procedures.[2]

With this proviso, the possibilities of Internet-assisted adult learning reducing the costs of lifelong learning significantly are considerable. This is despite the relative failure of earlier attempts to develop computer-assisted learning materials. The difference is the vast scale of the Internet, in comparison with anything that has been available earlier, and the dramatic reduction of costs of access to this medium. The main difficulty is that as well as reducing costs it changes the incidence of costs. Like all distance learning, courseware on the Net has to be prepared in advance, so decisions to put on a course are much more in the nature of investment decisions than in traditional labour-intensive teaching, where most of the costs are incurred as the teaching takes place. Given the financial state of most post-compulsory education and training establishments after 25 years of efficiency gains, the resources needed for UK contributions to this investment must either come from government or be raised commercially. The Open University and the University for Industry are both well placed to perform this role across a very wide range of learning.

Raising resources

While there is general agreement for the proposition expressed in the Report of the National Committee of Inquiry into Higher Education (1997) that paying for lifelong learning above the age of 18 should be a partnership between government, households and employers, there has been very little work to assess what the shares of each should be, either in general or in particular circumstances.

For economists there has long been evidence that the private financial returns to higher and further education (or net benefits to individuals) are considerably higher than the social returns (or net benefits to society) (Psacharopoulos, 1992). This is because traditionally a large part of the costs, including student living costs while studying in the case of full-time students in higher education, have been paid out of public funds. This is, in essence, the main economic argument that has caused governments in recent years to replace grants to students with loans and to charge fees to those students whose families are deemed to be able to afford them. It is too soon to know how far the private and social returns are now in line with one another but inevitably there will have been a shift in this direction.

Much less is known about the private and social returns to further education[4] and virtually nothing at all about the economic returns to later professional development and skills upgrading. However, the principles that might underlie future policy developments are fairly straightforward to grasp.

The financial responsibility of the state should be:

1. To encourage the expansion of education and training where there are public benefits over and above those that private individuals or organizations are willing to pay for. One classic example of this is research, many of the benefits of which spill over to benefit the community generally, even if they can be captured privately for a period through patenting exploitable findings. However, of more direct relevance to lifelong learning, recent theories of 'endogenous' economic growth provide

strong evidence that 'density' of highly qualified people has an independent effect on social and economic well-being over and above the benefits from each of them individually. A rigorous econometric demonstration of this effect is given in Rushnavand (1999). An example that illustrates this principle is that if only one person has the capacity to use e-mail, the benefits are few; as more people acquire the capacity to use it, the benefits grow exponentially.

2. To ensure that individuals who are likely to be excluded because of their personal or social circumstances have the opportunity to participate to the full extent to which they are able to benefit. Means testing is one way of trying to meet this criterion, but the moral hazard of misreporting personal financial circumstances creates some difficulties.
3. To ensure that the capital market necessary for 2 below is operating effectively and equitably.

The financial responsibility of households should, subject to 2 above, be to meet the costs of their own education and training up to the levels where the net private benefits are equal to the returns they could get from any other investment. They should pay either through:

1. current cash holdings; or
2. borrowing and repaying out of subsequent higher income.

Employers have a more ambivalent role. Their interest is in securing and maintaining the best possible workforce for their particular part of the market. They do this in part by remunerating their staff at levels that will prevent them from being 'poached' by other employers. At the top end of the labour market these market forces can easily be seen. Chief executives and finance directors of large companies are able to command huge salaries that discourage them from taking their skills elsewhere. Some leading professionals, especially those with financial and information technology skills, are able to do the same. However, even after the market reforms of the past two decades, there is still a large role for internal labour markets in which employers develop their own employees within the enterprise. Paradoxically, in a competitive global economy with rapidly changing technology, the advantages of internal staff development are more apparent than in less competitive sectors with relatively stagnant technology. Broadly, employers can contribute to the finance of lifelong learning in two ways:

1. by paying all or part of the costs of retraining and upgrading their staff;
2. by paying off all or part of the debts individuals incur in personally-financed continuing education – sometimes referred to as golden hellos.

Unfortunately, from some points of view, employers are usually much more willing to help meet the cost of further training of employees who already have a high level of skills.

A new way of reconciling these various objectives of lifelong learning and enlisting all the sources of finance is the experimental scheme of individual learning accounts that was launched in 1999 (DfEE, 1999c). These were initially proposed by the Commission on Social Justice (1994) and promised in the Labour Party Manifesto of May 1997 which stated that it would invest public money for training in Individual Learning Accounts (ILAs) which individuals – for example women returning to the labour force – could then use to gain the skills they wanted (Labour Party, 1997). It was proposed to kick-start the programme for up to a million people using £150 million of TEC money that would provide a contribution of £150 per person alongside individuals making small investments of their own.

The beginnings of this scheme were implemented almost immediately and in May 1999 the DfEE announced that in that year it intended to open accounts for up to one million people. The aim was to provide a mechanism that would enable people to *invest their own money in their account to pay for learning. We want people to see opening a learning account as a natural part of planning their future. We also want to establish a system that will encourage employers to invest jointly with their employees'* (DfEE, 1999c: 2).

A full discussion of the current state of play with respect to individual learning accounts is contained in Chapter 10. The aim in this chapter is to suggest how the idea could develop from being a relatively small add-on in the total expenditure on lifelong learning to being the major unifying concept for the funding of learning throughout the lives of all individuals.

A vision for the 21st century

It must be recognized that no education or training is free. All education and training uses resources that could otherwise be available for current consumption or other investments. The basic question for policy makers is always, 'Who pays for it, how and when?'

The purpose of this concluding section is to summarize how the principle of individual learning accounts can be combined with personal pension schemes to release potentially much greater funds for investment in lifelong learning from both employees and employers than is likely if individual learning accounts are seen as a separate form of private saving.

One of the most helpful ways of looking at the financing of lifelong learning is in terms of life cycle analysis. Everybody starts life in an economically dependent state and nearly everyone becomes dependent again before the end of his or her life. Early on in life, borrowing tends to be higher and savings lower, since earnings are lower. Later, savings rise as earnings rise. Finally, savings are run down (see, for example, Berthoud and Kempson, 1992). Measures of poverty and need are more useful for policy if they take account of lifetime income profiles. The transfer of resources from the long-term affluent to the long-term poor needs to be based on different criteria from transfers of spending power within the life cycles of individuals.

Personal pension schemes enable people to build up wealth during the relatively high earning stages of their lives and to use it when their earned income declines. Their pension funds are built up while they are working and run down after they retire. Individualized learning accounts can facilitate the reverse process. Individuals can borrow in advance of higher earnings and repay when they materialize.[3] Education and training are some of the most effective ways for most individuals to increase their earning capacity. In a well-administered, information-rich society, such as the UK, it would be possible for each individual to open a single individual human capital account which could serve both as a personal pension fund and as an individual learning account.

There is no doubt that if an average individual were given the cost of his or her higher education when he or she reached the age of 18, he or she would benefit over his or her life and finish his or her working life with a larger pension as a result of investing it in higher education than if he or she put it in a fixed-interest account in the bank. This is what the rate-of-return studies already referred to show us. The later in life investment in education is left, the smaller are the gross lifetime returns, because the period of working life remaining to derive the financial benefits is shorter (Blaug and Mace, 1977). However, investing in full-time higher education remains financially worthwhile for average men and women until well into their 30s. The main real cost of blocks of full-time learning – the income forgone while studying – rises rapidly as individuals reach their full earning capacity.

However, even from a narrow financial point of view, the personal benefits of further learning continue much later in the life cycle if rapid technological change renders earlier education and training partly obsolete. Furthermore, it can reasonably be assumed that, after initial education, most learning episodes would be shorter and less expensive in time and direct financial costs.

With suitable professional advice, individuals could have the possibility of using part of their accumulated pension fund at any stage of their lives to undertake investment in learning that would be likely to enhance their learning capacity or even, with suitable safeguards, to enrich their lives in other ways.

One attraction of the lifetime income profile approach is that it could, in large part, be financed through the banking system and there should be no need to treat schemes that facilitate transfers of income throughout the lifetime of specific individuals as taxation, in the usual sense of the word. There would be some public costs. However commercially sound the scheme, public funding will always be necessary both to transfer some resources into those accounts where particular individuals, such as disabled people, have little chance of building up an acceptable fund by themselves and also to cover some of the risks involved. After all, not everyone will benefit financially from any particular learning experience and some 'insurance cover' would be needed. There would also need to be regulation to prevent any individual withdrawing more than a certain percentage of the lifetime learning/pension fund.

It is true that there would remain some excluded individuals and groups who would be unlikely to take advantage of the opportunities such a scheme would provide. However, if they knew they had funds that could only be accessed if used for useful learning, this might be expected to act as a positive incentive. The 1999 DfEE annual report claimed that their market research showed that people welcomed individual learning accounts as a means of overcoming cost, one of the main barriers to learning, and that ILAs would help and support a change in career direction (DfEE, 1999a).

Employers would be required to contribute to each individual's account just as they do for existing occupational pension schemes. In addition, both the government and employers could pay into any individual's scheme according to any criteria they considered appropriate. Individuals would always have the choice of withdrawing funds up to a prescribed limit, for purposes of learning, or of leaving them to accumulate for pension enhancement. Younger people would be able to borrow ahead of earnings and this would be facilitated if decisions to invest in learning were matched by contributions from public funds.

A scheme of this type would ideally include all education and training beyond the age of 18 and would encompass the existing student-loan scheme and the existing personal-pensions scheme. A comprehensive scheme of this type ought to be able to be attractive to commercial financial institutions, since very large sums of money would be involved.

In brief, the concept of lifelong learning can best be financed with the help of the concept of life-cycle earnings and savings.

Notes

1. In 1997/8, 41.3 per cent of all first year students in higher education were over the age of 24 (HESA, 1998).
2. There are, of course, dangers. There can be no suggestion of vetting the Net or regulating what is available on it. The task to be performed is advisory – to help guide learners through the ever-increasing number of Web sites and newsgroups so that useful learning can occur as opposed to mere information gathering.
3. One immediate response by some may be that few would be able to afford to pay for lifelong learning in this way *and* save for pensions *and* take out a mortgage on a house. The reply is that if these activities are

to happen they must be paid for somehow out of the income of those who are working. There is certainly a good case for subsidizing the ILAs of the less affluent. The issue is whether the life-cycle funding approach offers a mechanism that is potentially more equitable, efficient, consumer-friendly and flexible.

4. A recent report (Deaden *et al*, 2000) shows that the returns to many lower level qualifications are comparable to those in higher education.

References

Beinart, S and Smith, P (1998) *National Adult Learning Survey 1997*, DfEE, London

Berthoud, R and Kempson, E (1992) *Credit and Debt*, Policy Studies Institute, London

Blaug, M and Mace, J (1977) Recurrent Education – The new Jerusalem, *Higher Education*, **6** (3), 277–95

Coffield, F and Williamson, B (1997) The challenges facing higher education, in *Repositioning Higher Education*, ed F Coffield and B Williamson, SRHE and Open University Press, Buckingham

Commission on Social Justice (1994) *Social Justice: Strategies for national renewal*, Institute for Public Policy Research, London

Dearden, *et al* (2000) *The Return to Academic, Vocational and Basic Skills in Britain*, Institute of Fiscal Studies

Department for Education and Employment (DfEE) (1997) Department for Education and Employment and Office for Standards in Education: Departmental Report, DfEE, London

DfEE (1999a) Departmental Report: The Government's Expenditure Plans 1999/00–2001/02, DfEE, London

DfEE (1999b) *Learning to Succeed: A new framework for post-16 learning*, DfEE, London

DfEE (1999c) *Individual Learning Accounts: A summary of progress*, DfEE, London

Higher Education Statistics Agency (HESA) (1998) *Student Enrolments on Higher Education Courses at Publicly Funded Higher Education Institutions in the United Kingdom for the Academic Year 1998/99*, HESA, Cheltenham

Kennedy, H (1997) *Learning Works: Widening participation in further education*, Further Education Funding Council, Coventry

Labour Party (1997) *Labour Party General Election Manifesto 1997: Because Britain deserves better*, Labour Party, London

National Committee of Inquiry into Higher Education (NCIHE) (1997) *Higher Education in the Learning Society: Report of the NCIHE* (The Dearing Report), NCIHE, London

OECD (2000 forthcoming) *Finding the Resources for Lifelong Learning: Progress, problems and prospects*, OECD, Paris

Psacharopoulos, George (1992) Rate of return studies, in *The Encyclopedia of Higher Education*, ed Burton R Clark and Guy R Neave, pp 999–1003, Pergamon, Oxford

Rushnavand, A (1999) *Education Experience and Earnings: A multilevel analysis*, unpublished PhD thesis, Institute of Education, University of London

Smithers, A and Robinson, P (1996) *Trends in Higher Education*, Council for Industry and Higher Education, London

6

Quality and equality in lifelong learning: intersections and collisions

Louise Morley

Lifelong learning has become a dominant policy in education today. By disaggregating education from age there are agendas for opportunity, continuous development and change. Individuals and professional communities are in a permanent state of becoming. A policy challenge is how to ensure the maintenance of quality and standards in the midst of enhanced participation. This chapter will examine some of the arguments for and against concepts of quality as they are applied to higher education in particular, and to lifelong learning in general. It will trace the genesis of quality from its origins in the commercial world and raise questions about whether quality technologies from industry are appropriate to the complex social and intellectual processes of the academy. It will also interrogate the discourse in relation to equity issues and identify whether quality and equality are oppositional or complementary discourses in the framework of lifelong learning.

The genesis of the discourse

Quality became an issue with the advent of industrialization, relating to elimination of waste (time, materials, money) and safety requirements. Quality now relates to 'fitness for purpose' and measurement of outcomes in relation to product specifications, 'zero defect', effectiveness in achieving institutional goals and success in meeting customers' stated or implied needs (Green, 1995). Quality gained currency in Japanese industry in the 1940s and 1950s and was applied specifically to the public services in the USA and UK in the 1980s.

Japan appeared to make a significant economic recovery after the Second World War. The West attempted to decode Japanese economic success. Japanese work practices were imported into different sectors of British manufacturing production, starting with the car manufacturing industry. Some of the key aspects of the Japanese economic miracle were thought to be long-term planning, designing quality into products, and employee attitudes and relationships. However, there were also questions raised about whether some social and cultural characteristics were more conducive to productivity. According to Imai (1986), the key to the overall success of Japanese business and industry lies first in the philosophical concept of *kaizen*, which, he argues, provides the best means by which all aspects of Japanese production and management can be understood. *Kaizen,* literally translated, means continuous improvement *'involving everyone, including both managers and workers'* (Imai, 1986: 3). It is a generic term that penetrates all aspects of Japanese life. Imai (1986: 3) states that *'the kaizen philosophy assumes that our way of life – be it our working life, our social life, or our home life – deserves to be constantly improved'*. This ethos is reflected in the ideology of lifelong learning. The notion of continuous professional development, and the decoupling of education from chronological age, means that there is never an end point. This is strongly associated with neo-Fordist employment regimes and the politics of flexibility (Jessop *et al*, 1991).

In a period of rapid technological and social change, the world has become a riskier place (Beck, 1992). Skill requirements are constantly in flux. Power (1997) argues that quality assurance is about seeking comfort and certainties. In today's risk society, the ineffective public institution is seen to be as risky to the public as an engine falling off an aeroplane. Quality was originally associated with quality control and was part of Fordist production processes. It consisted of the detection and elimination of components or final products that were not up to standard. It was invariably undertaken by an inspector/controller, rather than by the workers themselves. In education, this translated into external inspections consisting purely of observations and judgements. The emphasis gradually moved away from control and towards quality assurance. Quality was designed into the process, with the aim of preventing faults from occurring in the first place. Systems were put into place throughout the production process. The goal was for 'zero defects' and the meeting of product specification. In education, this is often represented as the quest for excellence (DfEE, 1997). Institutions are not just evaluated on students' performance, but also on the provision that is made for getting them to that point.

Quality assurance rapidly developed into Total Quality Management (TQM). This involves the creation of a quality culture. Staff are expected to understand, internalize and live the message. The structure of the organization allows and facilitates this process. There is a commitment to continuous improvement, reminiscent of Japanese production processes. The concepts of TQM derived from the industrial model made famous by Deming and Juran during the 1950s and 1960s in the USA and centralized in the Japanese production model.

In 1991 the Further Education Unit (FEU) published what was to be become a highly influential document in the framing of the quality debate in British education. *Quality Matters* (FEU, 1991: 2) positioned the concept of quality in education within the framework of manufacturing industry's definition of *'fitness for purpose'*, which, it argued, is *'arrived at through conformance to specification'*. The FEU highlighted distinctions between the concepts of 'quality control' (TQC), 'quality assurance', 'quality systems' and 'continuous quality improvement'. Japanese and US work practices form an integral part of the process of TQM, which places emphasis on *'the search for opportunities for improvement rather than maintaining current performance'* (FEU, 1991: 2). In education, TQM transferred to the adoption of adequate measures *'to improve the quality of teaching and learning, to increase participation, and to improve attainment'* (FEU, 1991: 3). Central to the concept of TQM is the need to change working practices and to generate a climate of 'not being satisfied' within the organization. Learning organizations are required constantly to evaluate, research, analyse and measure needs, results and effectiveness and to feed these back as part of the process of continuous improvement (FEU, 1991).

Similar to the notion of original sin in Christianity, the construction of the individual and the organization as being in deficit and in need of continuous improvement can be a powerful regulatory device. The mindset of never being satisfied can create an urgency and compliance that shifts attention away from values and ideologies and towards technologies and competencies. Hence, vast amounts of energy are invested in enhancing effectiveness, quality, learning and productivity rather than questioning whose interests are being served. Indeed, the end point in the continuous improvement process is unclear. Strathern (1997: 307) argues that this lack of closure brings with it a 'morality of attainment':

> 'Improvement' is wonderfully open-ended, for it at once describes effort and results. And it invites one to make both ever more effective – a process from which the tests themselves are not immune; measuring the improvement leads to improving the measures.

However, continuous improvement can also represent opportunity and personal development. It challenges 'routinization' and staleness in the workplace. The opportunity/exploitation dilemma is a powerful part of lifelong learning. Ball (1999: 197) identifies how Labour's education policies can be understood and analysed as a *'synthesis between market and social democratic values'*.

The discourses of quality and of lifelong learning both contain a mixture of democratic and economic imperatives. Sallis (1996) argues that there are four imperatives embedded in the quality discourse: moral, professional, competitive and accountability. The multi-layering of imperatives, alongside the command economy, where funding is linked to external assessments, means that quality is difficult to contest and resist. For many, lifelong learning is not an option, but linked to continuing professional status and indeed, employment (Eraut, Morley and Cole, 1998).

The political economy of education

A key question is why quality was inserted into education at a particular political moment. The economy was in crisis in the 1970s and 1980s. In Britain, the economic crisis revolved around stagnant markets, low levels of productivity in the manufacturing sector, high levels of unemployment, lack of investment in the development of new products and, related to these, Britain's inability to compete successfully in an increasingly globalized economy. These difficulties within the economy contributed to a general reduction in the Gross Domestic Product (GDP). The most marked transformation in the economy during the 1980s was the shift from the manufacturing to the service sector (Massey and Allen, 1992).

The changes that were now taking place in the labour market impacted also on skills training needs, including business management and other job-specific skills requiring specialist short-term training, some of which were predominantly information based. According to research undertaken by the Institute of Employment in the UK, by the year 2000, 70 per cent of all jobs in Europe will require people with A levels and above (Day, 1997). The belief that Britain needs to overhaul its educational system in order to be more globally competitive has been a central theme in New Labour's first two White Papers (DfEE, 1997, 1998). It was also a dominant theme in the Dearing Review (NCIHE, 1997). Human capital theory is a major policy influence now. The increasing subordination of education to economic considerations means that there is now a well-established knowledge economy.

Values, as well as technologies and drive systems from the cultural world of business and commerce, have been imported into education, bringing with them new meanings, priorities and truths (Morley and Rassool 1999). For many, interpretative academic freedom in education was causally linked to low standards, and there needed to be an insertion of certainties and benchmarks. Indeed, by the time that the Conservative Government came to power in 1979:

> Education had come to epitomise much that was seen to be wrong with burgeoning state power. It was construed as expensive, not self-evidently adequately productive, insufficiently accountable, monopolistic, producer-dominated, a bastion of an entrenched professional elite, resistant to consumer demand and, at worst, self-generating and self-serving.
>
> (Fergusson, 1994: 93)

In relation to higher and further education, expansion also created a type of chaos in need of regulation. After the 1992 FHE Act, the number of universities in Britain increased from 46 to 112. There was a rise in the number of students from 900,000 to 1,800,000 (from 15 to 33 per cent). There are no nationally defined higher education qualifications, and considerable product variety across the system. Quality had previously been assured via the system of peer review and external examiners. Studies appeared demonstrating the precariousness of peer review (Silver, 1993). As Evans (1999: 147) indicates, *'peer review is clearly not an exact science'*. Furthermore, the notion of 'peer' excludes considerations of exclusion and discriminatory practices. It is often based on gendered networks and comradeship.

The insertion of the quality discourse into higher education is an example of the changing relations between universities and the state. In one sense, it represents a challenge to the medieval achievement of separating the idea of intellectual authority from political authority (Finch, 1997). For some, this is perceived as an intrusion into academic freedom (Peters, 1992). For others, it is a long-overdue attempt to make dominant organizations of knowledge production more accountable and transparent in their procedures (Luke, 1997). It is debatable whether the questions being asked about quality and standards within a mass system have promoted equity issues. Rather, the emphasis has been on value for money, public accountability, and the identification of standards, ie the requirement for reference points, benchmarks against which performance is measured (Elton, 1998).

Two basic models of quality apply to higher education: inspectorial – an external agency is sent in to make judgements (quality control), and self-regulation – shared purposes, tacit values and understandings, peer review. Quality applies to the level of academic discipline, the award bearing institution and professional and statutory bodies. Brown (1998) argues that the most critical aspect of the new quality framework is the relationship between external and internal assessments. For example, providers of academic subjects now compile a self-assessment document that reflects the areas open to external assessment. The external inspection has a four-point scale for six areas: curriculum design, content and organization; teaching, learning and assessment; student progression and achievement; student support and guidance; learning resources; and quality assurance and enhancement. Customer care has been an important feature of quality assurance in higher education, with the introduction of handbooks, guidelines, codes of practice, student opinion surveys, a students' charter and staff development. The customer, however, often remains a universal subject, without gender, social class or ethnicity.

The regulation and management of quality in higher education has been a fairly fragmented affair. In 1990, the Committee for Vice-Chancellors and Principals (CVCP) set up an Academic Audit Unit (which lasted for two years). In 1992, the Higher Education Quality Council was established. In 1997, after the Dearing Report, the Quality Assurance Agency (QAA) was set up. Teaching, as well as research, has been highlighted as a signifier of excellence and productivity. Research quality is regulated via the Higher Education Funding Council for England (HEFCE) Research Assessment Exercise (every four to five years). Teaching quality is regulated via the QAA. Academic Reviewers are appointed to visit institutions for their Subject Reviews. The system of auditing teaching has moved from Quality Control to Quality Assurance, ie the emphasis is now on how quality is embedded in systems, structures and mechanisms. The Institute of Learning and Teaching opened in 1999. This provides professional development for university teachers. Membership is not yet mandatory (not a licence to practice), but is sometimes built into lecturers' probationary period. It is developing a national accreditation scheme, a portfolio of Continuous Professional Development (CPD) programmes and a register of members.

The audit culture

Quality combines culture management (the creation of purposes and meanings) with performance management (measuring what really matters). Performance is now an organizational responsibility. Underpinning these interventions are issues of trust, democracy and risk. As Power (1997: 103) suggests, *'The performance culture of rewards and penalties is a refusal to trust'*. Ironically, we are invited to place total trust in the auditors, many of whom are drawn from the profession on trial in the first place. The meaning of quality in public services relates to performance auditing. It also applies to the values of the entitlement culture, encoded in documents such as student charters. Audit and the ensuing certification and grading mean that private in-house matters are now open to public scrutiny. This is often referred to as the 'evaluative state'. There has been a shift from process-based local forms of self-evaluation to standardized measures of output.

Generally, in the public services, the performance ethos has created an 'audit explosion', with a proliferation of evaluative procedures (Power, 1994, 1997; Strathern, 1997). Audit is based on a conflation of measures with targets. There is a modernist, rationalist belief that the complexities of the social world can be measured and recorded with the appropriate instruments and technologies. Specific performance indicators are selected to illustrate effectiveness and individuals and organizations are graded in relation to these signifiers. The results then provide a reified reading, which becomes a truth. These readings become the baseline data for the point of entry into the mechanisms for continuous improvement.

Schools, colleges and universities, like other public-service institutions over the past two decades, have been subject to 'human accounting'. The introduction of markets and managers has been a generic transformational device designed to restructure and reorient public-service provision. The common elements have involved site-based management, the language of improvement and budgetary devolution. Funding regimes have become structuring mechanisms. Decision-making, priorities and service provision are determined by financial considerations. There are also financial consequences to quality audits, with resources allocated and withdrawn according to performance. Power (1994: 36–7) notes:

> What is audited is whether there is a system which embodies standards and the standards of performance themselves are shaped by the need to be auditable... audit becomes a formal 'loop' by which the system observes itself.

There is an implied relationship between accountability and improvement. The auditing gaze is both internal and external, as educational institutions are subjected to inspection. There is also a strong element of self-scrutiny. This self-regulation is an example of how power can be capillary, rather than monolithic. A capillary notion of power suggests that power operates everywhere in everyday transactions. It is totalizing in so far as it is rehearsed in inter- and intra-personal relations, as well as in structures (Morley, 1999).

One way in which macro-policies translate into micro-practices is in the identification of performance indicators. These represent an encoding of values, priorities and prejudices. It is questionable what the appropriate performance indicators are for lifelong learning. For example, are performance indicators such as completion rates appropriate to the concept of lifelong learning? Does this represent a type of closure in a process that is meant to be open-ended? Another consideration is whether completion rates are deconstructed with attention paid to equity issues. For example, as long ago as 1983, Berg and Ferber discovered that women students tend to be more successful in completing postgraduate degrees where the proportion of female academics on the staff is relatively higher. Furthermore, success criteria in lifelong learning are not always immediately apparent in the short term, or in the reified academic environment, but are only visible when applied in the workplace or the community often many years after completion. Performance indicators can be fragmented and left unrelated to one another. They can also be highly contradictory. For example, institutions with very high Research Assessment Exercise (RAE) scores, such as Oxbridge, have some of the lowest participation rates of working-class students (McCrum, 1998). Performance indicators can also date rapidly, as organizations and individuals can just work to those measures and nothing else. As Strathern (1997: 308) indicates:

> When a measure becomes a target, it ceases to be a good measure.

Quality as a regulatory device

I wish to argue that quality is not a neutral notion. Quality is a subjective category of description and its meaning derives from its point of articulation. There are questions about who defines quality, and indeed, whose interests it represents. Furthermore, multi-dimensional concepts, such as quality, are often reduced to binaries, such as effective/failing organizations. There are important questions about what type of support is appropriate for failing institutions, or whether, indeed, failure is merely a social construction – a totem to assuage the fears of consumers and to demonstrate state power over standards (Carvel, 1999).

Quality is often socially decontextualized, with an emphasis on organizational scores rather than social structures. It can also be fairly reductive, as there are complex areas of the public services that are difficult to measure, quantify and capture, ie processes, the affective domain, attitudes and values. The gaps and silences in taxonomies of effectiveness are often where equity issues constellate (Morley and Rassool, 1999). Ball (1997: 327) believes that quality is 'a "relay device" effectively linking government "mentalities" and policies, with everyday organizational realities'. The emphasis on continuous improvement suggests a permanent deficit model. Tacit professional practices are bureaucratized and a panoptical culture is promoted (Foucault, 1979a, 1979b). The quality discourse is an effective way of ensuring the compliance and docility of employees by establishing a set of goals and objectives that are not always negotiable.

There is a tacit notion of what constitutes excellence. Behind judgements of quality are power relations and values. Quality increases bureaucratization and takes practitioners away from the interface with clients. In quality-assurance procedures, organizations have to represent their identities discursively and in a confessional manner. Quality audits encourage 'performativity' (Lyotard, 1984), as organizations tend to give aspirational accounts of themselves within certain prescribed parameters.

A further criticism of quality in relation to lifelong learning is that quality is being promoted at a time when public funding is decreasing. For example, public funding per student in higher education has fallen by more than 40 per cent since 1976. The student–staff ratios have moved from 9.3:1 in the old universities and 8.4:1 in the former polytechnics to an overall figure of 16.5:1 (Watson and Bowden, 1999). There is also an increasing 'casualization' of labour and decreasing employment conditions in higher education. However, the quality discourse attempts to demonstrate how standards can rise even when investments and employment rights decrease, thus demonstrating the profligacy of pre-managerial regimes. The euphemism 'efficiency gains' for the cuts in higher education asserts that cuts in unit costs have not lowered the quality of the education provided by British universities (Trow, 1998). Whereas the Government has pledged to support the extra 500,000 students generated by lifelong learning initiatives, this funding is not necessarily for the institutions (Court, 1998). Hence quality may be being audited in conditions of funding and employment that could be eroding it. Quality could well be seen as a massive displacement activity, distracting attention away from under-resourcing and focusing on naming and shaming of individual organizations (Carvel, 1999).

In defence of quality

An argument in favour of quality is that it condenses complex professional processes into easily identifiable information for consumers. The use of league tables, grades for teaching quality and RAE scores can be indicators to assist choice-making processes. Similarly, benchmarking is often seen as a type of classification and framing exercise in the midst of the potential chaos of expansion of lifelong learning. This can be seen as elite organizations being forced to become more user-friendly, particularly to those users who lack the cultural capital and social advantages often required for educational decision-making. The reconstruction of students as consumers and clients changes power relationships between the purchasers and the providers of the educational product. Quality audits could be said to privilege users' voices by measuring customer satisfaction via the use of evaluation instruments and consumer surveys.

In terms of equity, greater transparency of procedures can sometimes make discriminatory and exclusionary practices more visible. One view is that quality audits can be used by women as a mechanism for what Yeatman (1990) calls 'equity-oriented change management' (Luke, 1997: 437). The 'panoptic' gaze of audit can bring marginalized groups into the light. The emphasis on continuing professional development and on accountability can challenge expert power and routinization. There is the potential for organizational reflexivity, as preparation for quality audits can provide some discursive space for reflecting on practices, assumptions, and procedures. Quality audits can sometimes transform and update organizations. If one takes a Foucauldian analysis of power, quality can be both oppressive and creative. Quality is a complex and contradictory affair.

Quality and equality

The quality discourse has achieved authority in higher education when the equality discourse did not. To say that there has been an implementation gap between policies and practices might be an understatement. The Dearing Report noted that only one-third of higher education institutions with equal opportunities policies had plans directed towards their achievement (Watson and Taylor, 1998). Ironically, New Right educational reform (continued by New Labour) was able to effect more significant changes in the quantity and composition of the student body in higher education than two decades of equality legislation. Critics of the quality discourse often express a sense of loss of academic freedom. However, Luke (1997: 436) asks whether the 'Golden Age of Academic Autonomy Prior to Managerialism' was, in fact, *'an epoch of access, equity and enfranchisement for women and people of colour?'*

However, there could be an equity paradox (Morley, 1997) in so far as the transition from an elite to a mass system has produced considerable concerns about the quality of the higher education product. The policy framework of lifelong learning is accompanied by a moral panic over standards (the 'dumbing' down/more means worse debate), and inflation of certification. To some, quality assurance is compatible with equity concerns. The scrutiny of organizations is seen as a refreshing challenge to elitism and to disciplinary authority (Luke, 1997). Quality audits are also perceived as transformational devices, allowing questions to be posed about whether equity provisions are measures of excellence, for example, arrangements for students with special needs.

The standardization implied in quality assurance could also suggest normalization. It is questionable whether the diversity implied in lifelong learning is reflected in audits. There are dangers of homogenizing teachers and learners and creating a universal subject and organizational isomorphism. Currently, very diverse organizations are placed on the same continuum for research excellence, for example. This automatically disadvantages those organizations with diverse populations, as Wagner (1989: 36) points out:

> It is those who restrict access by accepting only students with the highest traditional qualifications which receive status, privilege, honours and resources.

The technology of quality assurance is perceived as a reductive input/output model. It is seen as a process of impression management and 'performativity', with performance indicators socially and politically constructed. The technology masks the ideology and value base of what is considered excellent at this particular political and historical moment (Ball, 1997).

As part of the modernization programme, the Government has invested large sums of money in quality assurance, with an aim to collect evidence and evaluate educational provisions. There is an implied relationship between accountability and improvement. Accountability has been linked to public information. The rhetoric of improvement is related both to organizational development and to individual learners in the context of lifelong learning. However, in spite of this vast machinery, there is little evidence to suggest that the quality of student or staff experiences has been enhanced, or that the role that lifelong learning plays in social reproduction has been interrupted.

It is doubtful whether the evidence collected via quality audits reflects wider social transformations and shifting student demographics. Many of these concerns have crystallized around the issue of value added, ie ensuring that people exit with better characteristics than they possessed at the point of input (Brennan *et al*, 1997). However, issues of diversity and equity are only superficially addressed. Multifaceted qualitative processes such as pedagogical relations and barriers to participation are reduced to quantitative indicators (Morley, 2000). Vexed political questions relating to power and knowledge are condensed into concerns about course documentation, waiting time for essay feedback and so on. It is dubious whether audit detects complex micro-processes of power in organizations (Morley, 1999). Meanwhile, the rhetoric of lifelong learning and continuous improvement are sending powerful messages to students and staff, informing them of their lack and deficit, in an attempt to make them more 'governmentable'. Quality has become a regime of truth in the academy, reinforced by performance tables and financial consequences. Concerns about the authenticity of the exercise abound. Yet auditors and those who are audited perform a type of comedy of manners. We speak the discourse and the discourse speaks us.

References

Ball, S J (1997) Good School/Bad School: paradox and fabrication, *British Journal of Sociology of Education*, **18** (3), pp 317–36

Ball, S J (1999) Labour, learning and the economy: a 'policy sociology' perspective, *Cambridge Journal of Education*, **29** (2), pp 195–206

Beck, U (1992) *Risk Society*, Sage, London

Berg, H M and Ferber, M (1983) Men and women graduate students: who succeeds and why? *Journal of Higher Education*, **54** (6), pp 629–48

Brennan, J *et al* (1997) An institutional approach to quality audit, *Studies in Higher Education*, **22** (2), pp 173–86

Brown, R (1998) *The Post-Dearing Agenda for Quality and Standards in Higher Education*, Institute of Education, University of London, London

Carvel, J (1999) Thames Valley: the inside story, *The Guardian Higher Education*, Tuesday July 20, pp ii–iii

Court, S (1998) Lessons for life, *AUT Bulletin*, No 209, pp 6–7

Day, C (1997) Teachers in the twenty-first century: time to renew the vision, in *Beyond Educational Reform*, ed A Hargreaves and R Evans, Open University Press, Buckingham

DfEE (1997) *Excellence in Schools*, HMSO, London

DFEE (1998) *The Learning Age*, HMSO, London

Elton, L (1998) Are UK degree standards going up, down or sideways? *Studies in Higher Education*, **23** (1), pp 35–42

Eraut, M, Morley, L and Cole, G (1998) *Standards and vocational qualifications in continuing professional development*, QCA, London

Evans, G R (1999) *Calling Academia to Account: Rights and responsibilities*, SRHE/Open University Press, Buckingham

Fergusson, R (1994) Managerialism in education, in *Managing Social Policy*, ed J Clarke, A Cochrane and E McLaughlin, Sage Publications, London

Finch, J (1997) Power, legitimacy and academic standards, in *Standards and Quality in Higher Education*, ed J Brennan, P De Vries and R Williams, Jessica Kingsley, London

Foucault, M (1979a) *Discipline and Punish*, tr A Sheridan, Vintage, New York

Foucault, M (1979b) Governmentability, *Ideology and Consciousness*, **6** (5) p 22

Further Education Unit (FEU) (1991) *Quality Matters: Business and industry quality models and further education*, FEU, London

Green, D (1995) *What is Quality in Higher Education?* SRHE/Open University, Buckingham

Imai, M (1986) *Kaizen (Ky'zen): The key to Japan's competitiveness*, Random House, New York

Jessop, B *et al* (1991*) The Politics of Flexibility*, Edward Elgar, Aldershot

Luke, C (1997) Quality assurance and women in higher education, *Higher Education*, **33** pp 433–51

Lyotard, J (1984) *The Post-modern Condition*, Manchester University Press, Manchester

Massey, D and Allen, J (1992) *The Economy in Question: Restructuring Britain*, Sage, London

McCrum, N G (1998) Gender and social inequality at Oxbridge: measures and remedies, *Oxford Review of Education*, **24** (3), pp 261–77

Morley, L (1997) Change and equity in higher education, *British Journal of Sociology of Education*, **18** (2), pp 231–42

Morley, L (1999) *Organising Feminisms: The micropolitics of the academy*, Macmillan, London

Morley, L (2000) Mass higher education: feminist pedagogy in the learning society, in *Identity and Difference in Higher Education: Feminist perspectives* ed P Anderson and J Williams, Ashgate, London

Morley, L and Rassool, N (1999) *School Effectiveness: Fracturing the discourse*, The Falmer Press, London

National Committee of Inquiry into Higher Education (NCIHE) (1997) *Higher Education in the Learning Society*, NCIHE, London

Peters, M (1992) Performance and accountability in post-industrial societies: the crisis in British universities, *Studies in Higher Education*, **17** (2), pp 123–39

Power, M (1994) *The Audit Explosion*, Demos, London

Power, M (1997) *The Audit Society*, Oxford University Press, Oxford

Sallis, E (1996) *Total Quality Management in Education*, Kogan Page, London

Silver, H (1993) External examiners: changing roles, CNAA, London

Strathern, M (1997) 'Improving ratings': audit in the British university system, *European Review*, **5** (3), pp 305–21

Trow, M (1998) The Dearing Report: A transatlantic view, *Higher Education Quarterly*, **52** (1), pp 93–117

Wagner, L (1989) Access and standards: an unresolved and unresolvable debate, in *Higher Education Into the 1990s*, ed C Ball and H Eggins, Open University Press, Milton Keynes

Watson, D and Bowden, R (1999) Why did they do it? The Conservatives and mass higher education 1979–97, *Journal of Education Policy*, **14** (3), pp 243–56

Watson, D and Taylor, R (1998) *Lifelong Learning and the University*, Falmer Press, London

Yeatman, A (1990) *Bureaucrats, Technocrats, Femocrats*, Allen and Unwin, Sydney

7

Bringing knowledge back in: towards a curriculum for lifelong learning

Michael Young

Introduction

The promotion of lifelong learning lies at the heart of the present Government's policies for post-compulsory education and training and was first expressed in the Green Paper *The Learning Age* (DfEE, 1998). However, what lifelong learning means, what types of learning should be emphasized and what it will be important for people to learn are far from clear. This vagueness about the meaning of lifelong learning means that the Green Paper seems to be pointing in two directions at once. It stresses that becoming a lifelong learner is an individual responsibility while, at the same time, recognizing that lifelong learning is too important to be left to individuals on their own and requires the intervention of government.

The focus on the responsibility of individuals for their own learning is not entirely new. It has been a recurring theme of policies for the 14–18 age group such as 'active learning', 'individual action planning' and 'records of achievement'. Furthermore, the emphasis on the individual also reflects elements of the Government's 'Third Way' approach that aims to improve services and provision without significant increases in expenditure. What is new in educational policy is the shift to promoting learning throughout people's lives and, in particular, in contexts other than those associated with formal education. It is this shift that reflects what might be called a new type of 'collectivism' in government policy. While recognizing that the market is far from being an adequate distributor of learning opportunities, the Government seeks forms of intervention that involve minimum extra public spending. These tensions are reflected in the Prime Minister's view, quoted in the Green Paper, that 'education is the best economic policy that we have' (DfEE, 1998: 9). This is an indirect way of admitting that the Government is leaving a major aspect of the context in which individuals take up learning opportunities – the investment decisions of individual companies –

up to the market. At the same time, it is a recognition that the expansion of lifelong learning is too important to be left to the market and individual choice. What the Green Paper proposes, therefore, is a 'policy' on learning that seeks to 'educate the market' and persuade more people, especially those who have not been learners in the past, to become lifelong learners. One of the problems of the Government's approach, which I shall return to, is that investment decisions of companies and individual decisions to continue learning are nothing like as separate as the policy assumes.

The shift in the focus of education policy to learning (and, specifically, lifelong learning) represents a break from traditional policies that have emphasized new systems of funding, new organizations or new qualifications and assumed that improved learning will follow. There are new arrangements implied in the Green Paper and made quite explicit in the later White Paper *Learning to Succeed* (DfEE, 1999) that propose the setting up of a National Learning and Skills Council and a new inspectorate. However, the distinctive feature of both documents, and what I want to concentrate on in this chapter, is their new focus on promoting learning, both in formal education and elsewhere. It is a recognition not only that learning does not necessarily follow directly from new programmes, new qualifications or new funding arrangements, and that important learning can go on independently of any formal provision. However, what this new approach does not do is to follow through the implications of its own emphasis on promoting learning. The focus on the responsibility of individuals recognizes that, unlike new schools or new qualifications, learning cannot be directly funded or legislated for; it is an activity and a process in which people consciously decide to engage. However, individuals do not engage in learning activities in isolation but in specific contexts for specific purposes. It follows that if the new policy focus on learning is to become more than rhetoric, a number of issues have to be addressed that have not been seen as central to government policy to date. These include the contexts in which learning takes place, the nature of learning and that which distinguishes it from other activities, and the purposes and types of learning that are being promoted – in other words, the curriculum. Before discussing these issues, the chapter makes some brief comments on the main strategies endorsed by the Green Paper.

The Green Paper's strategies for promoting lifelong learning

The strategies designed to promote lifelong learning in the Green Paper aim to stimulate individuals to become or to continue to be learners. Three of the specific initiatives are the University for Industry, Learning Direct and Individual Learning Accounts. Before commenting on the initiatives themselves, it is worth stressing a point to which I will return in more detail later in the chapter. The problems with the proposed initiatives arise because policy makers have not grasped the implications of this new focus on learning. First, and unlike virtually all other educational policies, lifelong learning is an educational goal that is not directed to any specific group of learners. This means that if lifelong learning is to be more than a slogan, what is meant by it has to be made explicit. In practice, much of the focus of the Green Paper is not on lifelong learning, but on the narrower aim of persuading more adults to return to study. However, if the Government were really serious about promoting lifelong learning, there are issues of equal and arguably even greater importance. A key question, if we seek to create a society of lifelong learners in the future, is how to encourage those still in school or college to continue with their learning. There is an assumption that somehow this problem will be solved by the drive to raise standards in the primary and secondary schools. Second, if encouraging learning as an activity is a goal of policy, creating the social (and sometimes the institutional) space and time for people to try out and develop new learning activities and to rethink existing activities, in terms of their learning potential, will be as important as defining and identifying learning outcomes. Third, a one-sided stress on the responsibility of individuals for their own learning can lead to learning being treated in isolation from the contexts in which people find themselves. Moreover, a focus on individual responsibility does not take into consideration the extent to which the opportunities for learning are far from evenly or equitably distributed.

The main initiative referred to in the Green Paper is the University for Industry (UfI), which is concerned with brokering the 'market for learning'. The UfI rests on two assumptions. The first is that the main cause of the relatively low level and uneven distribution of lifelong learning is that many people lack information about learning opportunities. There are, it assumes, many potential lifelong learners and many providers eager to make learning opportunities available in more transparent and flexible ways. The role of UfI will be to bring these providers and potential learners into contact. Complementing the UfI, Learning Direct provides telephone advice to potential learners and Individual Learning Accounts will assist people in 'purchasing learning' and building up 'learning accounts'; both are designed to support individuals seeking to invest in their own learning. The Government's hope, as expressed in the Green Paper, is that these initiatives will encourage more of those who leave school or college to continue with their education and more adults to return to study or take up part-time or online learning.

From the point of view of this chapter, there are two questions that need to be asked about this essentially supply-side approach to promoting learning. The first is whether the Government's diagnosis is right. In other words, is a lack of information about learning opportunities the basic cause of low levels of lifelong learning? The evidence seems to be that there are other, more important factors that lie behind low levels of lifelong learning (Keep, 1998; Coffield, 1999; Keep and Mayhew, 1999). These are the low levels of attainment reached by the end of compulsory schooling and the lack of demand for higher levels of skills and knowledge by employers. It seems unlikely that efforts to make the learning market for adults more flexible will have much effect without major improvements in the levels and quality of learning in schools and a major restructuring of the economy that stimulates higher levels of demand for learning (Keep, 1998; Robertson, 1998).

The second and related question concerns the learning that is likely to be encouraged by these initiatives. There is no reference in the Green Paper to what type of learning is seen as important, or the kind of knowledge and skills that people should be encouraged to acquire, or, except in the references to basic skills, to the different needs of the potential learners whom the policy addresses. In the absence of a more explicit curriculum vision that is linked to the identification of new demands for learning, it seems likely that the proposed initiatives will repeat the all too familiar pattern of previous educational policies. Those with high levels of initial education will not only continue to benefit from existing opportunities, but will be in the best position to take advantage of the new learning opportunities that result from Government programmes such as UfI. Those with poor levels of achievement at school are likely to be in jobs that offer few direct incentives for them to become lifelong learners and the long-term unemployed will find themselves directed towards basic skill courses that offer few guarantees of employment.

A policy for learning?

The Green Paper's emphasis on promoting learning rather than just improving the provision of education is undoubtedly a significant change that reflects a genuine attempt to create a 'learning society' in which learning pervades every aspect of society. However, it relies on a fairly traditional view that learning is about 'getting qualifications', 'registering for part-time courses' or 'getting online access' to some learning package. None of these options, despite their individual merits, addresses the issue of what learning is being encouraged, who the new lifelong learners will be and why more people might be encouraged to continue their learning.

From the point of view of government, it is possible to see the attractions of these 'institutional' or 'outcome' definitions of learning. Whether the emphasis is on more people gaining qualifications, more people registering 'online' or more people taking part-time courses, all are quantifiable and can be used as evidence of higher levels of lifelong learning and as some indication of how public funds are being used. The examining and awarding bodies, the course providers, such as colleges, and the online providers of learning materials can use such measures to show increases in their productivity. Qualifications certainly provide evidence of learning; they can undoubtedly motivate people to learn and reward them for their learning achievements. However, contemporary learning theories (eg Lave and Wenger, 1991; Engestrom, 1994) have a much broader and more 'expansive' view of learning than that which is expressed by qualifications. They see it as an essentially social activity that involves changes in people's relationships and identities. In learning, people discover that they can act in (and on) the world in new ways. If people are learning, workplaces, families and communities must be learning and therefore changing. Measures such as the numbers of qualifications gained or numbers of learners registered on part-time courses say very little about such changes and, therefore, say very little about learning as it is increasingly understood by research.

On their own, 'outcome' measures tend to affirm the view that learning is a simple transmission process between teacher (or online provider) and learner. The acquisition of skills and knowledge by individual learners is of course an essential aspect in any genuine learning process. However, it is only one element abstracted from the complexities of actual learning. Because governments are concerned with the accountability and control of public funds, policies inevitably concentrate on outcomes and focus on what is easily measurable. However, when the main policy goal is to promote new kinds of learning activity, a narrow focus on outcomes may be counterproductive. Equally, a one-sided view of learning that overemphasizes learning as a social activity and neglects the skills and knowledge that learners need to acquire is equally an abstraction and can end up by neglecting what distinguishes learning from other activities. As I shall argue later in this chapter, the two aspects of learning, that it is both a social activity and a process of acquiring knowledge and skill, can be linked, if the purposes of the learning are defined through a concept of the curriculum.

I want next to consider in more detail a number of the factors neglected in both the Government's Green and White Papers, but which are crucial in developing a 'policy for learning'. These can be summarized as follows:

- the context in which learning *as an activity* takes place, including the incentives for learning and space needed to engage in it;
- the pedagogic expertise that is needed to enable the *learning potential* of different activities and contexts to be realized;
- the *content and purposes of the learning that are seen as important*; in other words, what kind of model of the curriculum is needed to define the purposes of lifelong learning for both learners and teachers?

The significance of each of these factors can only be touched on briefly in this chapter. Context is a broad concept that refers to the way in which any activity involves people in relationships with others; it is these relationships that give meaning to the activity, whether or not it involves learning. In the Green Paper, context has a more limited meaning; it is primarily its economic aspects that are focused on, and, as I have already suggested, it rests on some questionable assumptions about an untapped demand for learning. Although there are hints that the Government also recognizes the importance of stimulating employers' demand for learning in the recent Department of Trade and Industry's White Paper (DTI, 1998), there are fewer signs that such a recognition has reached the DfEE. This is partly, no doubt, because it poses a genuinely difficult issue for a government with an economic policy based on the belief that investment decisions are best left to the market.

A minority of the National Skills Task Force (not identified but likely to be the trade union members) recommends a flexible form of government intervention to stimulate employer demand for learning (DfEE, 2000), but this is unlikely to become official policy. The alternative approach, which the Government is adopting, is to try to encourage, on a voluntary basis, various types of education/business partnership. Leading edge firms in knowledge-intensive sectors, such as financial services, already treat learning as a key investment priority. In the same way that science-based industries invest in research and development, knowledge-intensive sectors invariably have strategic training partnerships with educational providers. However, it is difficult to see how, without more explicit government intervention, this pattern will be extended to many of the smaller firms that provide the bulk of employment in this country.

The context in which people find themselves is crucial to whether they are motivated to learn. Current policy focuses on qualifications and more flexible access to higher education as key contextual issues. Both are important; however, they are both examples of how external factors may motivate learning and, therefore, do not necessarily enhance learning as an activity in itself. Furthermore, the focus of recent qualifications reform has been primarily on the more rigorous specification of outcomes, not on the activities that might generate the outcomes. Another problem with placing too much reliance on qualifications in promoting learning is that much learning, especially at work, is not tied to qualifications. Given the opportunity, people often learn, both as a way of tackling problems at work or elsewhere, and because they enjoy learning 'for its own sake'. Although both these sources of motivation – workplace context and the appeal of learning for its own sake – could be more important than qualifications for lifelong learning, neither is emphasized in the Green Paper.

The second issue a policy for promoting lifelong learning has to address, but which is given little emphasis in the Green Paper, is the role of teachers and workplace trainers. The idea that significant lifelong learning can be promoted without higher levels of pedagogic expertise, especially in workplaces, can be traced back to the influence of the National Council for Vocational Qualifications (NCVQ) and the priority it gave to the assessment and verification of learning outcomes, rather than enhancing learning processes. The NCVQ approach was based on two assumptions – that opportunities for learning would be enhanced if a qualification (an NVQ) could be gained without undertaking any additional programme of learning; and that much important learning, especially workplace learning, is 'experiential' – in other words, it takes place incidentally to other workplace activities and does not require the intervention of a teacher or trainer. Both assumptions play down the key role of pedagogy in enabling people to move beyond the specific context within which they find themselves. Recent research on learning challenges these assumptions and stresses the crucial role of teachers in promoting any but the most limited forms of learning (Engestrom, 1994). Furthermore, new approaches to pedagogy are not just an issue for researchers to develop: they have to be tested and revised in context and by teachers or trainers. This requires space and time that are free from the immediate pressure to provide evidence of learning outcomes.

The need to make available 'free' space and time for teachers and trainers to develop and test new approaches to pedagogy poses problems for policy makers when they are also looking for ways of limiting or at least gaining greater control of public expenditure. In the public sector, the answer to this problem would be likely to involve:

1. more research on pedagogy, which links learning activities and learning outcomes;
2. improved further professional training for teachers and trainers based on the new research on learning and pedagogy;
3. encouraging professional bodies for teachers and trainers to be more responsible and accountable;
4. changing the balance of government policy from the current focus on tighter inspection priorities and control of funding to placing more trust in professional skills and knowledge.

In the private sector, these strategies would need to be complemented by various combinations of tax incentives and support for Investors in People along the lines suggested in the Third Report of the National Skills Task Force (DfEE, 2000).

The neglect of pedagogy is brought into sharper focus by the links made, as in the Green Paper, between lifelong learning and creating a future 'knowledge economy' in which increasing numbers of jobs are seen to involve either the application of knowledge or the creation of new knowledge. Some forms of lifelong learning will always take place as a part of other activities and without any explicit pedagogy or any intervention from teachers or government. However, the major form of learning that will be needed in a knowledge economy will require people to go beyond their experience and to explore alternatives by drawing on knowledge generated by research. It is the ability to make available such knowledge that lies at the heart of successful companies in a knowledge economy and that must, therefore, become integral to a lifelong learning policy. Promoting learning that goes beyond specific contexts needs not only pedagogic expertise but a concept of a curriculum to define the kinds of knowledge and skills that are needed. Without a curriculum that defines the purposes of lifelong learning, it is difficult to see how the concept of lifelong learning will move beyond rhetoric. Despite references to a knowledge economy in both the Green and White Papers, the question of knowledge itself and the kinds of knowledge implied in the idea of a 'knowledge economy' are largely absent. A possible approach to conceptualizing such a curriculum for defining the purpose and content of lifelong learning, whether it takes place in workplaces, communities or formal education, is considered in the next section.

Lifelong learning and the curriculum

The Green Paper contains no view of the curriculum, in the sense of a specification of the possible content of the lifelong learning that it seeks to promote. Nor, beyond a general endorsement of a knowledge economy and the need for more learning, is there a view of the kind of society the Government wants the UK to become or the skills and knowledge that might be needed by its future citizens. This lack of curriculum vision reflects two assumptions underlying Government policy on post-compulsory education and lifelong learning. First, there is a general reluctance to specify curriculum priorities for post-16 education. The often-quoted view of the DfEE is that the post-16 curriculum is (at least legally) the responsibility of individual schools and colleges, not government or the Qualifications and Curriculum Authority (QCA). Colleges and schools therefore can, in principle, offer any post-16 curriculum they choose provided it recruits students and is in accordance with the framework of existing qualifications. Second, there is a widely held assumption that the idea of a 'curriculum' only really applies to institutions of formal education with an identifiable group with responsibility for its delivery – teachers. From this perspective, it makes no sense to talk about a curriculum for lifelong learning. Lifelong learning is something that people should do and, if possible, get accredited for, but it is not the responsibility of government to prescribe it.

The alternative view, and the one that is adopted in this chapter, is that there are powerful reasons why the question of a curriculum for lifelong learning (ie what learning is important?) cannot be avoided. First, all contexts embody some learning resources and priorities that will influence what learning is possible, even if they are not made explicit or formally taught. Lifelong learning can be seen in terms of a continuum between the learning that individuals pursue on their own initiative, either at work or in local communities, and that is of no direct concern to government, and the learning that a democratic society sees as important to promote as a way of achieving its own goals, values and future. In the 20th century, the latter forms of learning became increasingly associated with the curriculum of schools, colleges and universities and the importance of the informal learning that take place in every part of a society tended to be forgotten.

Government encouragement of lifelong learning recognizes for the first time that it is not only the learning associated with formal education that is important. The idea of lifelong learning asserts that learning that takes place in contexts such as workplaces and communities, and which would not in the past have seen themselves as sites of learning, also constitutes valuable learning. It follows, therefore, that if learning in such contexts is important enough to be part of government policy, a concept of the curriculum appropriate to defining its purposes is needed. As with the curriculum for schools and colleges, the goal of a curriculum for lifelong learning would be to give learning a sense of direction and some clear priorities. In addition, and of equal importance, such a curriculum could provide a framework for people to link their informal learning activities with their participation in formal education.

The absence of a curriculum vision poses a number of problems for a policy designed to promote lifelong learning. First, it is difficult to see where potential learners, and especially those who have been unsuccessful at school, will turn to for guidance in linking their learning needs to any new learning opportunities. Colleges and other providers are limited in the extent to which they can take on such a role by the competitive context in which they find themselves. Careers advisers might be in a position to undertake such a guidance task. However, they would still need a curriculum framework within which to work. Second, without a curriculum that relates possible new learning needs to changes in the economy, colleges and other providers are likely to continue with their current offers, even if there are changes in the system of qualifications. One consequence could be that, while more people gain qualifications, less attention is given both to the skills and knowledge that people need that are not expressed in qualifications and to the problems of motivating students to continue learning when they no longer have links with formal education.

What then might be involved in a 'curriculum for lifelong learning'? I suggest it will need the following features:

- a definition of learning goals that is broad enough to include the aspirations of the enormous diversity of potential learners implied by the idea of lifelong learning;
- a way of relating the knowledge and skills that people need to acquire to an idea of how society, and in particular the economy, is changing;
- a framework that is flexible enough to encourage learning in a wide variety of sites, both formal and informal;
- criteria and strategies for linking learning needs generated in specific contexts and the acquisition of specialized knowledge through formal education.

Lave and Wenger's (1991) concept of a 'learning curriculum' is a useful starting point. It begins with the learner and conceptualizes an approach to the curriculum that is not defined by institutional attendance or formally prescribed programmes or content. For Lave and Wenger a 'learning curriculum' is 'a field of learning resources in everyday practice *viewed from the perspective of learners*... It is essentially situated. It is not something that can be considered in isolation, manipulated in arbitrary terms in isolation from the social relations that shape... participation. A learning curriculum is thus characteristic of a community' (p 23, emphasis added).

They distinguish a 'learning curriculum' from a 'teaching curriculum' which for them '[supplies] – and therefore limits – structuring resources for learning, the meaning of what is learned [and control of access to it...] [a teaching curriculum] is mediated through an instructor's participation, by an external view of what knowing is about' (p 23).

Even where there is a 'teaching curriculum', as in didactic situations which are typically found in schools and colleges, Lave and Wenger argue that the 'learning curriculum' is the foundation of all learning and that it *'evolves out of participation in a specific community of practice engendered by pedagogic relations and by a prescriptive view of the target practice as a subject matter'* (p 23).

Their model is useful in stressing the social foundation of learning and in emphasizing the idea of the resources available to learners in any situation, even those where no one is formally a teacher. It also points to how people acquire the 'knowledge' necessary to become members of a community that may be a peer group in a workplace or a school. However, it has a number of limitations as a basis for a curriculum for lifelong learning from the point of view being argued in this chapter. First, it is implicitly negative about a 'teaching curriculum', which is presented as 'limiting' and 'prescriptive'. It is as if a 'learning curriculum', in linking knowledge to specific contexts, is not itself limiting and, in its own way, highly prescriptive, albeit in very different ways to a 'teaching curriculum'. Second, in treating knowledge as embedded in specific contexts, the model is limited as a basis for expressing learning goals that go beyond such contexts, as is frequently the case in modern workplaces. Third, though Lave and Wenger's model of a curriculum from the learner's perspective is a valuable corrective to the highly prescriptive models of the curriculum that have characterized much curriculum theory, it has a profoundly limited view of the learner as only located in a specific context or community. A curriculum for lifelong learning has to encourage learners to go beyond the contexts in which they find themselves and, if this is so, a 'teaching curriculum' is anything but prescriptive or limiting. A broader definition of the possibilities of a learner's perspective is needed which goes beyond what he or she perceives as his or her needs at a particular point in time and indicates what a learner might need or want to know to achieve particular goals.

Some writers on the curriculum who have taken up Lave and Wenger's analysis argue that its particular value is in presenting learning as 'a knowledge construction process' (McCormick and Paechter, 1999). From this point of view McCormick and Paechter suggest that *'lifelong learning takes on a quite different character... the separation of work and learning diminishes and the equation of 'learning' and 'courses' (in or out of educational institutions) becomes less significant'* (p 23).

The idea of learning as 'knowledge construction' stresses the active role of the learner in the curriculum and recognizes that learning is not just a process of participation or an activity; it also involves 'the construction of knowledge'. However, such a view can easily take for granted the question of knowledge itself. The idea of 'knowledge construction' emphasizes how people create new meanings for themselves when they learn; however, many of the new meanings that learners need to acquire are already 'created' elsewhere. It is precisely because much knowledge is 'pre-constructed' and what learners can construct in the contexts in which they find themselves is always limited, that lifelong learning needs a curriculum that makes this explicit. Lave and Wenger's concept of the 'learning curriculum' refers to knowledge only in the sense of the knowledge that is embedded in particular contexts and acquired in the process of participation in such contexts. They are not interested in what is sometimes referred to as 'codified' or 'abstract' knowledge that transcends specific contexts. This bias reflects the pre-industrial locations of much of their fieldwork on apprenticeship on which their theory is based and where embedded knowledge was all there was. In modern and increasingly knowledge-based societies, a lifelong learning curriculum has to enable people to acquire knowledge that is not embedded in the specific contexts in which they find themselves, but which enables them to understand the forces shaping those contexts.

To summarize, Lave and Wenger's concept of a 'learning curriculum' is valuable as a basis for a curriculum for lifelong learning in two ways. First, it establishes the idea that all learning has a social foundation and links the idea of a curriculum as an activity much more closely into a theory of learning than is true of traditional models of the curriculum which stress only the knowledge transmission aspect of learning. Second, it frees learning from any automatic link with teaching or schools and offers the basis for conceptualizing such notions as a 'curriculum of the workplace' or a 'curriculum of the community'. In each case, it points to the learning resources that are features of contexts with no formal curriculum. However, by implying that all knowledge is located in specific contexts, Lave and Wenger's model neglects the extent to which the 'embeddedness' or 'situatedness' of knowledge is itself a variable. Some knowledge is almost entirely 'situated'; in other words it has virtually no meaning outside a particular 'community of practice'. Other knowledge, such as that represented in academic disciplines and subjects or within professional communities, is also based in specific communities (of specialists). However, the power and significance of the latter types of knowledge extend far beyond the communities in which they are generated. A curriculum for lifelong learning needs to encompass both types of knowledge and their interdependence. It needs to involve a model of learning as the acquisition of context-specific knowledge and as a process of re-contextualization of knowledge produced in other contexts.

As mentioned earlier, despite stressing the importance of learning, the Green Paper makes very little reference to knowledge. It is as if, like learning, its meaning is obvious. However, the concept of a 'knowledge economy' that emerged in the past decade represented a break both with earlier phases of industrialization and with the ideas of knowledge associated with them. Instead of the workplaces of the future consisting of increasingly intelligent and powerful machines operated by fewer people, the idea of the knowledge economy envisages that workplaces of the future will consist of teams of increasingly knowledgeable people, often, but not always, using intelligent and powerful machines capable of carrying out routine tasks of communication and analysis (Zuboff, 1988). It is this 'new knowledgeability' that lifelong learning must enable people to develop.

The last section of this chapter introduces a number of approaches to the question 'what is this new "knowledge of the future"?' It identifies some common themes underlying these approaches, which it proposes as the basis for bringing knowledge back into a lifelong learning curriculum.

Bringing knowledge back in

The previous section made two closely related arguments. The first was that any policy that seeks to encourage lifelong learning needs a concept of the curriculum. The second was that central to any curriculum is the knowledge that people will need to acquire in the future. A number of attempts have been made to conceptualize what might be called the 'knowledge of the future'. They have their origins in a variety of different intellectual fields: in organizational theory – Morgan's (1986) 'holographic model'; in political economy – Reich's (1991) 'connective, collaborative, conceptual and critical skills'; in higher education – Gibbons *et al*'s (1994) 'transdisciplinary knowledge'; in curriculum theory – Young's (1998) 'connective specialisation'; and in approaches to workplace skills and learning – Zuboff's (1988) 'intellective skills' and Griffiths' and Guile's (1999) 'connective model' of learning through work experience. Despite their different origins, common themes can be found in all these attempts to conceptualize 'knowledge for the future'. They all challenge traditional divisions between knowledge and skills, between academic and vocational learning, between subject boundaries and between theory and practice. All stem from the recognition that, as the rate of emergence of new knowledge increases, certain capabilities that transcend existing knowledge boundaries need to be developed among as wide a proportion of the population as possible. All stress the importance of people:

- being able to *contextualize* what they do and know by seeing it as part of a whole;
- having an intellectual basis for *criticizing* existing knowledge and practice and conceiving of alternatives;
- being able to *apply* what they know in new situations (and in the process being able to review their previous knowledge);
- being able to *connect* what they know to the knowledge of other specialists, whether in educational institutions, workplaces or elsewhere.

Developing these capabilities, I suggest, can be viewed as the curriculum aims of lifelong learning. However, they are not themselves a curriculum, at least in the conventionally used sense of a learning programme and its aims. They are better seen as criteria for evaluating existing learning, whether in schools and colleges, in workplaces or elsewhere. They assume that though learning potential is unevenly distributed across different contexts (especially workplaces), there are learning priorities and possibilities in all contexts. They assume that all contexts embody both a 'learning curriculum', in the sense of being resources for learning, and a 'teaching curriculum', in the sense of embodying ideas about the knowledge that needs to be acquired (whether at the organizational or national level) – though the extent to which one or the other is explicitly recognized will vary. Potentially, the criteria apply at any level of learning and in relation to any content and context. They are not a replacement for subjects, disciplines, broad occupational fields, workplace competences or national occupational standards. They are a set of criteria that expresses:

- the social, political and economic goals of a future society;
- a concept of learning as a social activity that has clear purposes and a distinct role for pedagogy, whether in formal education or elsewhere;
- a concept of knowledge that emphasizes the interdependence of different areas and types of knowledge;
- the basis for a critique and development of alternatives to current policies, provision and resources for learning.

How useful they are to policy makers, researchers, teachers or learners will depend, in part, on how they are used. They are generic, not specific. Without exemplars based on the learning resources and curricula of existing contexts, formal and informal, and without detailed analyses of changes in the global economy and the organization of work, they are at best only guides. As generic criteria they need to be used in relation to actual programmes and in specific contexts. Given the diversity of learning needs and demands that are included in the concept of lifelong learning and the speed of change in the global demand for knowledge and skill, a curriculum for lifelong learning can never be more than a set of generic criteria. However, they represent an attempt to link curriculum criteria to global economic and political change and are based on a distinct approach to relating learning and knowledge. They embody an approach to learning that focuses on developing new relationships between 'learning as an activity' and 'learning outcomes'. Their assumption about learning outcomes is one that links learning to the acquisition of knowledge and embedded knowledge, which people acquire in practice, to the codified knowledge they need to understand the factors shaping that practice. In making these links, the criteria aim to shift the debate about lifelong learning from questions of access and participation to questions of pedagogy and knowledge. A policy for lifelong learning that avoids the question of knowledge lays itself open to Coffield's (1999) criticism that it is little more than a sophisticated exercise in social control.

References

Coffield, F (1999) Breaking the consensus: lifelong learning as social control, *British Educational Research Journal*, **25** (4), pp 479–99

Department for Education and Employment (DfEE) (1998) *The Learning Age: A renaissance for a new Britain*, DfEE, London

DfEE (1999) *Learning to Succeed: A new framework for post-16 learning*, DfEE, London

DfEE (2000) *Tackling the Adult Skills Gap: Upskilling adults and the role of workplace learning*, Third Report of the National Skills Task Force, DfEE, London

Department of Trade and Industry (DTI) (1998) *Our Competitive Future: Building the knowledge driven economy*, London, The Stationery Office

Engestrom, Y (1994) *Training for Work*, International Labour Organisation, Geneva

Gibbons, M *et al* (1994) *The New Mode of Production of Knowledge*, Sage, London

Griffiths, T and Guile, D (1999) Learning and pedagogy in work-based contexts, in *Understanding Pedagogy and its Impact on Learning*, ed P Mortimore, Sage, London

Keep, E (1998) Changes in the economy and the labour market: we are all knowledge workers now, in *Work and Education*, Post-16 Education Centre, Institute of Education, University of London

Keep, E and Mayhew, K (1999) The Assessment: knowledge, skills and competitiveness, *Oxford Review of Economic Policy*, **1** (Spring), pp 1–15

Lave, J and Wenger, E (1991) *Situated Learning: Legitimate peripheral participation*, Cambridge University Press, Cambridge

McCormick, R and Paechter, C (1999) *Learning and Knowledge*, Paul Chapman (for the Open University), London

Morgan, G (1986) *Images of Organisation*, Sage, London

Reich, R (1991) *The Work of Nations*, Simon and Schuster, London

Robertson, D (1998) The University for Industry – a flagship for demand-led training, or another doomed supply-side intervention? *Journal of Education and Work*, **11** (1), pp 5–22

Young, M (1998) *The Curriculum of the Future*, Falmer Press, London

Zuboff, S (1988) *In the Age of the Smart Machine*, Heineman, London

Part 3

The policy focus under New Labour

8

Developing a national qualifications framework for lifelong learning: England's unfinished business

Ken Spours

Introduction

The Labour Government sees qualifications playing a central role in supporting lifelong learning.

> Qualifications are important to us all... Qualifications are a goal to strive towards. They are a visible sign of achievement and a passport to progression. A society that sets store by rigorous and respected qualifications is one committed to learning, to developing the talents of all its citizens and to playing a leading role in the global economy.
>
> (DfEE, 1997: 2)

In the Green Paper, *The Learning Age* (DfEE, 1998), the Government emphasized the importance of qualifications and the National Qualifications Framework (NQF) for both the individual learner and the education and training system. For individuals, qualifications are seen as a way of promoting individual employability, encouraging motivation and providing a means of progression. For the education and training system, the NQF is seen as a key instrument for developing nationally recognized qualifications, for maintaining high standards, for recognizing and valuing different types of qualifications and for creating a qualifications system that is understandable.

This chapter will examine the Government's approach to qualifications reform and, in particular, the role of the NQF as a means of supporting lifelong learning. It will be argued that the Government is in the process of developing an NQF based on 'standards and linkages' that aims to promote consistency and comparability between different qualifications. Such an approach still retains the three qualifications tracks while, at the same time, attempting to create links between them (Raffe *et al*, 1997).

A 'standards and linkages' based approach to qualifications reform contrasts with policies promoted by parts of the education profession and a range of national agencies, all of whom have favoured the development of a single 'unitized' and credit-based framework from 14+ (AfC *et al*, 1994; NAHT, 1995; NUT, 1995; AoC *et al*, 1997). Furthermore, qualifications developments in Scotland and Wales appear to be moving towards the creation of a single unitized qualifications framework with an emphasis on 'seamlessness' between qualifications for younger and older learners (Welsh Office, 1998; COSHEP *et al*, 1999).

The analysis of a standards-and-linkages-based NQF begins with a historical perspective which traces the development of the NQF through different stages of reform since its inception in the mid-1980s (see Table 8.1). It will be argued that while the 'new' NQF being developed by the Government will be more comprehensive and inclusive than in past phases, it will still retain barriers to achievement and progression and may also be introducing new age-related obstacles. Historical analysis will suggest that an NQF that aims to support lifelong learning has to remove barriers to qualification and achievement, not only for adults but also for younger learners. Any all-through qualifications system has to address serious barriers in the 14–19 age group, where qualifications have been traditionally designed for selection to higher education and to the labour market.

The historical development of the NQF – from the 'qualifications jungle' to the triple-track system

The development of the NQF in England has, over the past 20 years, been intimately related to rises in post-16 educational participation. It is this relationship that makes the future development of the NQF a key feature of a system to support lifelong learning. As more learners have sought to participate in the education system beyond 16, either as the result of youth unemployment or because of rising educational aspirations, governments have responded by developing new qualifications. A continuous process of proliferation has created pressure to rationalize all qualifications into a system that is understandable to both learners and end-users. What emerges from the following historical analysis is that, to date, the main strategy for managing the expansion of qualifications has been to organize them into qualifications tracks while, at the same time, responding to pressures for flexibility to improve learner participation, attainment and pro- gression.

The *Review of Vocational Qualifications* (MSC/DES, 1986) led to the formation of a National Vocational Qualifications Framework (NVQF). The NVQF, based on National Vocational Qualifications (NVQ) levels, units and outcomes, aimed to support the introduction of NVQs and to convert all existing vocational qualifications into this competence-based model. During this phase of the NQF, academic qualifications, such as the GCSE and A

Levels, were part of a separate reform process. The *Review of Vocational Qualifications* had indicated that linkages would be forged with other types of qualifications, but the dominance of a competence-based approach meant that this failed to transpire (Cross, 1991). In retrospect, the NVQF could be seen as both divisive and potentially radical. Although it was confined to vocational qualifications, the framework employed design features (eg units, levels and outcomes) with the potential to embrace a wider range of qualifications which, beyond government, would become a reference point for blueprints for a unified and unitized qualifications framework (see Finegold *et al,* 1990; FEU, 1992; AfC *et al*, 1994).

A second phase of the NQF began with the 1991 White Paper *Education and Training for the 21st Century* (DfE/ED/WO, 1991), which proposed that there should be a qualifications framework based on A Levels, GNVQs and NVQs. The main motivation for its formation was to find a place for the newly created General National Vocational Qualifications (GNVQs) in order to stimulate post-16 participation while preserving the role of selective A Levels (Williams, 1999). Despite the policy emphasis on 'qualifications distinctiveness', the triple-track qualifications system marked an advance on the previous vocational phase because it sought to embrace different types of qualifications. However, the degree of alignment between academic and broad vocational qualifications was not sufficient to encourage mixing and matching of academic and vocational study which had been one of the policy aims associated with the introduction of GNVQs (FEU/IOE/Nuffield, 1994). Moreover, the triple-track NQF, based on A Levels, GNVQs and NVQs, was far from inclusive, with most qualifications remaining outside the framework (Dearing, 1996). This divisive and partial system was sustained not only by government policy but by the separate 'cultures' of the two regulatory organizations – the Schools Curriculum and Assessment Authority (SCAA) and the National Council of Vocational Qualifications (NCVQ) (Spours *et al*, 1998).

By the mid-1990s, three qualifications reviews – the Beaumont *Review of 100 NVQs and SVQs* (1995), the Capey *Review of GNVQ Assessment* (1996) and the Dearing *Review of Qualifications for 16–19 Year Olds* (1996) – signalled an attempt to make the triple-track qualifications system more flexible and more aligned so as to reduce poor successful completion rates in advanced level qualifications. In his influential report, Sir Ron Dearing (1996) suggested that the NQF should comprise four levels – Entry, Foundation, Intermediate and Advanced – to be applied to both academic and vocational qualifications. He still insisted, however, on qualifications distinctiveness, while stressing the need to create opportunities for transfer between qualification 'pathways'. Dearing also proposed the merger of the SCAA and the NCVQ to manage and regulate what would be a more flexible but still divided system.

New Labour's 'standards and linkages' based NQF

The Labour Government is ushering in a third phase of the NQF. In its consultation paper on advanced level qualifications, *Qualifying for Success* (DfEE, 1997), and in its Green Paper, *The Learning Age* (DfEE, 1998), the Government stated that it wanted to see a simplified and high-quality framework of qualifications.

By September 2001, a new NQF will be launched to contain all publicly funded qualifications. It aims to provide a framework of qualifications that can be easily understood by all learners and end-users and which will combine qualifications standards and inclusion. The Government believes that a qualification is more likely to be taken up by learners if it lies within a clear and trusted framework. Moreover, if all qualifications have to meet accreditation criteria in order to enter the NQF, it is thought that they can be equitably linked and legitimately compared.

This approach to the NQF has emerged since the 1997 General Election. Prior to coming into office, New Labour had proposed a qualifications framework based on a system of unitized and credit-based qualifications (Labour Party, 1996) rather than on the comparability of whole qualifications. During the mid-1990s, New Labour's post-14 education policy was influenced by its relationship with progressive sections of the education profession and a range of educational researchers who supported the development of a flexible and unified qualifications system (Hodgson and Spours, 1999). It is possible to see the Government's current approach either as a rejection of this past and representing a closer affinity to Dearing or as an interim stage of development on the way to a more flexible and unified system. There is evidence to support both interpretations.

The Government is developing its standards-and-linkages-based approach through five strands of reform:

1. accrediting a wider range of qualifications to the NQF;
2. creating a closer relationship between general and general vocational qualifications;
3. making a distinction between qualifications for young people and qualifications for adults;
4. undertaking a modest reform of NVQs so that they can achieve a better 'fit' within the NQF;
5. undertaking research and development work on unitization and credit for adult learners, but without a policy vision of an all-through framework.

Over the next few years the regulatory authorities in Wales, Northern Ireland and England (ACCAC, CCEA and QCA) intend to bring a wide range of qualifications into the NQF. Currently, there are more than 17,500 publicly funded qualifications and more than 250 awarding bodies. One-third of these – GCSEs/A Levels, GNVQs and NVQs – have been part of the tri-ple-track NQF and closely regulated, though much less is known about the other two-thirds. The launch of the new NQF will see all accredited qual-ifications placed in one of three categories – general, vocationally related/vocational and occupational – and allocated to a level of attainment. However, qualifications that seek inclusion may incorporate characteristics of one or more categories and may span one or more levels (QCA, CCEA and ACCAC, 1999). Qualifications can enter the framework and be publicly funded when they are judged to meet the necessary accreditation criteria. These include the identification of opportunities for developing and assess-ing key skills and provision for quality assurance and external assessment. This expansion of the NQF can be seen as a huge 'tidying up' operation as the regulatory authorities attempt to guarantee standards 'by getting to know what is out there' (Cassidy, 1999).

A second feature of the new NQF is a clearer emphasis on qualifications linkages than in the previous triple-track phase. In contrast to Dearing, the Labour Government places more emphasis on the relationship between qualifications than on their distinctiveness (Hodgson and Spours, 1999). This is most clearly illustrated in the case of advanced level qualifications, where the *Qualifying for Success* reform process is creating smaller qualifica-tions blocks of identical size and structure (ie six- and three-unit blocks) and a common grading system between AS/A Levels and Advanced GNVQs. Other qualifications that seek to enter the new framework may also be head-ing in a similar direction with the requirement that they should consist of units and should indicate how they support the development of key skills and the understanding of moral, ethical, social and environmental issues (QCA, 1999a).

A particularly problematical part of the linkages approach is the attempt to integrate NVQs more clearly into the NQF. At present, NVQs comprise sets of competence-based outcomes of different volumes and size which pre-vent them being easily combined with other qualifications. In an effort to encourage a closer relationship between NVQs and other qualifications, the QCA has conducted a consultation process to explore how NVQs can be uni-tized. The consultation, however, has come up against a tension between meeting employer needs for specific training and assessment and ensuring that individuals can gain a transferable qualification. Nevertheless, there appears to be sufficient agreement around the role of unitization in facilitat-ing both customized employer training and individual accreditation to be able to proceed to a further phase of research. This next phase will focus on allocating size to units; creating smaller packages of units and investigating how qualifications can use a mixture of units (QCA, 1999b).

A fourth feature of the Government's approach to qualifications reform is to make a sharp distinction between qualifications for young people and for adults (DfEE, 1998 and 1999). The main aim of its qualifications reform for young people is to promote both breadth and depth of study through the reforms to AS/A Levels and GNVQs and, in the longer run, through the possible development of overarching certification. The approach to qualifications for adults, on the other hand, aims for greater access and flexibility of study, with proposals to create a range of new Entry Level or 'starter' qualifications (DfEE, 1998). While the NQF itself is not age related, it is possible to see the distinction between the learning and accreditation needs of these two groups diluting the Government's commitment towards unitization and credit and the concept of an 'all-through framework'.

While the Government is firmly focused on creating a standards-and-linkages-based NQF, it wants to keep open the door to the development of more flexible and unitized qualifications for adults that, in time, may open up a further stage of development of the NQF itself. A cautious programme of research and development is taking place focusing on links between unitization and funding, the 'sizing' of units, the place of freestanding units within the NQF, and transitional arrangements to a fully unitized system (QCA, 1999a). However, ministers not only make a distinction between qualifications for 16–19 year olds and adults, they also distinguish between unitization and credit-based systems. They want to push ahead towards a unitized system, which they see as commanding a broad consensus, but they also wish to see more research and development work on the issue of credit, which consultations have revealed as being more controversial.

See Table 8.1.

Is the standards-and-linkages-based NQF a framework for lifelong learning?

The Labour Government's standards-and-linkages-based NQF constitutes a framework for lifelong learning in so far as it seeks to create public confidence in a wide range of qualifications that are linked by common quality-assurance criteria. It is thought that individual demand for learning and for qualification can be stimulated by people knowing where a qualification is located within the framework and what it is worth (DfEE, 1998). However, in this next section of the chapter, it will be argued that this 'tidying-up operation' that allocates qualifications to 'equivalent homes' within the NQF does not sufficiently address the barriers of the existing qualifications system. Moreover, it might even compel lifelong learning oriented qualifications, which currently reside outside the NQF, to become more exclusive.

Table 8.1 Historical phases of the National Qualifications Framework

National Vocational Qualifications Framework (1986–1991)	Triple-track national framework (1991–2000)	New Labour's 'Standards-based' NQF (2000–?)	A 'Lifelong Learning' NQF (the future?)
originated with the *Review of Vocational Qualifications* (1986)	originated with White Paper *Education and Training for the 21st Century* (1991)	originated with *Qualifying for Success* (1997) and *The Learning Age* (1998)	originates in national systems in Wales, Scotland and local experiments in England
aimed to rationalize qualifications provision and to organize competence-based vocational qualifications	aimed to create a qualifications framework containing three distinctive qualifications tracks	aimed to create an expanded but consistent NQF based on 'linkages' between qualifications and 'common standards'	aims to create a 'seamless' and 'all-through' qualifications framework for lifelong learning from 14+
designed around a framework of NVQ levels and units of competence-based assessment outcomes	NQF contained A Levels, GNVQs and NVQs, but over 50% of qualification registrations remained outside the NQF	not a 14+ concept of NQF – distinctions between 14–16, 16–19 and adult learners	based on units and credit and increased number of qualifications levels from access to higher degrees to assist progression
contained newly created NVQs and aimed to provide a framework for all vocational qualifications that were to become NVQs	limited alignment between different qualifications – A Levels, GNVQs and NVQs allocated to NVQ levels 1, 2 and 3	linkages strategy based on smaller aligned qualification blocks at advanced level and the acquisition of key skills	NQF is unit based rather than qualifications based and organized through a national unit bank
excluded academic track and did not promote the 'linkages' between different types of qualifications outlined in original NVQ report	unification of SCAA & NCVQ into QCA to create a more consistent NQF and to police the awarding bodies	emphasis on comparability of whole qualifications; external assessment and occupational standards tend towards exclusion, not inclusion	qualifications to meet different needs are rebuilt from the unit bank – qualifications in the 14–19 area are broad, unified and flexible
separate regulatory authorities – NCVQ, SEAC and NCC	triple-track NQF failed to work efficiently – high A Level drop-out rates, low GNVQ completion rates and low uptake of NVQs	pragmatic reform programme aimed at limited unitization and credit	credit arrangements created across the framework to promote access and inclusion
failed to transform other vocational qualifications and to meet the needs of rising full-time participation	Dearing, Capey and Beaumont reviews aimed to create more flexible track-based NQF	single regulator; a number of awarding bodies and development of more common-funding mechanisms	administered by single regulator/awarding body with regional structure to balance national reliability, with local responsibility and 'social partnership'

Do the qualifications categories lead to a track-based NQF?

The means by which qualifications are to be organized within the new NQF is by allocating them to one of three categories – general, vocationally-related/vocational and occupational. The new NQF categories closely resemble the three tracks (A Level, GNVQ and NVQ) of the triple-track NQF and Dearing's three distinctive 'pathways' based on academic, applied education and vocational training (Dearing, 1996). The emphasis of the new NQF, however, is less on the distinctiveness of qualifications, which was the rationale behind the triple-track NQF, and more on *'clarifying the relationships between qualifications, including broad equivalences and routes of progression'* (QCA, CCEA and ACCAC, 1999: 6). The prime function of the qualifications categories is regulatory because they are a means by which accreditation criteria can be applied to all qualifications entering the NQF. While the principal function of the categories is not to 'separate sheep from goats', they, nevertheless, retain the language of the qualifications tracks; they impose restrictions on currently flexible qualifications which need to enter the NQF in order to be publicly funded and they inhibit creative thinking about the development of fully unitized and credit-based systems.

Standards based on a divided-track-based system

A major purpose of the NQF is to promote public recognition of different types of qualifications so that people know what a qualification means and can rely on its quality (DfEE, 1998). This emphasis arguably leaves the development of the new NQF too dependent on divisive or outdated public perceptions of qualifications. A prime example of this is the claim of the 'public knowing where they are with A Levels' (Smithers, 1998). Awarding bodies that wish their qualifications to enter the NQF have to satisfy the rules of the two fundamental tracks. From the general or academic track there is the stress on external assessment and from the occupational track an insistence on a high degree of match with occupational standards. The rules of these two fundamental tracks, which the Labour Government have uncritically embraced, were designed and honed under the Conservatives to safeguard the selection of elites in full-time education or to meet immediate and narrow employer training needs. They were not designed to promote access and progression, to produce a broad educational foundation, to promote personal transportability of qualifications or to encapsulate new combinations of knowledge and skill, all of which can be seen as integral to a lifelong learning qualifications system.

Downplaying the importance of broad and inclusive qualifications

The insistence on adherence to accreditation criteria based on the two fundamental tracks also creates problems for the middle category of 'vocationally related' qualifications. It will probably end up containing the bulk of qualifications, but will be in danger of becoming a 'non-category' because the rules of the NQF are being developed elsewhere. Many of the qualifications in this category, for example BTEC and Open College Network qualifications, are flexible, broad and multifunctional, and successfully span categories and levels. Ironically, the effects of their inclusion in the NQF could be to undermine their inclusiveness and diminish their capacity to motivate learners and to provide them with a broad range of vocationally related knowledge and skill (NCFE, 1999). Moreover, successful qualifications, such as various baccalaureates and vocational group awards, which aim to provide a broad curriculum as well as specialization, also do not fit within the type of track-based thinking that still underpins the new NQF.

The reform of qualifications for young people: a halfway house?

Qualifications from 14+ form an important part of any lifelong learning system. At present, the Government is focusing on broadening advanced level qualifications and offering more opportunities for 14–16 year olds to study vocational education. These can be seen as steps to provide a better foundation for further learning and to motivate more young people to stay in education. However, important barriers remain which demoralize young people and frustrate achievement. The five GCSE A*–C grade threshold at 16 continues to act as a sieve for access to advanced level qualifications. For those who fail to pass this threshold by the end of compulsory education, there is the option of one-year full-time 16+ provision – GNVQ Foundation, Intermediate and GCSE resits – which all have very poor attainment and progression rates (Spours, 1995). Another example is the 'voluntarist' reforms of A Levels and Advanced GNVQs, which result from *Qualifying for Success* (DfEE, 1997). These reforms may lead advanced level students to take one more AS subject or to mix academic and vocational subjects, but may not sufficiently secure other dimensions of breadth such as broad and lifelong learning related skills, because of the lack of recognition of these by selector universities (Hodgson and Spours, 2000). The reform of qualifications for young people has, therefore, the look of a halfway house. It is a limited attempt to introduce more flexibility and broadening, but not a systematic exercise in removing barriers to increased attainment by the cohort as a whole.

The continued separation of higher education

The Learning Age (DfEE, 1998) proposed that a national framework for higher education qualifications (HEQF) should be introduced to be accompanied by a higher education system of credit accumulation and transfer. This, it was suggested would improve linkages with adult-related credit accumulation and transfer systems in further education. The development of a separate qualifications framework for higher education is a pragmatic move to improve access to higher education but without having to undertake root-and-branch reform. However, the aim of widening participation in higher education through the development of a Foundation Degree (DfEE, 2000), which will be located at Level 4 of the NQF and which spans further and higher education, may be inhibited by the creation of separate qualifications frameworks overseen by separate agencies – QCA for the NQF and the Quality Assurance Agency for the HEQF.

A piecemeal approach to unitization and credit

In *The Learning Age* the Government indicated its support for a unit-based credit system for adults, though it considered that the six-unit and three-unit qualifications proposed by *Qualifying for Success* provided sufficient flexibility for 16–19 year olds in full-time education. In 1998, a QCA consultation on unitization and credit revealed strong support for access to individual units by adult learners, but with more divided views on credit. Responses from further and higher education tended to support the concept of credit, whereas employers and NVQ awarding bodies had significant reservations about ascribing numerical values to units and qualifications (QCA, 1999b). In the light of these findings, the QCA has found itself treading carefully as it tries to inch its way towards a more unitized system. The first steps will be to require all vocational qualifications submitted to the framework to be made up of units and to support unit-based funding in a revised funding methodology. The QCA also hints at taking a more relaxed attitude to credit-based and credit-rated qualifications entering the new NQF. In the medium term, the QCA will evaluate the case for the introduction of a credit-based system and will keep in close touch with parallel developments in other parts of UK.

Standards-based linkages – falling short of a coherent lifelong learning system

The Government's strategy for the NQF, therefore, has been to stress the themes of educational standards and external assessment, the 'improvement' of existing qualifications and the promotion of consistency across different qualifications in order to secure parity of esteem. Its current concept of 'inclusive qualifications' is based on the relationship between 'standards' and 'trust' of different qualifications, rather than on the accumulation of achievement and transportability of credit for all learners.

The Government acknowledges the existence of a strong professional consensus for a 14+ unitized and unified NQF (QCA, 1999a), but refuses to be driven by it on the grounds that it holds too many political risks. It is possible that the Government's reluctance to declare an end-goal of an all-through 14+ unitized and credit-based qualifications system is influenced not only by complex design issues, but also by a concern that a declaration of this sort would trigger a debate about radically reforming GCSE and pushing ahead with the development of unitized overarching certification. The Government views these developments as being too far ahead of public consciousness with the potential to alienate powerful interest groups amongst employers, independent schools and the selector universities (Hodgson and Spours, 1999). A single unitized and credit-based qualifications system is viewed by government as something that will gradually emerge from seeing out the current qualifications reforms, together with detailed development work on sections of the framework, rather than redesigning its overall architecture.

A 'Lifelong Learning Framework' – the next stage of development?

An all-through and inclusive qualifications framework may gradually emerge from the current English reforms, though this is by no means guaranteed. On the other hand, all-through systems are emerging much more clearly in Wales and Scotland as these increasingly politically devolved systems pursue more advanced or different approaches to qualifications reform (Raffe *et al*, 2000 forthcoming).

Wales

Wales has traditionally been seen as part of the English system. In recent years, however, the distinctiveness of Welsh institutions has contributed to the potential for autonomous policy making which will be boosted by political devolution and the promotion of 'Welsh needs'.

The Welsh Green Paper on lifelong learning, *Learning is for Everyone,* argued for a seamless system reflecting the distinctive needs and circumstances of Wales and for a 'single, unitised, credit-based framework from 14 onwards as a cornerstone of lifelong learning' (Welsh Office, 1998: 25). It went on to state that the single framework would build upon the CREDIS initiative (a post-16 credit framework for education and training below higher education) and the Higher Education Credit Initiative in Wales. In a separate but related development the Institute of Welsh Affairs, with the support of the Welsh Assembly, has launched a £1 million pilot of the *Welsh Baccalaureate* (IWA/South East Wales TEC, 1999) in several Welsh schools and is seeking recognition of its future outcomes from higher education institutions in both Wales and England. It remains to be seen how far the Welsh Assembly will be able to develop these distinctive practices and whether they will be viewed as a threat by the DfEE or regulatory authorities, or as blazing a trail that can be slowly followed by Wales's larger neighbour. There are a number of factors that restrain Wales from diverging too far from qualifications developments for England (Raffe *et al*, 2000 forthcoming). The most significant is the amount of 'cross-border traffic' between Welsh schools and English higher education institutions and the problem of any new qualifications being recognized by selector universities in England.

Scotland

Developments in Scotland share many features with those in Wales, but are further advanced, owing to the fact that the Scottish post-compulsory system won a level of autonomy in the 1980s to develop along more unified lines (Howieson *et al*, 1997). The Scottish Qualifications Authority (SQA), in partnership with a range of other national agencies, is in the process of establishing a Scottish Credit and Qualifications Framework (SCQF) which will arrange a number of qualifications (eg higher education degrees; HNCs and HNDs; Higher Still Qualifications and SVQs) into a single and integrated framework. Initially, the SCQF will comprise 11 levels ranging from access to higher degree level. Each of the qualifications, units or groups of units will be allocated credit points based on 10 notional hours of learning time and credit points will classified into 'general' or 'specific' credit to be transferred by agreement within the framework (COSHEP *et al*, 1999).

The partners promoting the development of the SCQF see the gaining of units of credit by both younger and older learners as supporting lifelong learning because the process can be viewed as an end in itself, as a means of accumulating achievement towards a larger award or as a tool to transfer credit from one programme of study to another. The Scottish approach towards credit is both forward-looking and pragmatic because it involves a range of 'credit links' by agreement rather than imposing a system of credit transfer (COSHEP *et al*, 1999). Furthermore, the creation of the SCQF is seen as a developmental process, in which transferring all students and courses to the new system will take a number of years. Scotland will face similar design challenges to England in relation to the inclusion of SVQs, because of the differences between these qualifications and others within the framework. However, in a classic act of Scottish accommodation, SCQF credit points will be allocated to SVQs on the basis of each SVQ being equated with a 'standard notional learner year'. This first move will immediately include SVQs within the SCQF and, at the same time, allow refinement of the relationship, based on practical experience of implementation. This strategy of pragmatic 'incrementalism' within a visionary framework may avoid the considerable problems encountered in the New Zealand experiment, which undermined educational consensus by adopting a more ideological, competence-based and top-down approach to their NQF (Smithers, 1997; Tobias, 1999).

Table 8.2 The English National Qualifications Framework

Quals/levels	Entry	Foundation	Intermediate	Advanced	4	5
Vocational	common	eg Level 1 NVQ	eg Level 2 NVQ	eg Level 3 NVQ	eg level 4 NVQ	eg level 5 NVQ
General vocational	to all	eg GNVQ Foundation	eg GNVQ Intermediate	eg GNVQ Advanced		
General	families	eg GCSE (grades D–G)	eg GCSE (grades A*–C)	eg GCE A/AS level		
			Key Skills			

The Framework will also include NVQs at levels four and five, and HNCs and HNDs awarded outside higher education. QCA will consider and approve other

Table 8.3 The Scottish Credit and Qualifications Framework

SCQF level	Standard Grade	Other National Qualifications (Higher Still)	Higher Education	SVQs
11			Masters/postgraduate	SVQ 5
10			Honours degree	
9			Ordinary degree	
8			Dip HE/HND	SVQ 4
7		Advanced Higher	Cert HE/HND	
6		Higher		SVQ 3
5	Credit	Intermediate 2		SVQ 2
4	General	Intermediate 1		SVQ 1
3	Foundation	Access 3		
2		Access 2		
1		Access 1		

Tables 8.2 and 8.3 highlight important differences to the creation of NQFs north and south of the border. First, the Scots, like the Welsh, have a vision of an all-through qualifications system with common rules that include young and older learners. In England, a 16–19/19+ divide is being cemented by age-related distinctions highlighted in *Learning to Succeed*.

Second, the Scottish framework comprises 11, possibly 12, levels, while the English NQF is confined to six. Third, the SCQF is allocating credit points to all qualifications, whereas in England credit systems are being developed separately in higher education and adult qualifications. Finally, the reform process is being conducted in different ways. In Scotland, aided by a more consensual educational political culture, difficult design issues, such as the credit rating of NVQs, are being addressed in a staged approach within an all-through framework vision and development programme. In England, the political difficulties of a more fragmented system with entrenched vested interests have resulted in a reform strategy that postpones the vision of the future until current design problems have been resolved. This approach is unlikely to succeed, however, since the root of the problem is, more often than not, ideological rather than technical.

Going beyond the English reform tradition

While they are at different stages of development, the Welsh and Scottish approaches to qualifications and credit frameworks share a number of features and background factors (Raffe *et al*, 2000 forthcoming). First, both qualifications strategies are inspired by a sense of national identity – the notions of 'Scottish educational tradition' or 'Welsh needs'. Second, reforms are taking place within small educational systems in which there is a high degree of personal interaction between the institutions and agencies involved in the policy process. Finally, both countries are building on existing unitization initiatives or unitized qualifications. This is particularly the case in Scotland, where this process has been accelerated through the implementation of *Higher Still* (SOED, 1994).

The English reform tradition in the area of qualifications, on the other hand, has been a mixture of radical critique and local experimentation shaped by opposition to track-based expansion of the system (Howieson *et al*, 1997). Moreover, the growth of institutional autonomy in further education colleges and the continued autonomy of higher education institutions have provided space for the development of local unitization and credit-based initiatives throughout the 1990s (eg FEU, 1992; HEQC, 1994) and their theorization into a system of qualifications for lifelong learning (Wilson, 1999). The recent reform of the UCAS Tariff can also be seen as part of this process of institutional voluntarism. As a credit-based initiative, the reformed Tariff is attempting to quantify achievement across different qualifications for access to university education on a UK-wide basis. However, it is not a government scheme and will not be recognized by all universities (Carvel, 1999).

The standards-and-linkages-based NQF is a step in the direction of a lifelong learning qualifications system. Its development, however, is being inhibited by political ambiguity and a lack of vision of a holistic system. What is required is that the current development work which litters the qualifications landscape (eg vocational qualifications at KS4, reform of advanced level qualifications, the introduction of an Foundation Degree, development of unitized qualifications in the NQF, and various credit-based initiatives) be encapsulated within a 'strong framework' of an all-through NQF from 14+. Such a vision for development would mean that all the current initiatives could be viewed and connected within a single framework; the relationship between qualifications and units could be understood and appreciated by all learners, not just adults, and the fundamental qualification barriers that lie across the 14–19 age range could be coherently addressed.

An all-through framework would also signal the development of a philosophy of achievement and not just standards, of levels aimed at progression rather than selection, and a more prominent role for units to encourage breadth of achievement as well as accumulation. Such a framework to support lifelong learning would, inevitably, have organizational implications. It would produce both a national and local 'climbing frame' that could be fully utilized by Local Lifelong Learning Partnerships and the Local Learning and Skills Councils, and would spur on a further phase of unification of the regulatory and awarding bodies. Furthermore, this phase of development would place England on a convergent rather than divergent path with our immediate neighbours. The 'home international' systems of Scotland and Wales are showing the way and there will be pressure for us to follow. It will be in the interests of all learners and end-users of qualifications that this is sooner rather than later.

References

AoC et al (1997) *Key Principles for Curriculum and Qualifications Reform from 14+*, Post-16 Education Centre, Institute of Education, University of London

Association for Colleges (AfC) et al (1994) *Post-Compulsory Education and Training: A joint statement*, AfC, London

Beaumont, G (1995) *Review of 100 NVQS and SVQS: A report submitted to the DfEE*, DfEE, London

Capey, J (1996) *Review of GNVQ Assessment*, NCVQ, London

Carvel, J (1999) A Level points switch row, *The Guardian*, 11 December

Cassidy, S (1999) Doubts voiced over sixth form curriculum, *Times Education Supplement*, 17 December

COSHEP et al (1999) *Adding Value to Learning: The Scottish Credit and Qualifications Framework*, SQA, Glasgow

Cross, M (1991) The role of the National Council for Vocational Qualifications, in *Post-16 Education: Studies in Access and Achievement*, ed C Chitty, Kogan Page, London

Dearing, Sir Ron (1996) *Review of Qualifications for 16–19 Year Olds*, SCAA, London

Department for Education and Employment (DfEE) (1997) *Qualifying for Success: A consultation paper on the future of post-16 qualifications*, DfEE, London

DfEE (1998) *The Learning Age: A renaissance for a new Britain*, DfEE, London

DfEE (1999) *Learning to Succeed: A new framework for post-16 learning*, DfEE, London

DfEE (2000) *Foundation Degrees Consultation Paper*, DfEE, London

Department for Education/Employment Department/Welsh Office (DfE/ED/WO) (1991) *Education and Training for the 21st Century*, HMSO, London

Finegold, D et al (1990) *A British Baccalaureate: Overcoming divisions between education and training*, Institute for Public Policy Research, London

Further Education Unit (FEU) (1992) *A Basis for Credit? Developing a Post-16 Credit Accumulation and Transfer Framework: A paper for discussion*, FEU, London

Further Education Unit, Institute of Education and Nuffield Foundation (1994) *GNVQs 1993–94: a national survey report: an interim report of a joint project – The evolution of GNVQs: enrolment and delivery patterns and their policy implications*, FEU, London

Higher Education Quality Council (HEQC) (1994) *Choosing to Change: Extending access, choice and mobility in higher education*, HEQC, London

Hodgson, A and Spours, K (1999) *New Labour's Educational Agenda: Issues and polices for education and training from 14+*, Kogan Page, London

Hodgson, A and Spours, K (2000) *'Qualifying for Success': Towards a framework of understanding*, Institute of Education/Nuffield Foundation Project Working Paper No 1, Institute of Education, University of London

Howieson, C et al (1997) Unifying academic and vocational learning: the state of the debate in England and Scotland, *Journal of Education and Work*, **10** (5), p 35

Institute of Welsh Affairs (IWA) and South Wales TEC (1999) *The Welsh Bac: From Wales to the world*, IWA, Cardiff

Labour Party (1996) *Aiming Higher: Labour's proposals for the reform of the 14–19 curriculum*, Labour Party, London

Manpower Services Commission/Department of Education and Science (MSC/DES) (1986) *Review of Vocational Qualifications: A report by the working group*, HMSO, London

National Association of Headteachers (NAHT) (1995) *Proposals on 14–19 Education*, NAHT, Haywards Heath

National Council for Further Education (NCFE) (1999) *Report of FE Focus Group Meeting*, 12 January, NCFE, Newcastle

National Union of Teachers (NUT) (1995) *14–19 Strategy for the Future: The road to equality*, NUT, London

Qualifications and Curriculum Authority (QCA) (1999a) *Unitisation and Credit in the National Qualification Framework: A position paper*, QCA, London

QCA (1999b) *Improving the Value of NVQs and Other Qualifications: A report on the outcomes of consultation*, QCA, London

QCA, CCEA and ACCAC (1999) *A guide to the arrangements for the statutory regulation of external qualifications in England, Wales and Northern Ireland*, QCA, London

Raffe, D et al (1997) The unification of post-compulsory education: towards a conceptual framework, *British Journal of Education Studies*, **46** (2), pp 169–87

Raffe, D et al (2000 forthcoming) Unifying academic and vocational learning: current policy developments in Wales, in *The Education Systems of The United Kingdom*, ed D Phillips, Symposium Books, Oxford

Scottish Office Education Department (SOED) (1994) *Higher Still: Opportunity for all*, HMSO, London

Smithers, A (1997) *The New Zealand Qualifications Framework*, The Education Forum, Auckland, New Zealand

Smithers, A (1998) View from here, *The Independent*, 9 April

Spours, K (1995) *Post-Compulsory Education and Training: Statistical trends, Learning for the Future Project, Working Paper No 7*, Post-16 Education Centre, Institute of Education, University of London, Centre for Education and Industry, University of Warwick

Spours, K *et al* (1998) *Regulation, Awarding Bodies and the Process of Unification in England and Scotland*, Unified Learning Project Working Paper No 4, Universities of Edinburgh and London, Edinburgh

Tobias, R (1999) Lifelong learning under a comprehensive national qualifications framework, *International Journal of Lifelong Education*, **18** (2), pp 110–19

Welsh Office (1998) *Learning is for Everyone*, HMSO, London

Williams, S (1999) Policy tensions in vocational education and training for young people: the origins of General National Vocational Qualifications, *Journal of Education Policy*, **14** (2), pp 151–67

Wilson, P (1999) *Lifelong Qualifications: Developing qualifications to support lifelong learners*, NIACE, Leicester

9

The case for a regional dimension to lifelong learning in the UK

Simon James

... we find the regional level to be highly suitable for organizing vocational training at all levels. Because of the increasingly distinctive skills needs of regionally specialized economies, probably only the regional level now has the appropriate purview of labour market demand and supply relationships in the current period

(Morgan and Rees, 1998: 15)

Introduction

The purpose of this chapter is to consider some of the issues raised by the concept of sub-national learning economies – local and regional – in the context of the lifelong learning debate and the government policy framework for post-compulsory education and training. Although the prime focus is further education, this should be seen as a case study – there are clear implications for all agencies concerned with the strategic planning and delivery of learning to individuals.

In the first part of this chapter, I map the background to the regional debate, exploring the concept of the region and how it has come to be charged with fostering and exploiting connections between economic revitalization and lifelong learning. Two issues of contemporary debate, which I explore briefly in the first part of this chapter, are the comparatively democratic nature of the region and the special relationship between regional arrangements and the knowledge economy.

The second part of this chapter discusses emerging regional structures in more detail and identifies the tensions and challenges that must be resolved. One of my purposes in the latter part of the chapter is to distinguish between the local and the regional and to test the implications of that distinction.

However, in order to do that I must define the two main axes of my case – 'learning' and 'region'.

Lifelong learning

The phrase 'lifelong learning' trips off every policy document in sight at present. Its meaning slides between two or three different (but not necessarily exclusive) models in current policy debates and it will be useful to outline those and to be clear about the meaning of the concept in this chapter.

The 'remedial' model of lifelong learning

The lifelong learning sector (as it will soon become) has a long and admirable tradition of encouraging adults whose under-achievement during their initial education has left them unqualified and without confidence. Most, if not all, colleges brim with stories of adults whose lives have been transformed as a result of their experiences on college courses – often as a result of a first step made through community education provision. Colleagues in colleges often cite this tradition in debates with ministers, civil servants and other post-16 learning opinion leaders. The 'second chance' tradition is an honourable one. But lifelong learning for the new economic age cannot be synonymous with structures and provision aimed at making up to people for the shortcomings of their early education. That model would imply that those who experience 'successful' education during their first 20 to 25 years have little need for further continuous learning.

Specific skills updating as a model of lifelong learning

Another model of lifelong learning envisages individuals occasionally dipping back into learning as their skills become outdated or as a new job demands different skills. Typically this model points to training in IT, management, customer service, medical technology, health and safety, new employment legislation and, most recently, key skills.

A learning culture

An even more ambitious vision – a learning culture – has been described by several commentators, perhaps most vividly by Bob Fryer (1997). In this scenario, opportunities for learning are available throughout people's lives at times and places that integrate well with other commitments and activities. The workplace and the home, in particular, become as significant as dedicated educational institutions, in terms of locations of learning. A lifelong appetite for learning is encouraged. Individuals certainly build upon their basic and key skills and acquire specific skills and knowledge sets. But they also deepen their broad capabilities, their abilities to be focused, to think forward, to think analytically and imaginatively, to work flexibly, to collaborate well with others and to adapt to new contexts and new demands.

In this chapter, I recognize that while there is a family resemblance between these models, it is this third broad concept of lifelong learning that will most effectively enable people to enjoy the risks and challenges of the 21st century economy.

Why learning *regions*?

Fostering sub-national learning economies is an important thread in this Government's policies for promoting lifelong learning. A series of new arrangements, including Regional Development Agencies, local Lifelong Learning Partnerships, and Local Learning and Skills Councils, are predicated on an analysis that the sub-national agency is the right unit for connecting strategies for economic revitalization to opportunities for individuals to develop capabilities that will ensure their employability and self-empowerment. 'Funding should follow individuals and employers and the wider community should decide the mix of opportunities which are made available, so as to meet the needs of local, regional and national labour markets and reflect the wishes of *local* communities. Improved employability will be the result' (DfEE, 1999: 22, emphasis added). This connection between the economic sphere and that of education and training can, such arrangements imply, work most effectively in the regional/sub-regional setting. Why?

Regions are not natural phenomena; nor is there necessarily consistency in the characteristics that define a region. Regions derive their identities from different sources. One source of regional identity springs from what is held in common by the people of a region, though what it is that is shared will vary. A region may be defined by its history, or by a language, by common or related economic activities, or by unity against external threat. Whatever a region's defining characteristic, it lends a loose, shared identity to its population. Other regions may have a less 'organic' identity than the sort defined above, which may be engendered by, for example, a unifying economic base. Where boundaries are the outcome of national administrative decisions, for example local Learning and Skills Council areas, and where these are not coterminous with more organic boundaries, or with people's perceptions of what constitutes their patch, discontents will surface.

Regional organization is also perceived as potentially more democratic, more 'bottom up', more inclusive, and nearer to the ground than the nation state. It is thus considered less likely to impose and more likely to hear all the voices and views that need to be heard. This function of subsidiarity is threaded through emerging policies on lifelong learning; the role of regional arrangements in securing economic revitalization is underpinned – lent detail, accuracy, depth, focus – by the more democratic nature of regions.

So the first bit of the answer to my question – why are regions and localities considered the best context in which to connect economic revitalization with the matching pattern of learning opportunities? – lies in the capacity for regional arrangements to engage, map and respond to the detail of social and economic geography.

In continuing to examine the policy emphasis on joining up learning opportunities with employment opportunities at the sub-national level, it is important to consider a concept fundamental to current policy developments: the knowledge economy.

Perhaps traditionally the word 'knowledge' implies a grasp of facts or theories. But in its new usage – the knowledge economy – it has taken on a wider, stronger meaning and embraces creative thinking, imagination, foresight, innovation, problem spotting and solving (Leadbeater, 1999). The 'knowledge economy' refers to an analysis that asserts that 'knowledge' is replacing unskilled labour and raw materials as the *primary* factor in economic production (Rees, 1997).

This is not to suggest that labour and raw materials do not continue to count significantly in creating our material world and the services we consume. The swiftest of glances around the office and kitchen – including the 'made in' labels on everyday products – provides evidence of their continued and significant presence. But, it could be argued that the value of the contribution of raw materials and unskilled labour to production has diminished in comparison with the value of the knowledge input (Rees, 1997).

Electronic technology is the most dramatic contemporary example of an industry where the catalytic process at the heart of production is the creation of knowledge that will be metamorphosed into products. Industries, such as pharmaceuticals, fashion and the media, provide further examples of the primacy of knowledge in comparison to unskilled labour or raw materials. However, if we look at products less obviously knowledge intensive in their manufacture – cars, aeroplanes, music systems, washing machines, food processors – we find that their manufacture too is increasingly knowledge rich. A comparison of the different values of the inputs will demonstrate the dominance of the knowledge element – often embedded on a microchip – and the shift towards the knowledge input.

The implication of the knowledge economy for economic policy makers, for educationalists, and for all of us is this: the capabilities and up-to-date skills of the population will be important as never before in determining economic competitiveness and success. 'Education is the best economic policy' (Blair cited in DfEE, 1998: 9) is not simply a platitude that most of us feel we have always known anyhow. In the knowledge economy, it does have a fresh meaning. In this context, it becomes essential to encourage the normalization of learning throughout individuals' lives.

People who are skilful, who are knowledge rich, and, in particular, those people with broad capabilities that equip them to be nimble and imaginative in the application of their skills and knowledge, will be highly employable; such skills are likely to be in high demand. This type of insulation from economic insecurity brings a sense of authorship to other aspects of people's lives beyond the means to a wage. After all, broad skills are an asset to individuals beyond their working lives; they do not recognize a boundary between work and personal life. Broad capabilities enhance all aspects of people's lives from their enjoyment of their children, their tactics for staying well, to leisure.

Knowledge economies thrive on a consistently high level of learning and achievement across the work force. In a knowledge economy, a distribution of learning opportunities that fosters the widest pool of capabilities makes sound economic sense (Green and Steedman, 1997).

Conversely, where significant numbers of people are shut out of learning, their potential contribution is lost; the price of that exclusion is suffered most keenly by the individual and her/his family, but the wider community also pays a price. At its sharpest, learning disadvantage leaves individuals stranded without even basic skills. In the knowledge-driven economy, the policy goals of social inclusion and economic competitiveness are closely stitched together The economy demands individuals who are focused, multi-skilled, flexible, thirsty to learn; the individual offered such personal-development opportunities is empowered and included.

The current skills profile of the UK reveals a wide gap between the knowledge rich and the knowledge poor. The performance of the UK's skills elite – in the pharmaceutical, creative, and scientific research industries – has been well documented and analysed (Green and Steedman, 1997). The low skills levels of a substantial proportion of the population – the long tail end – has been sharply revealed in rigorous detail by the findings of the 1998 Moser enquiry into adult basic skills. The volume of exclusion demonstrated by that survey was sobering, even startling. Moser has estimated that around seven million adults have poor literacy skills (Moser, 1999). This means that one in five adults reads and writes less well than an average 11 year old.

A plethora of current policies – New Deal, New Start, Right to Study, Education Action Zones, Youth Support Service, Graduation, more childcare places for single parents who want to study, Education Maintenance Allowances, Individual Learning Accounts, University for Industry (Learn Direct) – are aimed at dismantling the obstacles to learning for those who do not identify themselves as learners.

The underlying purpose of all these initiatives is to help individuals to equip themselves with skills and qualifications that will produce good employment prospects and more general self-empowerment. The engine of this argument lies with the Treasury. This Government does not simply demand that educational institutions take learning opportunities to more people (DfEE, 1999). The condition of additional resources and a place in the sun is that educational institutions of all types reach out to those learners who are trapped out of the system: crucially to those learners who do not think of themselves as learners. To ensure the UK's competitiveness in the global markets, we need to realize the potential of all.

How does this analysis connect with the regional agenda?

In contrast to the nation state, the region/sub-region as a unit is better suited to stitching up the seam between the demand for present and future skills, and the capacity of the relevant population to take advantage of that demand. Why? Because the nature of the scale and focus of a region enables a wider range of relevant interests to be included in the decision-making processes than would be possible in a national context.

Furthermore there is something visible to the naked eye about a region that makes it clearer to all parties that planning and implementing successful economic regeneration demands partnership and cooperation as well as competition.

Two things are transparent: no single agency can successfully promote economic vitality; and area-wide regeneration promotes a win–win scenario. Regions are suppler than national arrangements, the benefits of collaboration more evident. In that framework and with access to detailed intelligence with which to inform planning, regions offer a fruitful context for planning local learning economies. Increasingly, knowledge generation is the key process in economic activity. But knowledge generation at its most fruitful relies not just on the skills and training of individuals but also on the exchange of knowledge and ideas between individuals. However, knowledge generation needs more than the individual imagination in which to thrive. It is dependent both upon capable individuals and the gathering together of those individuals in a particular context. Knowledge grows where the cross-fertilization of information, perspectives, analyses, ideas and knowledge is encouraged and valued. Characteristically, a fertile context for the promotion of innovation will emphasize collaborative working practices, networking, and exchange. Teamwork will be encouraged both within and across organizations; dialogue and thought will take place across structures.

The anatomy of regions offers a context in which knowledge generation can thrive. The variety of networks, meetings, local communication media, links, channels of communication (formal, informal, even social) and teams permit intelligence to travel at speed, and continually to charge up the ideas of individuals.

There is a certain irony to this. The renaissance of regions unfolded just as, gazing at globalization, we were all working hard at imagining knowledge-sharing networks laced across the planet. At that moment, it seemed possible that the power of the knowledge networks opened up by microchip technology would obviate the need for physical proximity. And it remains true that the potential for such transnational networks is powerful. But those developments will not eclipse the equal but opposite power of regional networks.

There is another irony of course. Globalization is a bit of a misnomer. It is often used to mean that the small scale is at the mercy of the large scale. The network approach enables localization – one doesn't have to be a global player to reach global markets – and puts the big and the small on the same footing.

This government commends cooperation and collaboration to us. However, this is far from an ideological or political commitment to collaboration for its own sake – a sharing, caring way of working. Nor is it only the long overdue recognition of the negative outcomes, the value lost, of excessive and unbridled competition. Rather it rests on a hard-headed recognition of the greater added value produced by collaborative working styles in a knowledge-driven economy (DfEE, 1999).

Territorial aspects of current government policy

Whilst in opposition, the Labour Party established the Millan Commission (chaired by EU Commissioner Bruce Millan) to investigate all aspects of regional policy, particularly as they would affect the Labour Party's Manifesto Commitment for the 1997 Election. The Commission reported in 1996 and the main recommendations in relation to Education and Training included (RPC, 1996: x–xii):

Regional skills strategies

Skills levels in the regions are unacceptably low, which hinders competitiveness and impedes growth. Current targets for skills are unambitious, and should be reviewed, with a view to reaching the levels of our international competitors. Particular attention should be given to regions and areas that are lagging behind. Training policy lacks a strategic approach. Regional skills strategies should therefore be prepared, to develop and co-ordinate provision for vocational education and training. Such regional skills strategies should be an essential component of regional economic strategies, and prepared after consultation with relevant regional vocational education and training interests.

Regional Skills Agencies

Every region should have a Regional Skills Agency, to co-ordinate and integrate training and vocational education, and to prepare the regional skills strategy on behalf of regional chambers. Regional Skills Agencies could be separate from, or might be integrated with, the Regional Development Agencies, and should represent wide vocational education and training interests in the regions.

Colleges of further education

Colleges of further education have been removed from local authority control and given operational independence, but are now completely dependent on a national quango for their funding. This funding is determined on the basis of national priorities, with little regional emphasis. In order to give colleges a greater regional focus, part of their funding should be allocated for regional purposes, on the advice of the Regional Skills Agencies, in line with priorities identified in the regional skills strategy. Local interests should also be strengthened by providing for local authority representation on college boards of governors, and by consultation of college development plans with relevant local interests.

When Labour came into power, the regional agenda was pursued (and continues to be so) with some vigour by John Prescott, the Deputy Prime Minister and Secretary of State for Environment, Transport and the Regions. In 1998, the Consultation Paper on Regional Development Agencies was produced (DETR, 1998) alongside a range of proposals for a devolved Scottish Parliament and Welsh Assembly and similar arrangements in Northern Ireland. These have all (to greater or lesser extents and with greater or lesser stability or permanency) come to fruition. [1]

However, at the same time, the Department of Education and Employment (DfEE), led by David Blunkett, was beginning to formulate its own plans for lifelong learning. Here we begin to detect a divergence. The Department of the Environment, Transport and the Regions (DETR) has a continuing commitment to regionalization (indeed, it established Regional Government Offices – of which more later). However, the DfEE, acknowledged to be one of the most centralizing of government departments, began to focus its thinking on the national and local levels and published *Learning to Succeed* in the summer of 1999 with its proposals for a National Learning and Skills Council and 47 Local (not regional) Learning and Skills Councils (DfEE, 1999).

The current situation, as far as I see it, contains a number of tensions that replicate the tensions between those two major government Departments of State. On the one hand, the DfEE is developing more *localized* support and funding structures for lifelong learning, widening the brief of the Learning and Skills Council to include further education and all other post-16 provision (with the exception of higher education) with a strong remit for local Learning and Skills Councils to meet national learning targets.

On the other hand, the DETR has established Regional Development Agencies that have been given a fairly limited role in relation to the determination of Learning and Skills Councils' boundaries, but a more broadly defined role in determining regional skills strategies, of which the Learning and Skills Councils are expected to take note. Whether they will do so is, of course, a separate question.

And, in parallel to the whole of this process, is the development of separate democratic infrastructures for governance on a regional basis with regions, led by local authorities, developing regional assemblies, regional chambers with an ultimate ambition (which is more strongly articulated in some English regions than others) to regional assemblies. We also see the election of a Mayor for London and similar aspirations being voiced for cities such as Liverpool. And against this whole background are the developments of the Welsh Assembly and the Scottish Parliament that focus the debate within the extended United Kingdom on the nature of territorialism, but also throw down particular challenges to the 'remaining' English regions.

The regional learning economy and further education

In a piece of research conducted by the Further Education Development Agency (FEDA) during 1996 (James and Clark, 1997) a number of key figures in further education locally, nationally and regionally began to come to some important conclusions about the further education sector and its post-incorporation role. These conclusions did not (in most cases) come in a Damascene flash of light, but were the result of mature reflection and the experience of working in and for further education over a number of years.

Broadly speaking, the conclusion can be described as 'there's an economic development party going on out there and further education hasn't been invited'.

This manifested itself in many forms. A few examples will suffice here:

- The Single Regeneration Budget (SRB) had been established and colleges, although playing some key roles in SRB design and delivery, were often excluded from the strategic planning process and direct engagement by other partners at that vital first stage.
- Anecdotal evidence suggested that where local and regional inward investment agencies existed, whether mediated by a local authority or a Training and Enterprise Council (TEC), colleges were often brought very late into the process of introducing a new inward investing client to a particular area.
- TECs had a clear remit to exercise the local strategic role, and while there was some creative engagement with further education on development projects and a variety of ways of handling the requirement for TECs to sign off colleges' strategic plans, there was a substantial amount of veiled (or not so veiled) criticism of further education colleges as deliverers of government training programmes.
- Post-incorporation relationships with local, borough, district and county authorities ranged from warm to tentative to non-existent. Yet, pragmatic working relationships between further education and local authorities still needed to be found.

- Across Europe there was an increasing trend towards regionalization and an awareness that tertiary institutions were playing a role in regional economic development. This was not uniformly the case across England and Wales.

As a result of these and other trends, FEDA established a major strategic research and development initiative entitled 'Furthering Local Economies'. The original aim of the work was to map the role that further education plays in economic development, not just as a provider of skills, but in all aspects of economic development activity, from business development through community development to physical involvement in the regeneration of local areas.

To make sense of this role, FEDA defined (and asked colleges to comment on) their roles as 'service provider', 'strategic partner' and 'stakeholder'. They concluded that the size of the further education sector's role as a service provider of skills and business support, combined with its stakeholder role as local employer and purchaser, added up to a strategic partnership role that needed to be more firmly recognized by local, national and regional partners.

At about the same time that the research was published, the (then) new Labour Government issued its consultation paper on Regional Development Agencies (RDAs). As we have seen, the original Millan Commission Report that forms the basis of the RDA proposals had envisaged a clear and distinct role for further education in regional development issues. However, the feeling within the further education sector from the consultation paper was that although further education was mentioned, its role as a strategic partner was somewhat underemphasized.

As a result of the research work by FEDA and others, the further education sector on an individual, regional and national level, through its representative organizations, was able to make a strong case for greater inclusion within Regional Development Agencies. This will lead directly to further education representatives filling the 'education' place on several RDA boards, while others include business representatives with a strong (governor) interest in further education.

With the advent of *Learning to Succeed* we need to ask where the findings of research like this leave the new (and widely inclusive) 'lifelong learning sector'. Is the new sector to be allowed to find its place as strategic and operational partner – or will it be consigned to the role of a network of providers directed at a local and national level by the Learning and Skills Councils?

It seems plain to me that the dynamics of lifelong learning support and strategic development are inevitably larger than the local. With the range of interrelationships that the new partners in the lifelong learning sector will have these are simply not containable within the area covered by a local Learning and Skills Council – even if that is a fairly large metropolis such as

Newcastle-upon-Tyne or Manchester.[2] Travel-to-work and travel-to-school considerations, the regional transport infrastructure and the operation of other regional authorities, such as the health service, inevitably both stretch and blur the boundaries between the local and the regional.

For this reason I argue that, whether formally defined in the new structure or not, as far as lifelong learning is concerned, the region and its dynamic will continue to have major strategic importance and Government ignores this at its peril. [3]

Opponents of regionalization would argue that the region is too ill-defined and uncertain a creature, with too many differing political drivers – and as many definitions as there are regions – and that what some see as a dynamic, others would see as approaching chaos. However, those opponents would still argue for the regional unit of administration to be maintained, even if simply as the Regimental Sergeant Major in a national Command and Control model.[4]

But to enhance this ecological description of the regional learning economy, I would also propose that the model of stakeholder/strategic partner/broker and provider, established in the earlier FEDA work (James and Clark, 1997), contains important features of inter-institutional collaboration on a regional basis as well.

In my view, in the 'Third Way' world of Blairite Britain, divisions between those who strategically plan and those who locally operate become increasing blurred. Indeed, I go further. I maintain that an organization working truly and effectively in partnership with others will move backwards and forwards between the four roles – stakeholder/strategic partner/broker and provider – in the course of a single dialogue (see Figure 9.1).

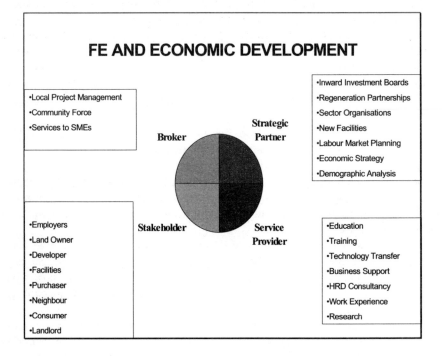

Figure 9.1 FE and economic development

The secret, therefore, is to understand the nature of the dynamic and, subsequently, to appreciate that the locality, as opposed to the 'regionality', cannot possibly contain such a dynamic – it is simply too small.

Wired-up regions

No discussion about learning and regions would be complete without reference to the regional uses of technology. In many ways I see the development of the World Wide Web giving the potential for the same sort of global learning market as I outlined earlier on the globalization of trade.[5] In my view though, a connection still has not been fully made on a regional basis between the development of learning, the regional economy and the use of technology to support that infrastructure.

What we need to look for is a way of regionalizing the technological use of the Web on a global basis to support and customize regional learning economies.

The question is: How does a region, wanting to make itself a learning region, make its presence felt in a global medium?

There are, of course, historical precedents – the meta approaches to the Web that have served non-geographically based interest groups so well through, for example, 'Web circles'. The secret will be to find protocols for linking local (ie ICT-based) learning, together in a way that makes sense as far as the regional customer is concerned. The mechanisms that will succeed are mostly like those of the Net itself, organic, incomplete, always in process – in other words, a dynamic.

So why does all this matter?

Regions will not go away just because of national government departmental tensions, although there is a separate debate about the nature of the 'natural' as opposed to the 'constructed' region and increasingly issues concerning peripherality in relation to some English regions and their proximity to either Wales or Scotland (or indeed Northern Ireland).

As Kevin Morgan says 'Some have argued that the regions in England are not "natural regions". This argument is, however, redundant in that the natural region does not exist anywhere in Europe; most regions are "artificial creations". Once regional institutions and budgets are introduced, regional action, focus and identity will follow'(Morgan and Rees, 1998: 15).

There is no doubt that regions do sometimes forge their unique identity on a learning infrastructure fairly bluntly and inaccurately, for example, the 'Industrial North' or the 'Resort-based Southwest'. Nevertheless, these descriptions and the sense of region contained within them do, in fact, infiltrate all aspects of local activity within that region: in terms of the new world of lifelong learning, these are ignored at no small risk.

So, in conclusion, national government departmental wishes cannot make regions go away – they are an essential part of the national learning development infrastructure and, therefore, a vital part of the national response to the globalization of trade and knowledge. But more than this, they are a macrocosm for what happens in local communities – a two-way filter between the national and the local. For this reason, institutions in the new lifelong learning sector need to find ways to develop services to respond to needs at both a regional and a local level.

The fundamental question that we will need to answer is: what's the lowest possible level of physical/economic control that is enough to give dynamism its head and grow whilst avoiding complete fragmentation – and to acknowledging the need of national government to assure public accountability. In other words, what does subsidiarity mean in terms of creating a learning society? For me, the combination of a tripartite relationship between technology, the economy and learning described within a regional context points towards the answer.

UK plc is dead, but is northeast.com the future?

Acknowledgements

I should like to thank my colleagues Nadine Cartner at ACM, Caroline Mager at FEDA and Ian Ground at the University of Newcastle Upon Tyne for their indispensable advice and assistance with this piece.

Notes

1. The case for an extension of the regional democratic remit to the English regions continues to be made by the English Regional Assemblies, but the debate is not sufficiently developed. This is primarily, I would argue, because of the regional vacuum that currently exists in national government policy that makes it difficult for us to understand the role that such a democratic tier might fulfil in regional learning policy. We watch Wales, Scotland and Northern Ireland with some interest.

2. See, for example, how the higher education sector, currently bypassed by the government's plans for lifelong learning, has continued to build on – indeed promote – it's regional branding in the face of a global knowledge economy – 'Universities should position themselves as able to contribute to regional development in a very broad way, synthesizing economic, social, cultural and environmental agendas' (CURDS, 1997: 8).

3. Indeed, there is some evidence that the Government is aware of this potential pitfall – see for example, PIU (2000).

4. In continuing to maintain a regional Government Office presence, the DfEE, in my view, is demonstrating its concern to maintain precisely this kind of overview. See North East Regional Assembly (1999), *Concordat*, p 5 – where the role of the Government Office for the North East includes: 'sponsor and regulate One NorthEast' (the RDA).

5. Indeed, as noted above, higher education is increasingly seeing this arena as its new trading base. Similarly, the development of the University for Industry recognizes a similar opportunity for the traditional lifelong learner.

References

Centre for Urban and Regional Development Studies (CURDS) (1997) *Annual Report 1997*, CURDS, University of Newcastle upon Tyne

DfEE (1998) *The Learning Age: A renaissance for a new Britain*, DfEE, London

DfEE (1999) *Learning to Succeed: A new framework for post-16 learning*, The Stationery Office, London

Department of the Environment, Transport and the Regions (DETR) (1998) *Building Partnerships for Prosperity*, The Stationery Office, London

Fryer, B (1997) *Learning for the 21st Century: First Report of the National Advisory Group on Continuing Education and Lifelong Learning*, NAGCELL, London

Green, A and Steedman, H (1997) *Into the 21st Century: An assessment of British skills profiles and prospects*, London School of Economics/Institute of Education, University of London

James, S and Clark, G (1997) *Investing Partners: Further education, economic development and regional policy*, FEDA, London

Leadbeater, C (1999) *Living on Thin Air*, Penguin, Harmondsworth

Morgan, K and Rees, G (1998) The Learning Economy – economic competition and colleges, in *FE: Aspects of economic development*, ed S James, Further Education Development Agency, London

Moser, Sir C (1999) *Improving Literacy and Numeracy: A fresh start*, DfEE, London

North East Regional Assembly (NERA) (1999) *Concordat*, NERA, Newcastle Upon Tyne

Policy Information Unit (PIU) (2000) *Reaching Out – The role of central government at a regional and local level*, The Stationery Office, London

Rees, G (1997) Vocational education and training and regional development: an analytical framework, *Journal of Education and Work*, **10** (2), pp 141–49

Regional Policy Commission (RPC) (1996) *Renewing the Regions – Strategies for regional economic development*, Sheffield Hallam University

10

Hopes, contradictions and challenges: lifelong learning and the further education sector

Norman Lucas

Introduction

In a recent survey of staff in 14 further education colleges (Lucas, McDonald and Taubman, 1999) it was found that the agenda of lifelong learning, particularly the issues raised by the Kennedy Report (1997), had stimulated a new debate about the strategic purpose of further education colleges. The research found that the concepts of lifelong learning, widening participation and social inclusion had caught the imagination and the mood of many of those who worked and taught in the further education sector. Initiatives concerning lifelong learning seemed, at last, to give further education colleges an agenda, which after incorporation in 1993 made some kind of sense, in terms of practice and policy goals. The vision outlined in the Green Paper *The Learning Age* (DfEE, 1998) seemed to acknowledge the further education sector's strengths, and saw further education colleges as institutions for social, economic and cultural regeneration.

However, the research also revealed concerns that behind the rhetoric of lifelong learning lay a number of barriers and contradictions that as yet seemed unresolved. Teachers and managers pointed out that the present funding arrangements favoured full-time and thus younger students. Concern was expressed about the cuts in course hours and the growing proportion of part-time staff being used. Furthermore, the funding regime did not, as yet, recognize partial achievement, which is so important for widening participation. Staff in the colleges welcomed the new stress on cooperation but expressed concern that the Government seemed to be leaving untouched an infrastructure that encouraged competition (Lucas, McDonald and Taubman, 1999). Generally staff in the further education college sector welcomed the moves towards national teaching standards in further education, but the myriad of National Training Organisations (NTOs), such as those of FENTO, the NTO for further education, ENTO for employment or PAULO, the NTO for youth and adult/community education, caused confusion because it duplicated and added yet more layers to an already unplanned and *ad hoc* system.

This chapter is going to focus on some of these concerns and will not discuss definitions of lifelong learning in any depth, which are covered elsewhere in the volume. For the purposes of this chapter the definition I shall work to is that lifelong learning for further education colleges is the creation of institutions that are flexible enough in their organization, curriculum, teaching and learning to meet the learning needs of adults throughout their life cycle. I shall trace the development of further education colleges from their early industrial beginnings, then trace the growth in the diversity of courses from the late 1970s up to incorporation in 1993. I shall show that during this period further education colleges, for the first time, began to look something like lifelong learning institutions in the sense that I defined above.[1] I shall suggest that the period of incorporation up to 1997 represents another phase towards further education colleges becoming more flexible institutions, albeit in a 'marketized' and unplanned context. I will critically analyse the Labour Government's initiatives concerning lifelong learning, particularly focusing on *Learning to Succeed* (DfEE, 1999a). The penultimate section will compare the strategic drift of further education colleges in England with community colleges in the USA, arguing for a fundamental realignment of further education colleges in relation to schools and higher education. I shall conclude with the suggestion that if further education colleges are going to become truly lifelong learning institutions, a far more strategic and less voluntarist approach needs to be taken by central government.

The historic context

Adult and technical education in the early 19th century was that of working-class 'self education', often organized through small associations and clubs and, on a larger scale, through the institutions of the labour and cooperative movements. In this political tradition, adult education took many different forms from the common reading circles of working men and women to the Owenite Halls of Science, the 'schools' organized by the Chartists, Christian Socialists, night schools and others. An example of the latter was the London Working Men's College formed in 1854 by the Christian Socialists to provide education for working men (Harrison, 1954). However, the principal precursors of the late 19th-century technical colleges, were the Mechanics Institutes, the first of which was founded in Edinburgh in 1821.

What was common to all strands of adult education and training was their predominantly voluntary and part-time character. The overall picture of technical education and adult provision in the late 19th century is one of a fragmented, *ad hoc* and marginalized learning opportunities. The state did not initially play a direct role in fostering industrialization either by directing capital into industry or by training in new skills (Green and Lucas, 1999). Companies were left to invest in training as they saw fit and many did not see it as a high priority (Barnett, 1986). Although there were some advances towards a more systematic approach by the end of the 19th century, the liberal, voluntarist creed dominated the approach. The British state generally preferred voluntary initiative to state intervention in education and training, particularly in the area of technical and adult education, which was seen as a low priority for government. This left an impoverished legacy, with technical and adult education existing somewhere between school and work, with a low status in comparison to other continental states, and with a lack of any notion of the relationship between general education and technical skills. It was a legacy that further education colleges would find hard to break out of throughout the next century (Green and Lucas, 1999).

Some initiatives were carried forward in public funding of technical education early in the 20th century and expansion did take place. Following the First World War, steps were taken to set up day continuation schools, which, although enjoying some success, remained voluntary and floundered during the economic depression of the late 1920 and 1930s (Richardson, 1939). Despite this, the development of adult community education did expand. Women's Institutes were founded and the Workers Education Association grew in strength. In many respects, it was in community adult education that concepts of lifelong learning were being embraced. There was no state concept of lifelong learning as schooling, technical colleges and vocational education generally was geared to the needs of industry (Venables, 1967)

Despite the advances for schools in the 1944 Education Act, post-compulsory education and training emerged after 1944 as a highly uneven provision that varied substantially from one locality to another with close links with local industry (Gleeson and Mardle, 1980). Legislation had been permissive, allowing local education authorities wide scope for interpretation. Vocational education and training remained low in status and apprenticeships were dominated by the engineering and construction industries, which by the 1970s were in decline, along with other traditional industries such as shipbuilding and heavy engineering (Gorringe, 1996). With the decline in traditional heavy industry and the steady rise of unemployment in the 1970s, technical colleges began to transform themselves into colleges of further education which began to provide a wider range of academic, vocational, pre-vocational and general vocational courses. Further education colleges began to acquire a multi-purpose educational function (Tipton, 1973) and there was a movement from colleges being exclusively linked to industry to a position where they were providing for the learning needs of people from the wider community.

Throughout the late 1970s and 1980s, full-time participation in further education increased steadily and colleges were required to respond to the needs of new types of learners, including, notably, adults and school leavers who previously would have entered directly into the labour market. During this period there was a shift from the typical technical college focus on vocational day-release and evening study, to the far more complex offer of the new style further education college with its increased load of full-time students following a variety of vocational and academic courses. A 'new vocationalism' developed which emphasized preparation for work rather then training in work. Many of the curriculum reforms in the early 1980s reflect a clear and visible attempt to shift from narrowly focused 'preparation for work' towards some notion of preparation 'for life', for 'citizenship', 'for multi-skilled work' and for 'collaborative work relationships' (Bloomer, 1997: 14).

Up to incorporation in 1993, colleges were gradually becoming more diverse institutions, providing learning opportunities for younger and older people in employment, the unemployed, people seeking employment, and youngsters who came to colleges for a second chance (Spours and Lucas, 1996). Colleges increasingly saw themselves as 'responsive' institutions, catering for a diverse student population (Cantor, Roberts and Prately, 1995). They offered part-time, full-time, sandwich and evening class study. They began to offer access courses to adults responding to the growth of higher education during this period. They also began to offer academic courses, as many schools became unable to maintain viable sixth-form provision (Hall, 1994). During this time, the further education sector can be seen as constituting a bridge between learning and work, as a 16–19 year old provider and an adult route to higher education (Young and Lucas, 1999). In a local sense, the modern further education colleges of the early 1990s, unlike the technical colleges of the earlier period, were becoming somewhat like lifelong learning institutions, albeit in a rather haphazard and pragmatic way.

Incorporation: flexibility and incoherence

The incorporation of colleges came about in the context of a Conservative Government in its third term of office ideologically determined to introduce competition between education and training providers and to erode further the influence of local education authorities (Lucas, 1999). Colleges got some independence from local education authorities, with devolved budgets, arising from the 1998 Education Act and the incorporation of colleges in 1993. This was followed by a period of high growth targets, 'efficiency savings', redundancies, the growth of part-time staff and the dispute over contracts. During this period of growth and competition further education students became even more diverse. An important part of this growth in diversity was that further education colleges began to take over a lot of adult education, provision that would formally have been organized separately from colleges in adult education institutes.

The massive growth in student numbers and diversity during incorporation, however, raised some important problems in the context of colleges becoming lifelong learning institutions where considerations concerning the learner are of central importance. Under incorporation, growth was finance driven, where maximizing units of funding, not educational or social considerations, seemed to dominate every aspect of college activity (Leney, Lucas and Taubman, 1998). This inhibited curriculum innovation and risk taking (Lucas, McDonald and Taubman, 1999). A few years into incorporation, colleges and teachers were found spending vast amounts of their time and energy trying to meet FEFC requirements, whilst at the same time trying to maintain the integrity of their provision, particularly part-time courses for adults (Unwin, 1999), which attracted relatively small amounts of funding.

During the period of incorporation, change was dominated by the need to make savings and to bring down the average level of funding by expanding student numbers. Considerations concerning lifelong learning were secondary to maximizing units of funding. Whilst many colleges tried to find a balance between educational and financial considerations, the logic of the funding methodology and the lack of overall funding allocated to the sector (Education and Employment Committee, 1998) forced colleges to take steps that were not always in the best interest of the students (FEFC, 1996). This included rising redundancies of full-time staff and the increasing use of part-time agency staff to save money. More and more resources were being spent on meeting the audit requirements of the FEFC, which were considered 'out of control' (Leney, Lucas and Taubman, 1998). The Kennedy Report (1997) noted that there was evidence of potential learners being denied full access to information and a wasteful duplication of effort. Furthermore the Report said that the priority for some colleges was to improve their market share rather then to expand the market for learning, with the funding regime acting as a barrier to the type of collaboration that was central to engage groups of excluded learners and to provide lifelong learning opportunities.

When judged by quantitative standards such as increases in the participation rate, or efficiency savings, incorporation can be judged as successful (Lucas, 1999). However, when judged on qualitative and curricula criteria, some problems become apparent, such as the effects of cuts in course hours, and the difficulty in funding the part-time partial achievement that is all important for lifelong learning.

The period of incorporation up to the election in 1997 has been described as the 'marketisation of further education' (Lucas and Mace, 1999) and my analysis is that the consequences of this period have left real problems concerning further education's ability to respond to the agenda of lifelong learning. This is partly because of the relentless pressure to make 'efficiency savings' and partly because the 'units logic' of the FEFC encourages unit maximization and quantity to be put before quality (Spours and Lucas, 1996). In other words I am arguing that the legacy of incorporation has left a culture and framework that are fundamentally market-based and designed on a different ideological basis to the policy thrust of the present government (Lucas, McDonald and Taubman, 1999). I would suggest that a funding mechanism based upon competition is not conducive to meeting the agenda raised by lifelong learning, which requires cooperation (DfEE, 1999a) and planning, with the learning needs of the community as a central consideration. A marketized and competitive approach may work for business in the private sector, but there is no evidence that it leads to the social inclusion and equity that are so vital for lifelong learning.

Although at the time of writing the funding regime for post-16 education and training as a whole is being reformed, it remains to be seen whether this constitutes a radical change. The latest consultation document on funding (DfEE, 2000) does say that key features of the new funding system will be designed to complement the aims of *Learning to Succeed* (DfEE, 1999a). It proposes, amongst other things, to simplify the system of funding, to make it more responsive to the needs of learners and employers, and to fund four key elements – recruitment of learners, retention, achievement and disadvantage. There is also a further round of consultations promised, with a pledge to make the funding method flexible enough to ensure that it can facilitate moving unemployed people into work. However, there is, as yet, no proposal that partial achievement is to be recognized.

Furthermore, college incorporation after 1993 and the creation of the FEFC have done nothing to rationalize the overall structure of post-16 education and training. Far from creating a national sector (Green and Lucas, 1999), in many ways it has made any such rationalization more difficult. As Labour formed a new administration in 1997 it was hardly an ideal starting point to promote lifelong learning (Robertson and Hillman, 1997). There was an even greater diversity of controlling agencies in the post-16 sector than in the past. This included not only the FEFC for colleges, but also the local education authorities for schools, the Funding Agency for Schools for Grant Maintained schools and the Training and Enterprise Councils (TECs) for youth and adult training. Such a proliferation of overlapping control made the planning of a further education college system very difficult, since no one agency had sufficient authority to plan across a whole area. Although *Learning to Succeed* does rationalize some aspects of post-16 funding, from the point of view of the learner the picture is still one of confusion and barriers to learning (Hodgson and Spours, 1999). It would take some decisive strategic thinking to give the colleges, let alone other post-16 providers, a clear sense of direction based on the type of cooperation and planning that are so important if the interests of learners are to be put first.

From another point of view, however, the period of incorporation can be seen as having some positive benefits for colleges in their 'drift' towards becoming more responsive and flexible organizations. The effects of growth in the diversity of learner needs and the influences of community and adult education traditions (combined with the FEFC's pressure to make ever more 'efficiency savings') were to cause colleges to seek new, more flexible ways of delivering learning programmes. Incorporation has thus led to improved entry, guidance and learning support procedures and mechanisms (Leney, Lucas and Taubman, 1998). Further education colleges have learning centres and computer-learning facilities, they accredit prior learning, and they use a variety of new flexible learning techniques (alongside traditional ones). This, in turn has led to a re-examination of the professional role of the further education teacher and the development of national standards to improve the quality of teaching in the sector (Guile and Lucas, 1999). From this point of view, the period of incorporation up to the general election in 1997 represents a period of further diversity and innovation, albeit market driven, *ad hoc* and unplanned. Although in 1997 further education colleges were in financial crisis owing to the marketization of further education, from another view they were more flexible, innovative institutions, uniquely placed to develop further their role as central providers for the new government's initiatives concerning lifelong learning.

New Labour: hopes and contradictions

The election of a new government represented a turning point for the further education sector, which had reached a financial crisis in 1997. After a slow start with the Labour Government remaining pledged to stay within the spending limits of the previous administration, further education did extremely well in terms of increased funding. The dash for unplanned growth shifted to more tangible targets. The rhetoric of competition was replaced by one of cooperation and efforts are being made to bring about partnership at a local level (DfEE, 1999a). In terms of policy goals a single focus of competitiveness in the global economy was tempered with an agenda around social inclusion and lifelong learning.

According to government statements such as *The Learning Age* (DfEE, 1998) and *Learning to Succeed* (DfEE, 1999a), further education is vital for forging an inclusive society. Government policy has given further education an important role in the New Deal and in most recent initiatives on lifelong learning.[2] It has also been seen as having a major economic role to play in raising the country's economic strength and morale (Education and Employment Committee, 1998). Today further education colleges appear to be meant to cater for everyone, 16–19 year olds, both academic and vocational, adult returners, access students, higher education students, those with special needs, the socially excluded and those not involved anywhere else. As part of the new ethos of staying on in post-16 education and training, if you are not in a school sixth form, at work or at university, then you should be involved with the local college.

It is precisely the fact that further education faces in so many different directions that causes colleges anxiety within the context of recent reform proposals. Colleges welcome the new emphasis on lifelong learning, but they also point to a number of contradictions (Lucas, McDonald and Taubman, 1999). For example, the contradiction between the Government's encouragement to widen participation and the funding pressures to enhance retention and achievement rates. This has led some staff to be increasingly selective in their entry procedures, which militates against widening participation. Also, following the Kennedy recommendations, extra funding has been given to students from postcode areas identified as suffering from economic and social deprivation. However, sharp distinctions need to be made between the value of taking such an approach and its effectiveness in widening participation. In recent research (Lucas, McDonald and Taubman, 1999), inner city colleges welcomed the mechanism, whilst colleges in suburban areas were extremely dissatisfied with it. Suburban colleges pointed to rural deprivation, which is less visible and often exists in pockets alongside affluence, which the weighting of postcodes does not identify. Inner city colleges felt they had reached some sort of limit in widening participation and the extra units were rewarding them for what they were already doing. There is widespread agreement among college staff on the need for specifically targeted provision to attract under-represented groups, but, in their view, genuinely widening participation should not be about 'chasing units'. Widening participation is about establishing real links with hard-to-reach groups and this requires cooperation and planning, which are difficult in a funding system that still encourages competition and unit maximization.

Whilst some new patterns of collaboration are emerging in response to Government initiatives, they are contradicted by old, and some relatively recent, competitive habits. Recent research (Lucas, McDonald and Taubman, 1999) indicates that competition remains sometimes active and open, sometimes less overt, but in all cases with a crucial lack of strategic planning. In practice, competition between local providers is fierce, due to a rigid link between funding levels and student numbers, league tables and the like, where everything is still funding or achievement driven, rather than being driven by learner need. In other words, whilst there is a wish to cooperate, behind the rhetoric of cooperation lies a framework designed in a context of marketization and competition. This has produced and continues to reproduce a culture that is at odds with the present Government's emphasis on social inclusion, widening participation and lifelong learning. My argument is that to change the habit of competition to one of cooperation requires either clear funding incentives or penalties.

One of the problems for the Government in tackling some of these issues is balancing the politically sensitive issue of colleges being the major providers of 16–19 education and training with the fact that, as a sector this type of provision represents only a small part of what they do. With the exception of sixth-form colleges and some tertiary colleges, the average further education college is overwhelmingly an adult institution, offering a wide variety of courses providing access to universities, courses for the unemployed, employer-specific programmes and a large array of vocational courses. This diversity distinguishes further education from all other providers.

The White Paper *Learning to Succeed* (DfEE, 1999a) embodies Labour's strategic approach to post-16 education and training. In attempting to deal with the duality of further education provision it includes proposals for separate inspection regimes for 16–19 year olds and adults, as well as separate advisory committees along the same lines within the new Learning and Skills Council. This all points in the direction of separate arrangements for adults and 16–19 year olds and stems from a perception that the needs and requirements of young people are very different from those of adults. I would not like to argue against this approach, yet it is not explicitly stated and many of the proposals are voluntarist in nature. There is a danger that this voluntarist approach may reinforce old divisions between adults and 16–19 year olds along the academic/vocational division rather then providing different arrangements for preparatory education and for a more flexible lifelong learning curriculum (Young, 1999). The White Paper merely intimates that local Learning and Skills Councils will be allowed some autonomy and flexibility to vary funding arrangements to meet local circumstances – it does not give the clear steer towards cooperation (discussed above) that is needed to bring about lifelong learning.

Although *Learning to Succeed* heralds a new strategic direction in the sense of rationalizing post-16 education and training by creating national and regional Skills Councils, it is still unclear what the power at the regional level will be. This dimension is important, as it is at the regional level that planning and cooperation can take place to enhance lifelong learning. At present further education colleges have no clear institutional identity, they include diverse and competing institutions such as sixth-form colleges, tertiary colleges (some 16–19, some including adults), large and small further education colleges and specialized agricultural colleges. Introducing separate inspections for adults and 16–19 year olds will not help colleges to gain clarity. In fact many courses in further education have a mix of 16–19 year olds and adult returners. Institutions in local areas still compete for the same students, offering duplicate courses in the same catchment area.

Furthermore, formal links between further and higher education are proliferating, yet higher education does not really feature in *Learning to Succeed* or the *Learning and Skills Bill* (House of Lords, 1999). This does seem an oversight, as 34 per cent of further education students now go into higher education and most of the 'new students' in the 'new' universities come via further education (Melville, 1998). At the same time 52 higher education institutions are currently funded by the FEFC for students on further education courses. My argument is that at present further education colleges compete with school sixth forms on the one side, and an increasingly expansionist higher education sector on the other, yet the Learning and Skills Councils do not include the university sector. With the already diverse and fragmented nature of post-16 provision, excluding higher education not only makes it difficult to plan on a national level, but also is bound to cause considerable obstacles to local and regional planning. In many respects the regional dimension of strategic planning is one of the most important aspects of the White Paper, yet it is one of the least thought through aspects of the *Learning and Skills Bill*.

The setting up of Learning and Skills Councils represents, in my view, a step in the right direction and nudges the post-16 system towards greater coherence, with an emphasis on planning. The National and Local Learning and Skills Councils embrace local education authorities, schools, employers and further education colleges. However, the Government has taken a voluntarist approach to employers. Whilst the Chair of the National Skills Council and the majority of Chairs of Local Councils will have a business background, together with at least 40 per cent representation of business people being required at both levels (DfEE, 1999b), employers are under no obligation nor are they given any fiscal incentives to enhance opportunities for their employees to train.

The record of New Labour up to the publication of the White Paper *Learning to Succeed* was one of a series of laudable but uncoordinated initiatives (Hodgson and Spours, 1999). My argument is that although the Learning and Skills Bill makes some progress towards a rationalization of post-16 arrangements, it still lacks a strong strategic and integrated approach. It is too early to draw final conclusions. However, early indications suggest a lack of strategic thought, particularly concerning regional arrangements. For example, London is being divided into five local Learning and Skills Councils. The shape of these councils bears no relationship to the shape of Regional Development Agencies or the emerging Greater London Authority. Such an arrangement makes a coordinated approach across London very difficult. It remains to be seen how much overlap between agencies takes shape in other parts of the country. I wish to suggest that a far more strategic and less voluntarist approach would be more appropriate in achieving an infrastructure for lifelong learning, which I expand upon below.

From colleges of further education to lifelong learning institutions

As I have shown above, the Government sees the further education sector as a key sector for developing lifelong learning. Colleges are, despite incorporation, still embedded in local communities and historically have had good links with sectors of the community that are now seen as potential sites for the dispersed learning opportunities envisioned in *The Learning Age* (DfEE, 1998). They still have some connections with employers, professional bodies and community associations, as well as 'outreach' operations that extend their activities. Further education colleges have, in the past few decades, become diverse and flexible institutions, and are becoming more so. They have shown their capacity to change and, as such, are well placed to develop the new modes and forms of learning associated with the networked, flexible learning college of the future.

It would seem that until now the present drift of further education is positioning the sector towards the US community college model (Green and Lucas, 1999). The *Learning to Succeed* White Paper seems to strengthen the movement in that direction but as yet has not made the strategic position of further education colleges clear. US community colleges tend to be large, multi-sited institutions which dominate provision in their given area. Many further education colleges may approach a similar scale as financial exigencies force further rationalizations and mergers. US community colleges are notable for their commitment to open access and for the flexibility of their provision, with courses running, for instance, from seven in the morning to 11 at night, including Saturdays, and summer vacation schools. Further education colleges are also moving towards this level of flexibility, although without the resources that the community colleges enjoyed in their heyday of expansion in the 1960s and 1970s. Very importantly, US community colleges have long since developed a pedagogy that is explicitly geared towards student progression and have made the distinction between preparatory learning for 16–19 year olds and lifelong learning which needs to be more flexible in its delivery and assessment (Young, 1999). Community colleges in the USA are exclusively adult institutions and do not have to provide the pastoral, extra-curricular activities and protected environment needed by 16–19 year olds. They consequently do not compete with schools in the way that further education colleges in England and Wales do. Community colleges are adult institutions but not, generally speaking, in competition with the universities in the USA since their mission is clearly defined. They pioneered 'modularization' and credit accumulation and transfer, and have developed extensive systems of linkage with the university sector. The 'two plus two' degrees (where the Community College provides the first two-year Associate degree and the university the last two years of a four-year bachelors degree) have become the route to qualification for a substantial proportion of the Unites States' graduates since the 1960s. To a large extent and in an *ad hoc* way, further education colleges in England and Wales are developing similar bridges through access arrangements and franchised higher degree courses.

This clarity of the strategic role and mission of US community colleges is precisely what we lack in England and Wales (Green and Lucas, 1999). As outlined above, the present state of affairs could, with some nudging from Government (*Learning to Succeed* is a start), push further education colleges to become more like US community colleges and gradually to evolve into exclusively adult institutions. They could then devote their time to sub-degree level further education and training and incorporate all of the adult non-examination (non-schedule 2) work that local education authorities sometimes run elsewhere. If this were to happen, 16 – 19 provision would gradually be rationalized around sixth forms and sixth-form colleges, allowing a comprehensive tertiary 16–19 sector to emerge.

Whilst a comprehensive tertiary system would be difficult to achieve in the present political context, in the longer term such a rationalization may become possible and desirable. This, however, would require a more strategic and regulatory approach from government, defining the boundaries and responsibilities of schools, sixth-form colleges, further education colleges and higher education. It could rescue schools from trying to maintain non-viable sixth-form provision and allow them to concentrate on the pre-16 curriculum. Further education colleges could become more focused on providing the flexible provision and support required by adult learners, leaving the particular structures and provision that the younger age group requires to other institutions, which would probably be a mixture of sixth forms in schools, and sixth-form type colleges. Colleges could focus on lifelong learning for the local community; universities could become regional providers offering degree and higher-level education. Sub-degree provision, like foundation and access courses, would be largely provided in colleges. 'Two plus two' courses could be developed on a systematic nationwide basis, but with the respective roles of the further and higher education sectors clearly demarcated. Short-course vocational higher education might legitimately be run by universities if they could show that their facilities were required for adequate quality of provision and that they could run these courses as efficiently as colleges. However, there would be a general presumption that sub-degree work, including a greater proportion of level 4 courses such as HNDs, was the province of the college rather than the university. This would be good for maintaining the distinctive mission of universities, as well as for maintaining standards in further education colleges.

Such an approach would establish further education colleges as adult providers and, in addition, would clarify their boundaries. A realignment of this type would help to develop the further education colleges' identity, which has become even more blurred in recent years through their growing diversity of provision. It would allow further education colleges to address important questions concerning curriculum change (Young, 1999) and the implications of teaching and learning in the context of lifelong learning (Young and Lucas, 1999). Furthermore, staffing issues, teaching standards and the professionalism of further education teaching staff could be addressed in a more strategic way (Guile and Lucas, 1999). Colleges could still span the academic/vocational divide, although there is much to be said for them regaining their image as technical/vocational institutions alongside their role as broader lifelong learning institutions. Such a realignment, with further education colleges as part of a lifelong learning continuum, requires coordination and cooperation with local labour markets, schools, universities, professional associations and employers – a level of planning that is hard to see under present proposals.

Notes

1. I am not including sixth-form colleges in my analysis.
2. The New Deal for 18–24 year olds is a Government programme designed to help young people to gain access to employment (see chapter 3 of *New Labour's Educational Agenda: Issues and policies for education and training from 14+* by Ann Hodgson and Ken Spours and published by Kogan Page in 1999 for full details and an analysis of this policy).

References

Barnett, C (1986) *The Audit of War: The illusion and reality of Britain as a great nation*, Macmillan, London

Bloomer, M (1997) *Curriculum Making in Post-16 Education*, Routledge, London

Cantor, L, Roberts, I and Prately, B (1995) *A Guide to Further Education in England and Wales*, Cassell, London

DfEE (1998) *The Learning Age: A renaissance for a new Britain*, The Stationery Office, London

DfEE (1999a) *Learning to Succeed: A new framework for post 16 learning*, The Stationery Office, London

DfEE (1999b) *National Transition Plan*. Version – November 1999, Circular, DfEE, Sheffield

DfEE (2000) *Learning to Succeed. Post 16 Funding and Allocations*: First technical consultation paper, DfEE, London

Education and Employment Committee (1998) *Sixth Report of the House of Commons Education and Employment Committee*, 1, May 19th, The Stationery Office, London

FEFC (1996) *Quality and Standards in Further Education Colleges in England*. Chief Inspectors Report 1995/96, The Further Education Funding Council, Coventry

Gleeson, D and Mardle, G (1980) *Further Education or Training?* Routledge and Kegan Paul, London

Gorringe, R (1996), *Changing the Culture of a College*, Coombe Lodge Report, 24 (3), The Staff College, Bristol

Green, A and Lucas, N (1999) Repositioning further education: a sector for the 21st century, in *Further education and Lifelong Learning: Realigning the sector for the 21st century*, ed A Green and N Lucas, Bedford Way Publications, London

Guile D and Lucas N (1999) Rethinking initial teacher education and professional development in further education: towards the learning professional, in *Further Education and Lifelong Learning: Realigning the sector for the 21st century*, ed A Green and N Lucas, Bedford Way Publications, London

Hall, V (1994) *Further Education in the United Kingdom*, 2nd edn, Collins Educational and Combe Lodge, Bristol

Harrison, J (1954) *History of the Working Men's College: 1854–1954*, Routledge and Kegan Paul, London

Hodgson, A and Spours, K (1999) *New Labour's Educational Agenda: Issues and policies for education and training from 14+*, Kogan Page, London

House of Lords (1999) *Learning and Skills Bill*, HL Bill 14–16th Dec 1999, The Stationery Office, London

Kennedy, H (1997) *Learning Works: Widening participation in further education colleges*, FEFC, Coventry

Leney, T Lucas, N and Taubman, D (1998) *Learning Funding: The impact of FEFC funding: Evidence from twelve further education colleges*, NATFHE/Institute of Education, University of London

Lucas, N (1999) Incorporated colleges: beyond the Further Education Funding Council's model, in *Further Education and Lifelong Learning: Realigning the sector for the 21st century*, ed A Green and N Lucas, Bedford Way Publications, London

Lucas, N and Mace, J (1999) Funding issues and social exclusion: reflections on the 'marketisation' of further education colleges, in *Tackling Disaffection and Social Exclusion*, ed A Hayton, Kogan Page, London

Lucas, N, McDonald, J and Taubman, D (1999) *Learning to Live with It: The impact of FEFC funding, further evidence from fourteen colleges*, NATFHE, London

Melville, D (1998) Returner learners need quality, *The Times Higher Education Supplement*, 6 November, p 9

Richardson, W (1939) *The Technical College: Its organisation and administration*, Oxford University Press, London

Robertson, D and Hillman, J (1997) *Individual Learning Accounts and a Learning Bank*, Report No 13, National Committee of Inquiry into Higher Education, NCIHE, London

Spours, K and Lucas, N (1996) *The Formation of a National Sector of Incorporated Colleges: Developments and contradictions*, Post-16 Education Centre Working Paper No 19, Institute of Education, University of London

Tipton, B (1973) *Conflict and Change in a Technical College*, Hutchinson Educational, London

Unwin, L (1999) Flower arranging's off but floristry is on: lifelong learning and adult education in further education colleges, in *Further education and Lifelong Learning: Realigning the sector for the 21st century*, ed A Green and N Lucas, Bedford Way Publications, London

Venables, E (1967) *The Young Worker at College – A study of a local tech*, Faber and Faber, London

Young, M (1999) Reconstructing qualifications for further education: towards a system for the 21st century in *Further Education and Lifelong Learning: Realigning the Sector for the 21st century*, ed A Green and N Lucas, Bedford Way Papers, London

Young, M and Lucas, N (1999) Pedagogy and learning in further education: new contexts, new theories and new possibilities, in *Pedagogy and its Impact on Learning*, ed P Mortimore, Sage, London

11

Developing capability: part-time higher education and lifelong learning

Alison Fuller

Analysts of policy makers' attempts to develop a 'learning society' have noted how the role of the individual is consistently highlighted (see for example Keep, 1997; Coffield, 1998; Evans *et al*, 1999). The policy rhetoric suggests that learning societies can be attained by improving the education, training and qualification levels of individuals (see for example DTI, 1995; Ball, 1996; EC, 1996; DfEE, 1999). The underlying assumption is that the capability of the workforce as a whole will be raised if more individuals take responsibility for developing their knowledge and skills throughout their working lives. It is not the purpose of this paper to discuss the strengths and weaknesses of this assumption; such critiques have been developed elsewhere (see for example Keep, 1997; Coffield, 1998; Evans *et al*, 1999; Young, 1999). The intention here is to focus on one aspect of participation, mature student take-up of part-time HE, which has seen a substantial growth over the past two decades and especially since the late 1980s (Schuller *et al*, 1998; Davies, 1999; Fuller, 1999). Wider availability of opportunities and the expansion of individual choice for some adult groups have combined to raise the proportion of older students in the overall HE student population. For the year 1997–98, over four out of ten first-year HE students are known to be aged 25 and over (HESA, 1999).

In the UK, one manifestation of the individual focus is the Government's attempts to create a more 'credentialized' population (Young, 1998; Fuller and Unwin, 1999; Young, 1999). The setting of National Targets can be interpreted as a central plank of the 'credentialist' approach in the UK. The latest targets, referred to as the *National Learning Targets for England for 2002,* were introduced in 1998 and embrace 11–21 year olds, older adults and organizations employing more than 10 people (NACETT/DfEE, 1997). The targets are expressed quantitatively, with aims for levels of qualifications linked to specific proportions of the population at different ages. With regard to the workforce, the main policy vehicle for increasing qualification levels has been the development of the National Vocational Qualification (NVQ) system.[1]

The Government has been promoting take-up of NVQs in at least three ways. First, through the implementation of outcome-related funding for Government-sponsored training programmes, where a proportion of the training provider's fees are withheld until the candidate has successfully achieved the required qualification, usually an NVQ. Second, by exhorting individuals to take responsibility for their own learning through participating in the NVQ system (eg DTI, 1995; DfEE, 1999). Third, by exhorting employers to use NVQs to 'credentialize' their employees and, by so doing, to help create a labour force where increasing numbers of workers might be described as 'lifelong learners' (DTI, 1995; DfEE 1999). In relation to lifelong learning, Young (1999) has argued that it should not be assumed that producing a certificated population is the same as creating a learning society in that, particularly under the NVQ system, people may be able to achieve qualifications without learning anything new. Even if the focus is solely on the quantity of certificates awarded, it is not clear how effective the NVQ system has been in increasing the numbers of qualified adults. Robinson (1996: 4) conducted a detailed review of the quantitative evidence on NVQ take up. He concluded that 'NVQs have made only a marginal contribution' to the National Target for the proportion of the workforce qualified at level 3 (equivalent to A level, advanced craft or technician level).

It should be acknowledged that it is difficult to gain an accurate picture of individuals' take-up of NVQs. The Qualifications and Curriculum Authority (QCA) the current publisher[2] of take-up data publishes the number of NVQ certificates awarded.[3] It does not provide details of the number of individuals achieving the qualifications. As someone may achieve more than one NVQ, it cannot be assumed that for each certificate awarded there is a 'new' NVQ achiever. Another difficulty with the QCA data is that the characteristics of individuals pursuing or having achieved NVQs are not available. To address this problem, Robinson (1996) turned to the Labour Force Survey (LFS) to investigate the characteristics of people in employment pursuing or having achieved NVQs. He found that expressed as a proportion of the age group, the LFS data showed that 'in Spring 1994, 11 per cent of all 16–19 year olds in employment were working towards (*not* had achieved) NVQs compared with only 1.3 to 1.4 per cent of those in the prime age categories (25–34 and 35–49)'. While qualifications' take-up in post-compulsory education and training is generally skewed towards young adults (16–21), these results nevertheless suggest that take-up has also been greatest in the groups that are more likely to be in receipt of government-sponsored training, where, as I mentioned above, the undertaking of an NVQ is usually an obligatory component of the programme. The results do not indicate that NVQs have become a popular return-to-study choice amongst the working population. It is beyond the scope of this paper to discuss why this may be so, although from the perspective of learning it is not clear that a mechanism that aims to 'credentialize' large sections of the workforce for their *existing* competence is the best way of developing individual or group capability or, to put it another way, to promote lifelong learning (Fuller and Unwin, 1999).

Alternatively, evidence from the higher education sector suggests that in recent years there has been a dramatic rise in the take-up of undergraduate and postgraduate level courses by mature students and older adults (30+) (HESA various dates; McNair, 1993; NCIHE, 1997; Fuller, 1999).[4] The number of adults (21+) taking courses leading to qualifications at higher education level increased from approximately 255,000 in 1970 to 1,063,000 in 1995–96, an increase of nearly 320 per cent (Fuller, 1999). Moreover, the mature student population has been found to be more diverse in its socio-economic and educational profile than the traditional 18–21 student group (McGivney, 1996). A survey implemented by Hogarth *et al*, (1997) found that older students were more likely than their younger counterparts to come from lower socio-economic backgrounds, to have a lower terminal age of initial education and not to possess conventional higher education entry qualifications (A levels). In particular, the growth in the numbers of mature students participating in part-time courses is indicative of the appeal to many older people of combining a return to study with other domestic and/or employment commitments (Callender, 1997; Schuller *et al*, 1998; Davies, 1999; Mills, 1999). As Pat Davies (1999: 147) points out: 'Almost all part-time students are adult... Part-time provision is therefore about "lifelong" rather than "initial" learning'.

It is important to note that part-time participation has increased, despite the fact that, historically, students on part-time undergraduate and postgraduate courses have had to pay tuition fees. Moreover, mature student participation (as well as take-up by 18–21 year olds) in higher education increased substantially during the late 80s and early 90s, when the focus of the then Conservative Government's post-16 policy was on increasing take-up of vocational rather than academic qualifications (Wolf, 1997). In this chapter, I shall argue that if the policy goal is to create a society of lifelong learners (where people regularly participate and re-participate in education throughout their lives), it is sensible to look for ways of improving the availability of part-time higher education for at least two reasons. First, increasing take-up of part-time courses brings with it higher participation by older adults. Second, part-time courses in higher education seem to meet the return-to-study requirements of rising numbers of older people.

The chapter is organized into three main sections. In the first section, I shall identify some of the statistics that indicate the extent to which part-time higher education is being pursued by older adults. In the second section, I shall look at some of the issues that lie behind the figures and I shall suggest that insights into the formulation of future policies can be gained from considering the perspectives and motivations of mature students themselves and how these relate to the changing social and economic context in which they are making their return-to-study decisions. The chapter concludes by highlighting issues for future research and by calling for part-time higher education to be given a higher place on the lifelong learning policy agenda.

The quantitative picture

Age, level and mode of study

The Dearing Review of higher education indicated that, until the mid-90s, the proportion of part-time participation in higher education remained fairly constant in relation to the proportion of full-time take-up, at around 37 per cent of the total higher education population (NCIHE cited in Davies 1999). However, using more recent figures from the Higher Education Statistics Agency (HESA 1998), Davies has shown that in the late 90s, the proportion of part-time relative to full-time take-up of higher education is increasing at both post- and undergraduate levels (see Table 11.1).

Table 11.1 All UK domiciled students, level and mode of study, percentage change 1994–95 to 1996–97

UK	Postgraduate		Undergraduate [2]		All	
	PT	FT	PT	FT	PT	FT
Total[1]	+10	+3	+45	+2	+28	+3

[1] Percentages have been rounded
[2] Undergraduate includes 'first degree' and 'other undergraduate'
Source: compiled from Davies, 1999: 147, Table 3 using HESA, 1996; HESA, 1998

Tables 11.2 and 11.3 indicate that most mature part-time students at both undergraduate and postgraduate level are over 30 years old on entry to higher education. This finding reinforces the point that the part-time route attracts older participants who are returning to study more than a decade after completing their compulsory education (although not necessarily for the first time) and who, from the perspective of lifelong learning, are closer to justifying the label of lifelong learners than those returning to study in their twenties. Davies points out: 'part-time learners are lifelong learners: they are adults who are working and have wider social and familial roles and responsibilities' (1999: 153).

Table 11.2 All first year, undergraduate[1] UK-domiciled students, mode of study, percentage 21+ and 30+, 1997–98

Age	PT	FT
21+	95%	28%
30+	62%	10%

[1]Undergraduate includes first degree and other undergraduate level courses such as HNC/D.

Source: HESA, 1999

Table 11.3 All first year, postgraduate UK-domiciled students, mode of study, percentage 25+ and 30+

Age	PT	FT
25+	90%	46%
30+	68%	24%

Source: HESA, 1999

Major source of tuition fees, age and mode of attendance

I noted earlier in the chapter that participants on part-time courses in higher education historically, and unlike their full-time counterparts, have not had their tuition fees paid from public funds. It can be suggested, therefore, that take-up of part-time places, particularly where tuition fees are paid from the individual's resources, is likely to be an indicator of two things – individual rather than state-led demand and the strong link between employment and the student's ability to return to study. Where the fees are paid for by a student's employer, take-up may be linked to the employer's requirements as well as the individual's own perceptions about his or her learning needs. In some cases, it may be the case that employees feel that their employer is obliging them to participate (Schuller *et al*, 1998). Nevertheless, payment of tuition fees by the student's employer reinforces the relationship between economic activity and take-up of higher education by mature students. The following tables (12.4 and 12.5) allow us to gain insight into the major source of tuition fees for first-year higher education students aged 30 or over.

Table 11.4 First-year UK domiciled part-time undergraduates (first degrees and other) aged 30+, 1998–99

Major source of tuition fees	Number of students	Percentage
No award, pay own fees[1]	70,943	64
Student's employer	15,374	14
Central/local government, health, employment, agriculture bodies	9,813	9
Other [2]	14,173	13
Total	110,273	100

[1] The HESA notes state that this code is used where there is no award or financial backing at all. In other words, the student is paying his or her own fees.
[2] This line covers all the remaining codes used by HESA to identify major source of tuition fees, including Research Councils, UK/LEA awards and institutional waiver, as well as 'Absent for year' and 'Not known'.
Source: HESA Student Return December 1998, author enquiry

Table 11.4 confirms that the majority (nearly two-thirds) of mature students aged 30 or over studying on part-time, undergraduate level courses are funding their tuition fees themselves. The tuition fees of 14 per cent of this group are funded by their employers. The figures also show that the student's employer is more likely to pay for the employee to study for a first degree (19 per cent) than for other undergraduate level courses (13 per cent) (HESA Student Return, December 1998, author's enquiry).

Table 11.5 indicates that just over a quarter of the part-time postgraduate students (aged 30+) have their tuition fees paid by their employer. Nearly half of the students in this group pay their own fees.

Table 11.5 First year UK-domiciled part-time postgraduates[1] aged 30+, 1998–99

Major source of tuition fees	Number of students	Percentage
No award, pay own fees[1]	28,106	48
Student's employer	15,397	26
Central/local government, health, employment, agriculture bodies	3,221	6
UK/LEA awards	2,584	4
Other	9,023	16
Total	58,331	100

[1] Including those studying on research and taught courses.
Source: HESA Student Return December 1998, author enquiry

These statistics appear to confirm the findings of other studies that most students on part-time courses in higher education are economically active (Callender, 1997; Schuller, Raffe and Clark, 1997, cited in Davies, 1999). This helps to explain why such large proportions of older students, studying at either under- or postgraduate level can afford to fund their own tuition fees. The figures also indicate that the tuition fees for a significant minority of students aged 30 or over are paid for by their employers. Employed students may also receive assistance from their employers in other ways not shown in the HESA data, such as in the provision of study leave, or financial aid for books and travel costs.

In the next section I want to begin to look behind the statistics on older adult participation in higher education to ask why the size of this student population has been growing strongly in recent years. To do this I shall draw on a small-scale qualitative study of 10 older mature students who are currently completing or have recently completed first degrees (Fuller, 1999)[5]. In-depth, one-to-one interviews with members of this group elicited their perspectives on why they had returned to study, as well as on the meaning of their experiences. I have drawn on a wider understanding of social change and contemporary socio-economic conditions to interpret the data and to suggest why the perspectives of this small sample may provide insights that are relevant to the debate about ways of fostering lifelong learning in the UK.

Mature students' perspectives

The analysis presented below is based on interviews with five men and five women aged between 29 and 44 who were taking or who had recently gained a first degree in a range of social science and technical/engineering subjects. The sample was constructed broadly to reflect the social, economic and educational characteristics of the older, mature student population in higher education. Seven of the interviewees were over 36, two were aged between 30 and 34 and one was 29 years old. Eight of them were following or had followed part-time courses, and eight of them described themselves as coming from a working-class, although not from particularly deprived, background. All bar one of the sample had attained some qualifications prior to leaving school (usually CSEs) and all had gained vocational qualifications in their late teens and early twenties. In this regard, the interviewees were not first-time students in post-compulsory education and training, but were returning to study after a lengthy period. In line with increasing prospects of upward mobility for some working-class groups over recent years, these interviewees perceived their lives as 'better' than those that their parents or some of their peers had experienced. The eight students studying on part-time courses were all in employment and all 10 interviewees had long working track records and had experienced very little unemployment. Some were paying their own tuition fees, employers were paying the fees of others. All the interviewees had the range of domestic and financial commitments and responsibilities typical for adults in their 30s and 40s.

These mature students were prepared to take risks, or as one interviewee put it 'to take on challenges' to improve their material living standards and to promote their personal development. The interviewees recognized that the social and economic conditions under which they live have produced a new range of opportunities, as well as uncertainties, to which they can respond. Within this context, these adults were willing and able to take responsibility for managing their life courses and for developing their individual capabilities. Their participation in higher education was illustrative of this approach – higher education, particularly through the provision of part-time courses, appealed to this group because it offered a way in which they could develop personally and in their careers at the same time as fulfilling their existing domestic and financial commitments. Not surprisingly, the interviewees were quick to acknowledge that studying part-time is hard work and that the support required from family, friends and, preferably, employer should not be underestimated.

The interviews were wide-ranging, but two themes were highly relevant to the focus of this chapter on the role that education (particularly part-time) can play in developing capability and lifelong learning. The first relates to the interviewees' perceptions of their motives for pursuing a first degree as older adults; the second to the meanings they attributed to the experience of higher education.

Reasons for take-up

With regard to the concept of motives it is helpful to remember the clarification made by Wright Mills (1963: 440):

> Rather than fixed elements in an individual, motives are the terms with which interpretation of conduct by social actors proceeds. This imputation and avowal of motives by actors are social phenomena to be explained.

Mills' point is methodologically important, in that viewing motives as 'outside' the individual is relevant to how the researcher interprets his or her data on motives. In this regard, and following Mills, we can look for connections between the reasons these students gave for their participation and the underlying and changing social conditions that contextualize their motives. As Mills points out, 'motives vary in content and character with historical epochs and with societal structures' (p 452).

I would argue that changes in the social and economic opportunity structure over the past 20 or so years have produced a context in which more people perceive that they have the option to pursue education and qualifications in mid-life. As one expression of social change, I would suggest that some adults' relationship to participation is altering and this can be illustrated, at least partly, by the changing nature of the reasons they offer for taking courses leading to qualifications. In this regard, my interviewees gave largely vocational reasons for pursuing craft and clerical type occupational qualifications after they had left school. Their 'means to an end' reasoning was consistent with the limited scope for making personal decisions that they had experienced as young people. In contrast they saw their recent take-up of a degree course as an expression of expanding individual choice. The opportunity to go to university as a mature student was one example of an area for action in which the possibility of individual choice was perceived to have grown.

As one interviewee, William (aged 44), observed:[6]

> I mean there's much more choice, the whole of life is about choice now... I'd say retail exactly mirrors the way our lives work because before we went to a grocer's or we went to a florist's but now you go to a supermarket and you choose from an enormous range and no one tells you... now you can, you've got the choice and the amount of choice. That's one reason why I went to university because... I mean I don't think universities had taken in people in their 40s that time ago.

In some similarity with other recent studies on participation in higher education, the reasons these students gave for their take-up of degrees were both personal and vocational (Campbell, 1993; Lunneborg, 1994, 1997; Schuller *et al*, 1998). On the one hand, their motives for take-up were expressed through a vocabulary of self-betterment and material improvement relating to career progression. On the other hand, their reasons often encompassed a vocabulary relating to the goals of self-actualization and inner development.

For example, Paul's motives for taking a part-time degree were partly associated with improving his chances for promotion and partly with providing him with an opportunity to gain satisfaction at a more emotional level:

> In a couple of years time [I'll] have a degree, chartered status just at the right time where I could be put in another position but I don't really, I'm not really that ambitious to be honest with you... I feel as if I'm doing this for my own personal satisfaction.

Within the framework of vocational and personal motives for participation, the interviewees' reasons had two slightly different emphases. The first could be termed 'aspirational', in that the expressed motive appeared to relate to material enhancement and self-betterment. Anne, for example, perceived that she had the chance to have a 'better' life than her parents. She felt that fulfilling her lifestyle ambitions was conditional on achieving a degree and doing well at work.

I've got a chance to do something different – to lead a better life than my parents did. I want to try and see if I can do it and that's the most important thing to me... I mean this [higher education] is just the foundations of sorting out my life really. In the next five years [laughs] this should be interesting, I see a new house with a garden, I've always dreamed of a garden.

The aspirational motive included the perception that qualifications can open up opportunities for self-expression and fulfilment through enabling the individual to move into new areas, or more senior levels of employment. Peter commented:

It's [pursuing a degree] an opportunity to develop my career, uhm, it's given me a career I think. Before I was an electrician and I always would've been an electrician or some other trade work. Now I have got the opportunity to be as successful as I want to be.

The second motivational emphasis related more to inner, personal development than material choices. For example, Mary observed that taking a degree was part of a continuing quest for self-development and, in particular, fulfilment of her latent academic potential:

It's [studying at university] just proved to me that I can do things, and I s'pose when I started at secondary school I knew I shouldn't have been in the B group and I s'pose I've always been proving it to myself really.

I am not suggesting that degrees represent the sole return to study and qualifying route in which people in their 30s and beyond may express personal and vocational motives for take-up. Nor that degrees represent the only type and level of qualification likely to facilitate personal growth. On the other hand, it is plausible to suggest that the broader opportunities for intellectual development and stimulation involved in taking a higher-level academic qualification may mean that this type and level of course has special appeal to those wanting to develop their individual capability.

Meaning of their experiences

In terms of meanings, I recognize that the pursuit and attainment of a qualification cannot easily be separated from the experience of the educational process that leads to the attainment of that qualification (Antikainen *et al*, 1996). These interviewees interpreted their higher education experience as a resource for managing change, including its use in managing occupational transitions, facilitating personal growth, and for securing their position in an uncertain labour market. Some interviewees perceived their studies as a means by which they could broaden their career options, for example by going into management. For others, meanings were linked to the role of higher education in helping them to maintain their labour market position in the event of redundancy or company reorganization. In these two respects, the meanings expressed by my interviewees were consistent with those discussed by Lunneborg (1997) in her study of the meanings mature male Open University students gave to their experiences. In this regard, Paul made the point that:

> It's [the degree] a bit of an insurance as well, because where I actually live, if our company decided to actually close [his site]... I would feel that I wouldn't have to just move up to Scotland or wherever they wanted to put me. I would actually have a choice because... if you've got a degree behind you... you're going to be a lot better off in the labour market as well.

More generally, these individuals perceived higher education as a 'resource for life' in the sense that they felt empowered by the acquisition of knowledge and understanding. In particular, they had acquired the skills of 'finding out' for themselves:

> Knowing that knowledge is the key I don't need to be afraid y'know, I can go and find out something for myself because I can read, I can write, I can understand things fairly well, so to me – I think that you're, I'm capable of a lot more things. I can go and find out for myself, I'm independent, I can go and read about things and stuff like that [Janet].

Overall, the degree experience was perceived as a resource for responding to changing social and economic conditions, in particular to the risks and opportunities identified as characteristic of the contemporary labour market environment. As adults who had all been economically active for several years, these interviewees saw the contemporary labour market as being highly uncertain. They felt that through developing their knowledge and proving their willingness to learn, they would improve their chances of retaining employment and would put themselves in a stronger position to take advantage of opportunities created in some sectors of the economy.

Contextualizing adults' take-up

During the past 20 years or so, patterns of employment have changed dramatically (Reich, 1991). The demise of primary industries, the decline of manufacturing and the associated rise in male unemployment, combined with the emergence of new sectors based on microelectronic, information and communication technologies, the growth of the service sector and related part-time and temporary employment are some of the well-documented features of change (eg Reich, 1991; Aronowitz and Di Fazio, 1994). In this regard, Hutton (1995) has argued that fresh social and economic divisions have emerged from the past two decades of technological, economic and political change, and that new relationships have developed between the labour force and employers. He evokes the notion of the

30:30:40 society to describe the differences between the 30 per cent of the adult population who are extremely disadvantaged, particularly through unemployment or minimal part-time work, the 30 per cent who are 'marginalized' because they are recently self-employed or work in insecure jobs with no 'formal employment protection', and the '40 per cent whose market power has increased since 1979' (pp 106–08). Those categorized in the last group as 'privileged' include people in full-time permanent employment and those who have been employed for more than two years. It is not surprising that increasing numbers of adults are pursuing the sorts of actions that they perceive will help them to compete for places, or to remain in Hutton's 40 per cent bracket. I would argue, therefore, that rising take-up of higher education by those in their 30s and 40s in particular can be interpreted, at least in part, as a way in which these groups of people might gain advantage in the contemporary employment environment.

In addition, and particularly during the past decade, higher education has expanded for young people. This means that older adults looking to return to the labour market or to change occupations are having to compete with an increasingly well-qualified young workforce for the limited supply of 'good' jobs. I would suggest that recent economic and industrial change and the rising participation of young people in post-compulsory education have fuelled credential inflation and extended the role qualifications have traditionally played in the selection of job applicants. The observation that the recipients and users (including employers) of qualifications place more worth on academic and general qualifications than they do on occupational qualifications, such as NVQs, reinforces the growth in importance of qualifications gained in higher education to people across the age range. I would argue that it is contextual features such as these that help explain why increasing numbers of adults are taking up the opportunity to study in higher education. Their participation is facilitated by the expansion of more flexible ways of studying in higher education, for example, in terms of the provision of part-time and distance learning courses at both undergraduate and postgraduate level.

This section of the chapter has summarized some of the perceptions and experiences of a small sample of adults pursuing a first degree, mostly through taking part-time courses. I suggested that the reasons interviewees gave for entering higher education were symptomatic of at least two features of economic and social change. First, the development of an uncertain labour market characterized by a mix of threats and opportunities perceived by the individual, and second, the expansion of personal decision making to new areas of action. In this latter regard, these mature students perceived their decision to pursue higher education as an individual choice to participate in an activity that was not available to previous generations of older adults. Interviewees felt that their recent participation and achievement facilitated the fulfilment of their evolving career, material and inner aspirations. Put another way, higher education, and particularly part-time courses, appealed to this group because it provided an opportunity through which they could progress within the framework of their existing personal and employment commitments.

Concluding remarks and policy implications

From the perspectives of developing capability and lifelong learning, the policy debate needs to identify the social and economic benefits of adults' participation in part-time courses in higher education and then to review how public funds can be used to support and encourage a form of participation that has been chosen by increasing numbers in the adult population. From the perspective of policy, it may be necessary to ask hard questions about the relative levels of public funding going into promoting the take-up of NVQs to an adult population (including employers) that seems sceptical about their worth.

In her recent article, Pat Davies (1999) has argued strongly that a more positive view should be taken by policy makers of the role part-time higher education is playing in the development of lifelong learning in the UK. As she points out, there is enough quantitative evidence to suggest that part-time participation merits a position high on the policy-making agenda. I support her view that the quantitative perspective should be augmented with a better understanding of the qualitative issues surrounding the impressive increases in older adults' take-up of higher education, and particularly of part-time courses. Insights provided by the data reported here suggest that by increasing support to adults on part-time and/or distance-learning courses, public policy can be used to stimulate latent demand, particularly from employed adults in their 30s and 40s; demand that seems to stem from the sorts of concerns and aspirations expressed by the interviewees in my sample. I would argue that in so doing, policy could facilitate an increase in the proportion of over 30s participating in higher education. Davies has called for a research agenda designed to find out more about the characteristics of part-time (and *de facto* mature) students, the relationship between family, education and work in adults' lives, and the impact higher education has on participants' lives and the wider community (Davies, 1999: 153). The small-scale empirical study referred to in this chapter, suggests that further research comparing mature participants and non-participants in higher education with similar social, economic and educational characteristics would help to determine how best to target public policy and funds to increase take-up by older adults further. I recognize that the characteristics of my sample are not shared by the whole adult population and particularly by the unemployed, and that new opportunities, such as the chance to return to study or to qualify as an adult, are unevenly distributed. On the other hand, I would argue that insights on changing patterns of participation can be gained by focusing on the growing group of adults in their

30s and 40s who have opted to enter higher education, and whose take-up has already served to diversify the profile of the overall higher education population in terms of age, educational and socio-economic characteristics.

In conclusion, I would argue that New Labour's recent decision to expand the part-time places in higher education, for example at the Open University, is welcome (Elliot, 1999). However, in my view, the Government's emphasis on increasing participation in higher education amongst those in their 20s (Carvel, 1999) may detract from attempts to increase the proportion of part-time provision in the sector as a whole. Given that take-up of places on part-time courses appeals particularly to those who are over 30 years old, this begs the question of why an aspect of policy – the provision of more part-time places – which is highly relevant to the creation of more lifelong learners, is accompanied by policies that specifically aim to increase participation of those in their 20s.[7] Whilst the demand for higher education and the learning needs of this group should not be underestimated, an opportunity may be being lost to increase participation amongst older adults further by singling out those in the early stages of their working lives for special attention.

Notes

1. SVQs in Scotland.
2. The QCA has followed the lead set by its predecessor the National Council for Vocational Qualifications in only providing data on the number of certificates awarded.
3. Its focus is on the number of certificates awarded by broad occupational area and level. In the year to 30 June 1999, there was a 5 per cent decrease in the number of certificates awarded in the year to 30 June 1998 (QCA Web page, November 1999).
4. The vast majority of students entering part-time courses at undergraduate and postgraduate level are mature (ie 21 and over at undergraduate, or 25 and over at postgraduate level).
5. The empirical research to which I refer in this chapter formed part of the research for a PhD thesis entitled Qualifications, Adults and Social Change: A theoretical and empirical examination of the growth in importance of qualifications taken by adults over the last 20+ years (Fuller, 1999, Institute of Education, University of London).
6. To preserve anonymity all names were changed but interviewees' gender has not been changed.
7. The government's aim is for half of all 18–30 year olds to have followed a course at higher education level over the next eight years (Carvel, 1999; DfEE, 1999).

References

Antikainen, A et al (1996) *Living in a Learning Society: Life histories, identities and education*, The Falmer Press, London

Aronowitz, S and Di Fazio, W (1994) *The Jobless Future, Sci-Tech and the Dogma of Work*, University of Minnesota, London

Ball, C (1996) A learning society, in *For Life: A vision for learning in the 21st century*, ed P Maxted, RSA/Campaign for Learning, London

Callender, C (1997) *Full and Part-time Students in Higher Education: Their experiences and expectations*, Report 2, National Committee of Inquiry into Higher Education, NCIHE, London

Campbell, P (1993) *No Going Back: Women as university students*, Fernwood Publishing, Nova Scotia

Carvel, J (1999) Blair's Revolution for Learning, *The Guardian*, 8 March

Coffield, F (1998) A tale of three little pigs: building the learning society with straw, *Evaluation and Research in Education*, **12** (1), pp 44–58

Davies, P (1999) Half full, not half empty: A positive look at part-time higher education, *Higher Education Quarterly*, **53** (2), pp 141–155

Department for Education and Employment (DfEE) (1999) *Learning to Succeed: A new framework for post-16 learning*, The Stationery Office, London

Department for Trade and Industry (DTI) (1995) *Competitiveness: forging ahead*, Cmnd 2867, HMSO, London

Elliot Major, L (1999) Packed Agenda, *Guardian Higher Education*, 6 April

European Commission (EC) (1996) *Teaching and Learning: Towards the learning society*, White Paper on Education and Training, Office for Official Publications of the EC, Luxembourg

Evans, K et al (1999) *Working to Learn: Is New Labour learning? A critique of New Labour's policies for work-related learning*, Paper presented to the ESRC Seminar, November 19th 1999, Institute of Education, London.

Fuller, A (1999) *Qualifications, Adults and Social Change: A theoretical and empirical examination of the growth of qualifications taken by adults in the last 20+ years*, unpublished PhD dissertation, Institute of Education, University of London

Fuller, A and Unwin, L (1999) Credentialism, national targets and the learning society: perspectives on educational attainment in the UK steel industry, *Journal of Education Policy*, **15** (1)

Higher Education Statistics Agency (HESA) (1996) *Students in Higher Education Institutions 1994/5*, HESA, Cheltenham

Higher Education Statistics Agency (1998) *Students in Higher Education Institutions 1996/7*, HESA, Cheltenham

Higher Education Statistics Agency (1999) *Students in Higher Education Institutions 1997/8*, HESA, Cheltenham

Hogarth, T et al (1997) *The Participation of Non-Traditional Students in Higher Education*, HEFC Research Series, Institute for Employment Research, Warwick

Hutton, W (1995) *The State We're In*, Jonathan Cape, London

Keep, E (1997) 'There's no such thing as society': some problems with an individual approach to creating a learning society, *Journal of Education Policy*, **12** (6), pp 457–71

Lunneborg, P W (1994) *OU Women: Undoing educational obstacles*, Cassell, London

Lunneborg, P W (1997) *OU Men: Work through lifelong learning*, Lutterworth Press, Cambridge

McGivney, V (1996) *Staying or Leaving the Course: Non-completion and retention of mature students in further and higher education*, NIACE, Leicester

McNair, S (1993) *An Adult Higher Education: A vision*, NIACE, Leicester

Mills, C W (1963) Situated actions and vocabularies of motive, in *Power, Politics and People, the collected essays of C Wright Mills*, ed I L Horowitz, Oxford University Press, New York

Mills, J (1999) The fruitful harvest of a double life, *Guardian Higher Education*, 2nd November

National Advisory Council for Education and Training Targets (NACETT)/DfEE (1997) *Skills for 2000: Report on progress towards the National Targets for Education and Training*, NACETT, London

National Committee of Inquiry into Higher Education (NCIHE) (1997) *Higher Education in the Learning Society, Main Report*, NCIHE, London

Reich, R (1991) *The Work of Nations*, Simon & Schuster, London

Robinson, P (1996) *Rhetoric and Reality: Britain's new vocational qualifications*, Centre for Economic Performance, London School of Economics, London

Schuller, T, Raffe, D and Clark, I (1997) Part-time higher education and the student–employer relationship, *Journal of Education and Work*, **10**(3), pp 225–36

Schuller, T et al (1998) *Part-Time Higher Education: Policy, practice and experience*, Higher Education Policy Series 47, Jessica Kingsley, London

Wolf, A (1997) Growth stocks and lemons: diplomas in the English market-place 1976–1996, *Assessment in Education: principles, policy & practice*, **4** (1), pp 33 –50

Young, M (1998) *The Curriculum of the Future: From the 'new sociology of education' to a critical theory of learning*, Falmer Press, London

Young, M (1999) Two issues in rethinking qualifications for a learning society: Higher Vocational Qualifications and the emerging National Qualifications Framework, Paper presented to the ESRC Seminar, November 19th 1999, Institute of Education, University of London

12

Lifelong learning: challenging learning and teaching in higher education

Greg Light

Introduction

In 1999, following the key recommendations of the Dearing Report (NCIHE, 1997), a new national and professional Institute for Learning and Teaching in Higher Education (commonly abbreviated as ILT) was founded. Ostensibly established to raise the status and profile of university teaching, it is intended to ensure that the UK will be 'at the forefront of world practice in learning and teaching in higher education' (8.56). It is anticipated that it will play a key role in higher education's response to the advanced requirements and needs of a learning society setting forth in the new millennium, an ever-demanding lifelong learning agenda under its arm. The ILT may yet come to mark a critical watershed in our understanding and appreciation of academic practice as a whole. What is more clear, however, is its potential role in the development of a new paradigm of learning and teaching in higher education, a shift from a primarily skills-based paradigm towards that of a fully professional paradigm of understanding and practice.

This chapter will explore the key set of challenges at the centre of this move towards academic 'professionalism' in learning and teaching. The first section examines the context of the challenge within a wider lifelong learning agenda, arguing that this agenda has, in effect, drawn up a general 'knowledge specification', characterized by a flawed 'discourse of excellence', which it 'contracts' with higher education to deliver. The second section considers the economic and social features of the learning and teaching aspect of that 'knowledge specification', suggesting that it fails to provide space for disciplinary and professional critique of the prevailing discourse of 'excellence'. The third section explores the development of the ILT in terms of two contrasting models of 'professionalization', one wholly inadequate to the challenges identified, the other providing the potential for significant and substantial professional impact. Finally, the fourth section raises the concept of a professional 'language' (for the development of learning and teaching in higher education) which addresses not only the challenges specified by the prevailing lifelong learning agenda but that very agenda itself.

A discourse of excellence

The relationship between higher education and the 'learning' society in which it is situated has been one that has hitherto privileged the former. It has been governed by an almost one-way, linear relationship, through which academics defined and produced knowledge that was then imparted and distributed throughout society via its graduates and the dissemination of its research. This relationship characterized the university's separation and autonomy and lies at the heart of its oft-used description as an 'ivory tower'. The one-way nature of this relationship is epitomized by the phrase 'academic freedom', a concept central to the fabric of academic life, embedding 'separation' and 'autonomy' within individual academic practices. The customary social counterpart to this freedom, 'academic responsibility', however, was less clear and less frequently observed or understood. '*Academic freedom*', as Donald Kennedy, the past president of Stanford University, notes, '*is a widely shared value; academic duty, which ought to count for as much, is mysterious*' (1997: 2). This he suggests is due to a dissonance in the way in which society and higher education see their relationship. It is a dissonance, moreover, that has recently seen an escalation of public criticism and policy concern with respect to the accountability of higher education (Robertson, 1997).

This concern for accountability is constitutive of the wider change in the complex relationship between higher education and society. Higher education no longer simply resides 'in society', it is 'of society' (Barnett, 1994), and being of society it has increasingly become subject to its prevailing ideologies, social and economic transitions and ways of viewing the world. Higher education no longer simply informs society through its 'knowledge' contributions, but is, rather, shaped by society through what may be usefully called 'knowledge specifications' (in terms of both students and research), which the latter 'contracts' with higher education to deliver: the 'new bargain' (Robertson, 1997: 88). In the UK, these 'specifications' have, for example, become meticulously spelled out and quantified at disciplinary level in terms of both research and teaching: the former through the Research Assessment Exercise (RAE) – which, since 1992, has been closely linked to funding – and the latter through the Teaching Quality Assessment (or Subject Review) – which, while not yet directly linked to funding, has spawned a system of scores and rankings which can have a substantial effect on institutional status, student recruitment and the financial implications of that.

In this endeavour, moreover, society (primarily in the guise of the state) has not been content simply to compose a more explicit and hard-nosed set of specifications. In the drive to ensure more effective delivery of these specifications, it has also engendered changes in the traditional structures of higher education (primarily through funding mechanisms) that have reduced 'the autonomy for traditional universities' (Watson and Taylor, 1998: 10). It has generated a redefinition and transformation of higher education in a direction more clearly focused on issues of social and economic effectiveness and efficiency, exposing the sector to quasi-market and new 'managerialist' forces which conceive of 'the contemporary university as a bureaucratic corporation' characterized by a discourse of 'excellence' (Readings, 1996: 21). Indeed, in a relatively short space of time, the idea of 'excellence' has come to dominate higher education and the mission statements it now populates, mission statements so accommodating to the discourse that they are, according to Coffield and Williamson (1997: 1), 'ubiquitous, vacuous and inter-changeable'. Indeed, the very universality of 'excellence' makes its absence more telling than its presence. Not pursuing excellence is tantamount to an admission of failure.

Assessed in terms of inputs and outputs, 'excellence' is a measure of the way in which the university performs its social role, not of the role or the values inherent to that role. It is accountable to the terms of the 'knowledge specification' and defined in terms of performance indicators of both the efficiency with which higher education delivers the product and the quality of the product. Drawn up under a social and economic agenda characterized and energized by such issues as 'globalization', 'knowledge-based economy' and lifelong learning', the 'specification' is replete with notions of competitiveness in terms of number: expansion of knowledge base, expansion of student numbers, competitive advantage, efficiency gains, employee productivity and so on. And it is primarily to these 'numbers' that higher education is now accountable. It is a conception of accountability in which 'the quite proper demand that universities be *accountable* gets translated into the reductionist idea that everything is simply a matter of *accounting*' (Harvey, 1998: 115). This is clearly light years from how the university has traditionally understood 'academic duty', however mysterious it might be.

The knowledge specification

Despite the tenor of the above discussion, the 'discourse of excellence' is not entirely a negative phenomenon. Indeed, the nature of its challenge – embedded in what many regard as long overdue concerns and questions of social and economic accountability – plays a significant role in the development of 'professionalism' in teaching and learning. On the other hand, immersed as it is in an 'accounting' mode, this challenge of 'excellence' must remain deeply suspect, provoking issues that the very notion of the 'professional' in learning and teaching must critically address and contest. This section will briefly look at the nature of the challenge with respect to the new relationship with students it raises and the issues of knowledge at the heart of those relationships.

If, as suggested, 'knowledge' characterizes the 'specification' that the 'knowledge-based economy' contracts' with higher education to provide, 'economy' might be said to characterize the way in which that knowledge is increasingly developed, managed and disseminated. Knowledge is the 'product' of modern society and subject to the structures of its market 'economy': it is traded as is any other commodity or service. Indeed, it is increasingly traded on global communication and information systems that, by virtue of their growing impact, have themselves become a serious component of the knowledge market. In this model, universities no longer sustain the monopoly they once enjoyed. They are simply one of many social and corporate organizations developing, managing, disseminating and competing with knowledge. Indeed, they are often in partnership with corporate organizations that, by virtue of financial muscle, demand and are given 'knowledge control' (Chomsky, 1998). The academic relationship with knowledge is increasingly dominated by competitive economic structures that any dominant and powerful product ('knowledge is power') engenders.

Within such a framework, the nature of knowledge and our perception of what it entails inevitably change. Traditional elitist distinctions between 'high' knowledge (and related cultural concerns) and 'mass' or popular knowledge, for example, begin to dissolve (Usher *et al*, 1997). Produced, moreover, within new sites with different priorities and a wider set of organizational and technical goals, knowledge has 'mutated' and increasingly taken on an 'active voice'. Active forms of knowledge that can be employed to increase economic competitiveness and personal effectiveness are increasingly displacing the passive knowledge of truth, contemplation and personal awareness. Gibbons *et al* (1994) have described this change in terms of a move from mode 1 knowledge – primarily 'disciplinary' based and situated in an academic context – towards mode 2 knowledge, which is trans-disciplinary and located in a context of application. Echoing this distinction, Barnett (1997a: 30) describes the university as '*a site of rival versions of what it is to know the world*' embodied in the distinction between 'academic' and 'operational' competence. They are elucidated in a range of categories, the former with a focus on, for example, 'knowing that' and stressing 'propositions' evaluated by criteria of 'truth'. The latter, in contrast, focused on 'knowing how' and stressing 'outcomes' evaluated by 'economic' criteria. The pressures in the direction of the latter are, he suggests (Barnett, 1997b), changing our very epistemological existence.

If the lifelong learning agenda is, within this 'discourse of excellence', interrogating our traditional ways of conceiving and using knowledge, it is, in a related development, also contesting the academic relationship with the student. In particular, there is pressure to regard students as 'consumers' to whom we are accountable in terms of the product ('knowledge') that we are providing. Aside from the changing nature of this product (including calling it a 'product'), this has always been a role of the academy. Within the terms of the 'knowledge specification' presented to higher education, however, students have themselves now become more firmly regarded as a 'product' for which the university is accountable to society. In the language of excellence, and the ironic paradoxes that it raises, students have become a 'product' through consuming a 'product' in order to become 'productive' within our society! As such, it is precisely the nature of student-as-product that has recently become the focus of social and economic concern.

The 'knowledge specification', moreover, stipulates in some detail the main collective and individual features of this 'product'. The former is expressed by such terms as 'mass' and 'diverse'; the latter by such terms as 'transferable' and 'meta-learning'. Within a generation, the student body that higher education in the UK serves has radically changed from an 'elite' to a 'mass' system (Trow, 1970), student participation rates more than trebling and the number of institutions called universities more than doubling. Accompanying this enormous rise in student numbers has been an increase in the diversity of students, including growth in the participation of women, mature students, ethnic minority students, students from less privileged classes and overseas students (Watson *and* Taylor, 1998). Underlying the increase both in numbers and in diversity – and stressed in the Dearing Committee's recommendations 1 and 61 respectively (NCIHE, 1997) – has been the focus on widening access, again primarily '*to contribute to improved economic competitiveness and to local economic success*' (Robertson, 1997).

This economic imperative is also manifest in the individual features specified by society, more recently under the expression 'graduateness' (HEQC, 1996). Higher education should be aiming to 'deliver' to society individuals (graduates) who have developed both a range of 'transferable' or key skills and the more general ability and willingness to 'learn to learn' or meta-learning. The former – including personal skills, communication, teamwork, problem solving and information technology – underpin the economic requirement of flexibility and adaptability graduates might take into a range of different employment and life practices and activities. The latter – the 'core skill' of transferable skills – underpins individual 'lifelong learning' or the graduate's ability to continue to learn new knowledge, skills and practices. What this points to for teaching and learning 'is not a core "subject" curriculum so much as core characteristics, qualities and kinds of outcomes for all who enter and re-enter higher education' (Duke, 1997: 67).

In essence, then, the following features epitomize the nature of the lifelong learning challenge to teaching and learning in higher education:

1. the increasing numbers of students in our classrooms;
2. the increasing diversity of background, experience and needs that our students present;

3. the social requirement for a curriculum of transferability;
4. the conceptual shift in focus from teaching to learning, from delivering knowledge to facilitating students' ability to learn independently, to discover and reconstruct knowledge for themselves.

The challenge posed by this general teaching and learning 'specification' is situated, of course, within specific disciplinary (and interdisciplinary) fields of knowledge that will have their own particular curricula. The nature of the 'specification' (and challenge) will be contoured differently depending on the discipline, department, institution, student composition and so forth. And it will need to meet national *'benchmark information on standards (for individual disciplines) operating within a framework of qualifications'* (NCIHE, 1997: recommendation 25). Nevertheless, the generic character of this specification is pervasive, containing its own pedagogical significance. The prime focus of these benchmarks is *'on the intellectual attributes associated with successful study of a discipline'* (QAA, 1998: 11), attributes embodied in the third and fourth features described above, attributes, moreover, primarily coupled with an agenda of economic success. Such attributes are not, however, inherently linked with disciplinary and professional critique of the field, of its prevailing values or of its relationship to other fields and discourses. The deepest challenge to models of 'professionalization' encompassing learning and teaching in higher education will consist of its ability to dissent from and critique the above 'specification' and the 'agenda' underpinning it; indeed, to incorporate the capability for such critical dissent within the specification itself.

ILT: models of professionalism

The key national development with the potential to meet the above critical challenges posed to teaching in higher education is the Institute for Learning and Teaching in Higher Education (ILT), although it is far from clear how radical it will be in interpreting what is rather a tame remit. Drawing on a number of diverse, often competing sector-wide developments and influences, the overall purpose of the ILT is to improve both the practice and the status of learning and teaching in higher education.[1] It was formally proposed in recommendation 14 of the Dearing Report:

> We recommend that representative bodies, in consultation with the Funding Bodies, should immediately establish a professional Institute for Learning and Teaching in Higher Education. The functions of the Institute would be to accredit programmes of training for higher education teachers; to commission research and development in teaching and learning practices; and to stimulate innovation.
>
> (NCIHE, 1997: 128)

The Government's response was positive, seeing the ILT's role in the enhancement of the professional skills and status of teachers in higher education as central, and stating that its 'long-term aim is to see all teachers in higher education carry a professional qualification' (CVCP, 1998b). The implicit agenda of the ILT was to meet the above challenge: 'to inspire a new pedagogy, both more professional and reflective... to meet the needs of a more heterogeneous as well as a larger student body' (Watson and Taylor, 1998: 58).

In the two years following the Dearing report, culminating in the establishment of the ILT in the spring of 1999, interim committees were established and consultation papers/reports circulated across the sector. These primarily concerned the structure of the new institution and the nature of the professional accreditation framework for learning and teaching.[2] The lively, often controversial, national debate that ensued elicited a wide range of responses and concerns which revolved around a series of issues constituting two general models of approach to 'professionalization': 'autonomous' and 'prescriptive' (Light, 1998). These two models are described in terms of two categories of attribute: institutional attributes, concerning the relationship of the ILT to higher education institutions, and programme attributes concerned with the nature of accreditation programmes (see Table 12.1).

Briefly, the 'autonomous' model is distinguished from the 'prescriptive' model in terms of its concern to focus the national discussion and its subsequent developments in the context of both wider institutional autonomy and wider academic practice. In the first instance, this approach is concerned that the new institute not be set up with a host of centralized functions that undermine individual institutional autonomy: that the ILT does not, for example, become a sanctioning 'factory' for mandatory 'licences to practice', detached and oblivious to the diversity of distinctive institutional and disciplinary academic missions and practices. Similarly, there is a concern both that the funding for the ILT is not structured so as to weaken the influence of its academic membership in favour of external agencies and bodies and that the governance of the ILT reflect and be rooted in its membership. Secondly, this approach reflects a concern about the nature of the accreditation framework for which the ILT would be responsible. In particular, there is a concern that pressures from external agencies with differing agendas will result in a framework for promoting learning and teaching programmes that are viewed as detached from the other aspects of academic practice. There is an anxiety that these will be regarded as more of an irrelevant hurdle or obstacle to endure than as a legitimate opportunity in which to reflect upon and develop learning and teaching practices. Such a 'prescriptive' approach, it is felt, would add up to and consist of little more than a list of competencies and/or performance indicators to be measured and checked off.

Table 12.1   The Institute for Learning and Teaching:
professionalization: models of approach

INSTITUTIONAL ATTRIBUTES	AUTONOMOUS	PRESCRIPTIVE
Control	Decentralized: national policies and structures to encourage participation and diversity in HEI accreditation programmes	Centralized: ILT issues mandatory 'licence to practice' for teachers
Funding	Structured to develop academic 'ownership' of ILT	Structured to accent the influence and control of external bodies and agencies
Governance	Weighted towards its academic membership	Weighted towards external bodies and agencies
PROGRAMME ATTRIBUTES		
Perspective	Flexibly developed: perceived as an 'opportunity'	Inflexibly developed: perceived as a 'hurdle'
Academic practice	Teaching and learning integrated within a wider concept of 'academic practice': inclusive of scholarship, research, discipline	Teaching and learning skills developed without significant reference to the whole of academic practice
Learning focus	Focus on broad learning outcomes	Focus on competencies
Professional focus	Focus on reflective practice	Focus on performance skills/indicators

Source: Light, 1998

How the ILT will finally develop in response to the challenge is yet to be seen, although there are some positive indications. On the institutional front, universities will be encouraged to participate, but there is no suggestion of the ILT issuing 'licences to practice' – an early concern in some quarters. This has been rejected, at least for the medium term. Issues of funding and governance, moreover, have been structured around individual membership, the former aided in the first five years by HEFC monies and the latter being phased in to ensure that a majority of the governing council positions are allocated to individually elected academics (ILT, 1998). On the programme side, despite a 'draft' national framework proposing 24 learning and teaching outcomes, suspiciously detailed and prescriptive enough to suggest a national 'competencies' framework (ILT, 1999a), a vociferous sector response led to its withdrawal (although it remains on the ILT Web site in 'guideline' form). This framework has been replaced by a 'light-touch' approach to accreditation of institutional programmes, focused on five broad outcomes and with a diversity of routes, which are more sensitive to the diversity of institutional provision, disciplinary factors, teaching levels and so forth (ILT, 1999b).

It is, however, very early days for this new professional institute. The ILT is still regarded sceptically by a large number of academics, who see it inflicting yet another level of the externally imposed bureaucracy of 'excellence' upon them. The success and ultimate value of the ILT will finally rest on the extent and robustness of its autonomy. It has the potential to develop into a vigorous professional organization carving out a substantial 'space' for learning and teaching in higher education. Encouraging improvement and promoting good practice, however, are not sufficient. It needs to achieve such an undertaking in a fashion that allows for a wide range of diverse and creative approaches, which in its very practice, informed by research, critically examines the nature of the 'knowledge specification' itself, which convincingly confronts and challenges the lifelong learning agenda (particularly in its manifestation of 'excellence') and the agencies charged with delivering this agenda. Indeed, there is a case to be made that, without a critically robust ILT, issues of accountability, standards and quality could easily be dominated by the 'excellence' agenda and whatever the current political interpretations of lifelong learning demand of it. The ILT, under the regime of a prescriptive model, would merely reinforce this narrowly focused dominance. In a fully worked out, autonomous model, however, the ILT may have a significant role to play which goes to the heart of traditional academic values, combining academic freedom with a broad and more radical sense of academic duty, not struggling to maintain vestiges of such freedom under the barrage of academic 'accounting'.

The reflective professional

The challenge to learning and teaching within the above framework of 'professionalization' may be profitably illustrated by the distinction between the call 'for' professionalism and the call 'to' professionalism. The former is primarily a call from the discourse of 'excellence' for accountability, an external call for standardized professional organization, practice and evaluation procedures. It reflects the overall desire for increased efficiency and competitiveness within an 'accounting' framework of quality. The latter, on the other hand, is a call both 'to defend' academic values and practices from the excesses of externally imposed ideological discourses of excellence, but also 'to acknowledge' the challenge and to transform it. The 'call to' is a call towards a new way of thinking about teaching and learning, which neither falls back on traditional *laissez faire* academic versions of the benign 'amateur' (Ramsden, 1992), nor succumbs to newer versions of behavioural competence. In this respect, it is a call to change, but it is also a call to an ongoing transformation situated in the changing nature of the learning context as characterized above.

One of the corollaries of such a transformation is that any adequate model of practice must account for not only the events and situations that arise in practice, but also the changing social context and nature of that practice. In this respect, 'reflective practice' (Schon, 1983) is not sufficient. While stressing the practitioner's ability to employ professional knowledge, to reflect-in-action, in such a manner as to devise, choose and apply appropriate responses to unexpected and complex events and situations, 'reflective practice' is nevertheless primarily located in and bounded by those events and situations. It is a tacit defender of the 'status quo'.

Extending the concept of the 'reflective practitioner' to the 'reflective professional' embraces not only the locus of practice but the sphere of the profession as well. It encompasses what Barnett (1997b) refers to as 'professing-in-action', which includes an understanding of the wider professional and academic context. If the 'reflective practitioner' reflects on practice, the 'reflective professional' critically reflects on the profuse and diverse discourses constitutive of practice within the broader frameworks of her/his professional situation, however constituted or clustered: teaching–research–administration; discipline–department–institution; ethical–social–economic–political; local–national–international.

Professionalism resides in the ability to manage the intersections and inevitable collisions between these frameworks, to situate oneself and one's practice critically within an environment of changing academic roles, knowledge bases, ways of knowing, student needs, departmental requirements, institutional demands, external agency demands, professional accreditation demands and so on. It consists of the capacity to make sense of them, understand them, critique them and work within them as they happen. Of necessity this *'depends on having the appropriate language linked to theoretical ideas'* (Entwistle, 1998). It requires a 'language' that is critical, innovative and open, a language in which concrete 'problem solutions' (Kuhn, 1981) can be devised, implemented, evaluated, negotiated, modified and/or set aside in an ongoing cycle of critical and creative performance. Such a 'language' must be capable of sustaining and developing a range of practical 'genres' – that range of academic practices that teachers perform in their teaching, including, but not limited by, the five broad outcomes described by ILT. It is a 'language' that needs to be open and elastic enough to accommodate a diversity of individual circumstances within rapidly shifting curriculum expansion and development over a wide range of disciplines (and their interdisciplinary 'contours') set within a diverse range of higher education departments and institutions.

Language(s) of practice, finally, are the construction of teachers and students within situated interactions. They may be, usually are, delimited historically, socially, institutionally and by discipline and department. They are rarely, however, completely and utterly restricted and solidified. There are frequently chinks, often huge gaps, in the structures in which teachers and students engage one another, from which they can pry open practice and initiate substantial reflection and change. The approach to professionalism proposed here is that of mutual empowerment through an engagement with a 'language' of teaching and learning, through a critical understanding of its principles, and through its enhanced status. In this respect, it is a language of lifelong learning, not one that asks academics to submit to a barrage of techniques, tips and prescribed practices that they might 'inflict' on themselves and their students, but rather one that challenges them to engage in ways of critically and creatively thinking about their own practice. It is a challenge that, at the very least, should be both subversive and liberating.

Conclusions

It is worth mentioning that the use of terms such as 'subversion' and 'liberation' almost feels dated and old-fashioned in the global, 'end of history' culture that has steadily unfolded during the past few decades of our millennium. Indeed, 'fashion' is precisely that with which such terms increasingly feel out of step, other terms like 'inclusion' and 'empowerment' having overtaken them in the 'fashionable' victories of excellence and lifelong learning. These latter terms are modern and appealing, politically, ideologically and globally comfortable, and like 'learning' difficult to contest. Neither of these latter terms substantially critiques or challenges the prevailing social agenda. Indeed, they both signify an aspiration to be included and empowered by that agenda and all that it entails. In this respect, an essential element of the lifelong learning agenda has been the assimilation of opposition and the regulation of critique within its own terms and values. The very notion of change (and with it innovation and creativity) has been standardized and homogenized. By contrast 'subversion' and 'liberation' have become awkward and difficult terms, the unacceptable face of social justice, unwelcome unless they change their names and tailor their practices to the 'third millennium' agenda of the 'third way' (aspiring, perhaps, to last for a thousand years!)

In this chapter, I have briefly attempted to examine the nature of the post-millennial challenges to learning and teaching in higher education. These, it must be stressed, have been examined primarily from within the current agenda of lifelong learning. As significant as these challenges are, however, the greatest challenge lies in maintaining a vigorous sense of critique as 'subversion' and 'liberation'. Privatizing such a role in the present social market culture is by definition impossible. It may be that it is rapidly becoming impossible, even within the 'new' higher education that is taking hold of society. It is, nevertheless, a role that the university sector needs to strive to retain and reinvigorate. For an academic professionalism that is to be genuinely critical and reflective, for the students that lecturers are engaging with and for national institutions, such as the Institution for Learning and Teaching, that profess to promote and support both, this will be the greatest challenge, a challenge it is not at all clear higher education will be able to meet.

Notes

1. Developments here include, for example, those initiated by the Staff and Educational Development Association (SEDA) and the Universities' and Colleges Staff Development Agency (UCOSDA), the Higher Education Quality Council (HEQC) enhancement division, the Open Learning Foundation and so on.
2. The main consultation documents and reports here are: (i) *Accreditation and Teaching in Higher Education*, issued from the Planning Group for Accreditation and Teaching in Higher Education (chaired by Clive Booth), May 1998 (CVCP, 1998a); (ii) *The Institute for Learning and Teaching: A draft prospectus*, issued from the ILT Planning Group (chaired by Roger King), September 1998; (iii) *Implementing the Vision*, (ILT, 1998); and (iv) *ILT Consultation: The National Framework for Higher Education Teaching*, circulated in February 1999. See also current ILT documents on their Web site.
3. Currently the ILT requires accreditation to address the following five broad outcomes: (i) teaching and the support of learning; (ii) contribution to the design and planning of learning activities; (iii) assessment and giving feedback to students; (iv) developing effective learning environments and student learning support systems; (v) reflective practice and personal development (ILT, 1999b).

References

Barnett, R (1994) *The Limits of Competence*, SRHE/Open University Press, London

Barnett, R (1997a) Beyond competence, in *Repositioning Higher Education*, ed F Coffield and B Williamson, SRHE/Open University Press, London

Barnett, R (1997b) *Higher Education: A critical business*, SRHE/Open University Press, London

Chomsky, N (1998) Chomsky warns of corporate secrecy threat, in *The Times Higher Education Supplement*, November 20

Coffield, F and Williamson, B (1997) *Repositioning Higher Education*, SRHE/Open University Press, London

Committee of Vice Chancellors and Principals (CVCP) (1998a) *Accreditation and Teaching in Higher Education*, Booth Report, CVCP, London

CVCP (1998b) *The Institute for Learning and Teaching: A draft prospectus*, issued from the ILT Planning Group chaired by Roger King, CVCP, London

Duke, C (1997) Towards a lifelong curriculum, in *Repositioning Higher Education*, ed F Coffield and B Williamson, SRHE/Open University Press, London

Entwistle, N (1998) *Conceptions of Teaching for Academic Staff Development: The role of research*, Conference Paper on Development Training for Academic Staff, Goldsmith College, London

Gibbons, M *et al* (1994) *The New Mode of Production of Knowledge*, Sage, London

Harvey, D (1998) University, Inc, *The Atlantic Monthly*, **282** (4), pp 112–16

Higher Education Quality Council (HEQC) (1996) *Graduate Standards programme: Draft Report*, HEQC, London

Institute for Learning and Teaching (ILT) (1998) *The Institute for Learning and Teaching: Implementing the vision*, ILT, York

ILT (1999a) *ILT Consultation: The National Framework for Higher Education Teaching*, ILT, York

ILT (1999b) *The National Framework for Higher Education Teaching*, ILT, York

Kennedy, D (1997) *Academic Duty*, Harvard University Press, Cambridge, MA

Kuhn, T (1981) *The Structure of Scientific Revolutions*, University of Chicago Press, London

Light, G (1998) The Professionalisation of Teaching in Higher Education, *Learning Matters*, No 2, Institute of Education, University of London

National Committee of Inquiry into Higher Education (NCIHE) (1997) *Higher Education in the Learning Society*, The Dearing Report, NCIHE, London

Quality Assurance Agency (QAA) (1998) *Quality Assurance: A new approach*, Higher Quality: the Bulletin of the Quality Assurance Agency for Higher Education, No 4

Ramsden, P (1992) *Learning to Teach in Higher Education*, Routledge, London

Readings, B (1996) *The University in Ruins*, Harvard University Press, Cambridge, MA

Robertson, D (1997) Social justice in a learning market, in *Repositioning Higher Education*, ed F Coffield and B Williamson, SRHE/Open University Press, London

Schon, D (1983) *The Reflective Practitioner*, Basic Books, New York

Trow, M (1970) Comparative Perspectives on Access, in *Access to Higher Education*, ed O Fulton, Leverhulme Studies 2, SRHE, Guildford

Usher, R, Bryant, I and Johnson, R (1997) Adult Education and The Post-modern Challenge: Learning beyond the limits, Routledge, London

Watson, D and Taylor, R (1998) *Lifelong Learning and the University: A post-Dearing agenda*, Falmer Press, London

13

Building a lifelong learning system for the future

Ann Hodgson and Ken Spours

Introduction

As many of the chapters in this book indicate, the current Labour Government in the UK sees education as its number one priority, both because of the changing nature of society and the economy at the beginning of the 21st century and also because of the considerable and persistent problem of low levels of achievement and participation in the education and training system in this country. It could be argued that this Administration has a twofold strategy for tackling these challenges. First, it believes in improving the quality and performance of compulsory education from the early years upwards in order to enable more young people to succeed at 16 and thus to enter post-compulsory education and training. Hence the *Excellence in Schools* (DfEE, 1997a) agenda with its focus on literacy and numeracy targets, strong inspection systems, performance tables and benchmarking. Second, the Labour Government wants to stimulate the demand for learning among adults and particularly among those adults who have previously missed out on education or training or who have failed to gain the skills and qualifications required to meet the needs of a flexible labour market. Evidence of this approach can be seen in *The Learning Age* (DfEE, 1998a) with its emphasis on initiatives such as the University for Industry (UfI) and Individual Learning Accounts (ILAs). The first approach is seen as long term with the expectation that it will produce future generations with higher levels of basic skills and an improved capacity for learning. The latter is a desire to get something done now to address the acute problems of non-participation and social exclusion and to remedy some of the worst effects of the 'Conservative legacy' (Hodgson and Spours, 1999). But it can also be seen as a longer-term approach based on an assumption that there is a pent up demand for learning that can be released by a range of learner-led mechanisms.

We start this final chapter by recognizing that there is a strong rationale behind the Government's dual approach to lifelong learning in a first Labour Parliament. However, we will argue that it is now time that this was supported by an additional strategy to create an 'all-through' education and training system to support lifelong learning. Later in the chapter we identify three major dimensions of an all-through approach. First, there is a need for an all-through vision that sees lifelong learning as a building process starting at an early age and in which each phase of education connects with the next. Such a vision seeks to relate formal learning (eg in school, college or the workplace) with informal learning. Lifelong learning is thus conceived as a seamless web of progressive learning opportunities extending out of a strong foundation of successful initial education, rather than as a series of episodes in adulthood that remedy past failure. Second, 'all-throughness' seeks to address fundamental barriers to learning and achievement. English society still suffers from deep social divisions that prevent effective mass participation in lifelong learning and sustain an anti-educational culture in certain sections of the population (see, for example, Macrae, Maguire and Ball, 1997; Oppenheim, 1998). In this chapter, we will argue for the need to build a lifelong learning infrastructure to address factors that we believe work against the development of a lifelong learning system for the future: poor achievement in compulsory education, which diminishes the number of those participating in post-compulsory education (Gray, Jesson and Tranmer, 1993; Green and Steedman, 1997); a selective curriculum, qualifications and delivery system (Hodgson and Spours, 1997); a lack of widespread and sustained employer involvement in education and training (Senker *et al*, 1999); and inequitable access to both funding incentives (Callender, 1999) and rewards for learning (Robinson, 1998). A third dimension of 'all-throughness' as we see it is the development of 'personal capacity' for learning as an individual and as an active member of wider 'communities of learners'. In Chapter 7, Michael Young argues for the development of a range of skills and forms of connective thinking and a recognition that learning is a social and not just an individual activity. We support this view and suggest that a debate about learning needs to accompany policy debates on the development of an all-through system to support lifelong learning.

The UK Government's strategy for lifelong learning post-16

The Government's current approach to lifelong learning in the UK might be described as comprehensive and proactive but diffuse and potentially contradictory. At its core, it relies on stimulating individual demand for learning, based on a range of initiatives and incentives. *The Learning Age* Green Paper (DfEE, 1998a*)*, which provided the first and only comprehensive statement of the current Government's policy in this area to date, indicates a strong commitment to lifelong learning as a strategy for supporting national economic competitiveness, personal employability and social inclusion. It sets out an agenda for individuals, education providers, employers and trade unions around individual learning accounts, the University for Industry (now Learning Direct), basic skills, unitization of qualifications for adults, standards and inspection, learning in the workplace and collaboration at the regional and local level. Alongside *The Learning Age*, the Government stated its approach to further and higher education in two accompanying documents *Higher Education for the 21st Century* (DfEE, 1998b) and *Further Education for the New Millennium* (DfEE, 1998c), which outline its responses to the recommendations of Sir Ron Dearing's report on higher education (NCIHE, 1997) and Baroness Helena Kennedy's report on further education (Kennedy, 1997).

Six strands of policy in lifelong learning

From these documents and others listed below, it is possible to draw out six major strands of policy associated with lifelong learning in England. These strands arise from the work of different task groups or agencies, have different reform timescales and may be uncoordinated and even, at times, actively in tension with one another.

The first, which might be termed an 'adult learning opportunities strand', is the most prominent and diffuse. It emerges from *The Learning Age* itself, the Moser Report on basic skills, *Improving Literacy and Numeracy* (Moser, 1999), and the National Advisory Group for Continuing Education and Lifelong Learning (NAGCELL) Report *Creating Learning Cultures: Next steps in achieving the learning age* (NAGCELL, 1999). These developments form part of the discussion in Chapters 7 and 10 and elsewhere in this book. This strand has been the major focus of the Government's policies for lifelong learning, because it has been concerned to find ways of including those who have previously been excluded or who have not felt the need to participate in learning. *The Learning Age* is based on a vision of lifelong learning as a series of learning episodes throughout the lifespan and identifies a wide range of initiatives to support these, notably the development of individual learning accounts and Learning Direct.

NAGCELL was commissioned by the Secretary of State for Education and Employment, David Blunkett, to investigate the creation of the type of 'learning cultures' that would stimulate demand for learning, particularly in relation to the needs of mature adults. This is seen as the next step on from *The Learning Age*. The NAGCELL committee's work is, in some senses, more ambitious than *The Learning Age* because it seeks to go beyond an individualistic approach to lifelong learning by focusing on strategies for stimulating individual demand for learning, for improving the environment for learning, for providing incentives and for encouraging peer support and mutuality

(NAGCELL, 1999). It can be commended as an immediate and pragmatic approach to the issue of motivating more learners to take up opportunities to learn, although it does not address the complementary issue of lifelong learning system building because it works within the framework and constraints of *The Learning Age*.

Second, there is a social exclusion strand, which is extensively discussed in Chapter 4 and has been a major focus of the Government's reform agenda for lifelong learning. Initiatives include, for example, the development of the New Deal programmes, New Start, the setting up of the Social Exclusion Unit and the development of funding mechanisms for widening participation in further and higher education. This strand seeks to connect the work of the DfEE with other government departments, notably areas of government concerned with welfare and housing, so as to be able to target opportunities more effectively at the most excluded and marginalized.

A third strand is related to qualifications reform and emerges from *Qualifying for Success* (DfEE, 1997b), *The Learning Age* (DfEE, 1998a) and a review of the National Curriculum. As described in Chapter 8, this strand has three major thrusts. Currently, the two main areas of reform relate to broadening the advanced level curriculum and creating more flexibility for 14–16 year olds to undertake vocational education. The third area is about rationalizing the national qualifications framework by focusing on the development of credible whole qualifications. While all these reforms amount to important changes in each of their individual areas, there is, as Chapter 8 points out, no overall conception of building an all-through credit and qualifications framework for lifelong learning.

Fourth, there is a skills and work-based learning strand which is associated with the three major reports produced by the National Skills Task Force: *Towards a National Skills Agenda* (DfEE, 1998d), *Delivering Skills For All* (DfEE, 1999c) and *Tackling the Adult Skills Gap* (DfEE, 2000). This strand, which forms part of the discussion in Chapter 12, focuses largely on exhorting employers to support work-based learning and suggests a range of weak voluntarist incentives to underpin this development. This approach pays little heed to long-standing criticisms of low employer demand for skills within the UK (eg Keep and Mayhew, 1996). Nor does it address the lack of employer involvement in the work-based route for younger learners (Senker *et al*, 1999).

A fifth strand of work involves the broad area of post-16 funding and organization, which is associated with the *Learning to Succeed* White Paper (DfEE, 1999a). This is discussed in several of the chapters earlier in the book, particularly Chapters 5 and 10, and will be described and analysed in more detail later in this chapter.

The final strand concerns quality and standards. These issues are discussed extensively in Chapters 6, 8, and 12, permeate all the Labour Government's major policy documents and are likely to lead to quite significant changes to post-16 inspection regimes and the training of education professionals. However, policies focused on 'standards' are also likely to create difficulties for some of the other strands outlined above – the development of an inclusive national qualifications framework for lifelong learning, for example, and the Government's widening participation agenda.

A weak framework approach?

Despite the comprehensive nature of these strands of work and the plethora of policy initiatives they contain, elsewhere we have described New Labour's proposals for lifelong learning in its first two years of government as a 'weak framework approach' (Hodgson and Spours, 1999). We will argue that this type of policy approach places too much responsibility on the shoulders of individuals while not paying sufficient attention to overcoming wider system barriers or to building an all-through infrastructure for lifelong learning which genuinely empowers learners. In particular, we point to the Government's cautious approach to qualifications reform and to securing the involvement of employers in education and training. This Administration tends to place responsibility for change in the hands of individuals or institutions when it is apprehensive of alienating important interest groups. This has certainly been the case with A Level reform and is echoed in the Government's reluctance to consider a levy system to underpin vocational education and training.

Another feature of a weak framework approach is the absence of all-through system building and even the imposition of potential new barriers. One of the underlying assumptions behind *The Learning Age* is that there needs to be a different approach to policies for young people and to those for adults and that lifelong learning is largely associated with the latter. The problem with focusing on adults and young people as separate groups is that it draws attention away from the education and training system as a whole. Seeing younger as well as older learners as part of the same lifelong learning system, on the other hand, is more likely to result in an analysis that identifies the type of system barriers we outlined at the beginning of this chapter. These barriers begin in compulsory education, are exacerbated in the 14–19 phase and continue into later life and lifelong learning. We will see in the final part of the chapter that lifelong learning documents in Wales and Scotland have taken a different approach by connecting the problems of younger and older learners in a more overt way. These policy statements, unlike their counterparts in England, thus recognize the need to tackle education and training system barriers in order to create all-through lifelong systems. It is a radically different form of analysis that leads, we would argue, to a different reform emphasis.

A further feature of a weak framework approach can be seen in the Government's position on the role of the market in education and training. In *Learning to Succeed*, the Government recognizes the detrimental effects of institutional competition on learners and attempts to modify them by creating voluntarist partnerships at the local and regional levels. Within the rubric of personal responsibility already described, there is also an emphasis on the targeting of limited amounts of state funding to give incentives to certain groups of individuals to participate in learning rather than bringing in reforms that might make the system more attractive to all learners. It is also possible to see strong centralized structures (eg DfEE, QCA, Ofsted and sectoral funding bodies) as part of a weak framework approach, because they retain power at the centre to regulate market forces, rather than devolving real power and resources to regional and local levels to strengthen the type of strong collaborative planning structures required to assist the development of a lifelong learning system in the longer term. A key question is whether voluntarist partnerships will exercise sufficient power to overcome the dysfunctional effects of the market in education and training.

Finally, a weak framework approach attempts to address divisions within the education and training system by overarching rather than replacing divided structures. This is one way of looking at the emerging proposals for a graduation certificate for 18 and 19 year olds (SEU, 1999).

A weak framework approach, therefore, does not fundamentally alter the structure of the education and training system as a whole, although it may have a modifying effect on the way in which it works. Moreover, because the weak framework approach does nothing to counter institutional voluntarism (for example, decisions to implement or not to implement qualifications reforms), it places considerable power in the hands of education providers and end users such as universities and employers, which may work against equity and common learner entitlements.

The degree to which the Government deploys a weak framework approach differs across the six different strands of policy identified above. The approach to social exclusion might be characterized as less weak, for example, because it seeks to use 'joined-up government' to target resources and opportunities on those who need them most. On the other hand, the Government's approach to the reform of qualifications and work-based learning has been particularly weak because of its dependence on voluntarist arrangements. Yet, we would suggest that the qualifications system and the traditional lack of employer involvement in education and training constitute two of the deepest education and training system barriers to the creation of a lifelong learning system in this country.

Learning to Succeed: a move towards a strong framework approach to lifelong learning?

It is possible to interpret the recent White Paper *Learning to Succeed* (DfEE, 1999a) as marking a departure from this approach and a move towards a strong framework in the area of funding and organization, because of its emphasis on local planning mechanisms, common funding and inspection systems.

On the surface, this policy document appears different from earlier ones because it claims that it wishes 'to drive up standards and performance by removing structural barriers within the current (education and training) system' (DfEE, 1999a: 15). It then sets out new and more common arrangements for the funding and organization of all post-16 education and training (with the exception of higher education).

The creation of a National Learning and Skills Council with 47 local Learning and Skills Councils (LSCs) responsible for funding all post-16 provision with a single national tariff across all providers (schools are currently excluded but are expected to join this system by 2002/3) appears to constitute what we would describe as a strong framework approach to organization and funding. Similarly, the setting up of a common inspection system for all post-19 provision (although a different one for 16–19 provision) indicates a move towards such an approach. Undoubtedly, the development of local LSCs will create an impetus for planning, rationalization and collaboration at the local level.

However, closer scrutiny of *Learning to Succeed* from the perspective of building an all-through system for lifelong learning suggests that it is divisive, narrow in its focus and does not sufficiently connect with the other strands of reform outlined earlier. From this standpoint, it is possible to see this document not as an elaboration of a comprehensive vision of lifelong learning hinted at in *The Learning Age*, but more as a swift pragmatic reaction to immediate education and training system failings and an attempt to address some of the negative effects of the Conservative legacy of 'marketization'. As the document itself states:

> This is the case for change. There is too much duplication, confusion and bureaucracy in the current system. Too little money reaches learners and employers, too much is tied up in bureaucracy. There is an absence of effective co-ordination or strategic planning. The system has insufficient focus on skill and employer needs at national, regional and local levels. The system lacks innovation and flexibility, and there needs to be more collaboration and co-operation to ensure higher standards and the right range of choices.
>
> (DfEE, 1999a: 21)

This is damning stuff indeed, but it remains a very selective criticism of the current education and training system. First and foremost, it focuses on obtaining value for money from public funding – the *Learning and Skills Council Prospectus* (DfEE, 1999b: 9) claims that the new post-16 organization and delivery system set out in *Learning to Succeed* will save at least £50 million per year that will be invested in improving the quality of learning. There is no denying that this is important: public money wasted on bureaucracy is a legitimate cause for government concern, not least because it robs potential learners of scarce resources. A second rationale for change is to facilitate better individual access to relevant learning experiences. This again is a laudable aim and can be seen as carrying through part of the vision of *The Learning Age*. However, because *Learning to Succeed* does not take a system perspective and does not, therefore, look at some of the underlying barriers to access that continue to dog the education and training system in this country, it remains questionable whether its policy proposals will succeed in achieving its own aim of facilitating individual access to learning.

While *Learning to Succeed* holds out the possibility of creating networks of education providers and users at the local level, it does not make overt connections between the strands of policy at national level (eg qualifications and skills and work-based learning) that will allow these local learning systems to work flexibly and effectively. Moreover, *Learning to Succeed* introduces new barriers and distinctions that may undermine some of its own objectives.

First, it divides strategies and provision for 16–19 year olds from those for adults. We would suggest that this is on political rather than on educational grounds. There are areas where it might be important to make distinctions between the needs of younger and older learners, for example in relation to the curriculum. There are well-known educational arguments for making a distinction between the kind of broad foundation education that 16–19 year olds might require and the more flexible learning opportunities that adult learners might need or want to undertake as part of their continuing education or professional development. Indeed, this distinction is made in all other European countries. In *Learning to Succeed* differentiation between policies for adult and younger learners is, we would suggest, made along the wrong dimensions – inspection, qualifications and some aspects of funding – that, arguably, erect new barriers to an all-through system for lifelong learning.

Second, higher education remains outside the remit of the LSC and will continue to be funded through the Higher Education Funding Council and inspected by the Quality Assurance Agency. It is possible to have some sympathy with the practical problems that might arise from bringing higher education institutions into the new and already complex arrangements for other post-16 providers. Placing higher education institutions outside these arrangements, however, is also likely to be problematic. The work of higher and further education institutions is often both overlapping and mutually interdependent. If one of the major thrusts of the *Learning to Succeed* funding and organizational reforms is to make progression routes for learners more transparent, then the importance of local learning networks involving higher education institutions becomes immediately apparent.

Third, as we have mentioned earlier, the *Learning to Succeed* reforms are taking place on a different timescale from the *Qualifying for Success* reforms. This means that changes to funding are not being made at the same time as changes to curriculum and qualifications for 16–19 year olds. There is some emerging evidence that this might jeopardize the success of the latter reforms because schools, in particular, are concerned both about the cost of the qualifications changes that will be introduced as a result of *Qualifying for Success* and the potential impact of future funding reforms (Hodgson and Spours, 2000).

Fourth, in spite of its emphasis on learning in the workplace and learning for work, *Learning to Succeed* continues to take the type of voluntarist approach to employers that characterized *The Learning Age*. Employers are given *'a substantial stake in shaping what is provided in post-16 education and training'* (DfEE, 1999a: 22) through their representation on the LSCs at national and local level, but without commensurate statutory responsibilities for funding or providing education and training for their employees. Neither is regulation in this area supported by the Third Report from the National Skills Taskforce, *Tackling the Adult Skills Gap: Upskilling adults and the role of workplace learning* (DfEE, 2000). Indeed, this document overtly shies away from the idea of a statutory minimum training requirement, despite strong calls for proposals of this type from some of its members: '*A new statutory obligation on employers does not form part of our recommendations.*' (DfEE, 2000: 46).

Finally, *Learning to Succeed* lacks detail or clarity about the roles of and the relationships between the different layers of government – national, regional and local – in the funding, organization and planning of lifelong learning. Currently the arrangements look bureaucratic, complex and undemocratic. It also remains to be seen how the various different types of voluntary partnership at local level will function and to what extent learners' voices will be heard over those of all the competing providers, users and administrators. Under the proposed arrangements resulting from *Learning to Succeed*, who ultimately has either the power or the desire to forge a lifelong learning system at the local level?

Strong frameworks – towards 'all-throughness'

At the beginning of this chapter, it was suggested that an initiative-led approach to lifelong learning could be seen as a necessary early response to the Conservative legacy. Our principle criticism, however, is that to date this approach has tended to focus on the individual without providing mechanisms for constructing a holistic system to support lifelong learning and to address more fundamental underlying factors that inhibit educational participation and achievement. Towards the end of a first Parliament, and in consideration of a further term of office, the Government is now in a position to think about a longer-term strategy for England. In this respect, other parts of the UK education and training systems are already pointing the way.

We can contrast the approach taken in England with that taken in Wales and Scotland. Wales has traditionally shared the same education and training system as England, but now appears to be diverging. In both the Welsh

Green Paper on lifelong learning, *Learning is for Everyone* (Welsh Office, 1998) and the report from the Education and Training Action Group for Wales (ETAG, 1999) it is possible to identify an emphasis on building a comprehensive system for lifelong learning that is based on the development of integrated post-16 provision to support both young people and adults to *'fulfil their individual aspirations'*(ETAG, 1999: 3). These documents argue for a *'radical shift'* in the education and training system, but with *'phased progress over a longer time scale'* (ETAG, 1999: 13). They thus stress both a clear vision of what a future lifelong learning *system* should look like and propose a staged approach to its creation. Scotland, which has always had a more separate education system, takes a similar approach to Wales by linking the 'learning habits' of younger and older learners (Scottish Office, 1998) and by stressing the need for a credit and qualifications framework that embraces learners of all ages in post-compulsory education.

Earlier in the chapter, we suggested that the Government employed a 'weak framework approach' to lifelong learning with the emphasis being placed on individual responsibility without addressing fundamental barriers to participation and achievement. This can be contrasted with a strong framework approach that attempts to provide a clear vision of a future lifelong learning system in which individuals and organizations can see the staged development of different dimensions of a holistic system over the longer term. Crucially, it involves building common structures within the education and training system that support genuine individual empowerment and a planned approach to lifelong learning at the local, regional and national levels. A strong framework approach thus means reforming key areas of the education and training system (eg qualifications, the roles and responsibilities of employers, funding and organizational arrangements) to overcome long-standing system barriers and divisions. It also requires devolving governmental power away from the centre in order to strengthen regional and local collaboration to support the individual learner within her/his local learning context. In contrast to a weak framework approach, the aim is to provide a set of common rules or conditions within the education and training system that are designed to limit the harmful effects of institutional discretion and to maximize learner voice and entitlement. A strong framework approach to lifelong learning might, therefore, be built around three basic dimensions of what we have termed 'all-throughness' – a vision of a holistic, all-through system, the creation of an infrastructure for lifelong learning and the development of personal capacities for learning within the compulsory education system.

A vision of an all-through and holistic system

At this point we would argue that a vision of 'all-throughness' is absolutely crucial to counteract the potentially negative outcomes from the Government's 'standards agenda' that are in danger of creating an artificial divide between the needs of younger and older learners. The current focus on life-long learning as a set of learning experiences that take place beyond compulsory schooling is, in itself, too narrow. We believe that a lifelong learning system for the 21st century will need to secure connections between all phases of education so that learners develop early on the skills and motivation to undertake learning throughout the life cycle. The idea of a holistic and all-through system vision is equally important to policy makers as they try to implement 'joined up government' to ensure that different initiatives and strands of the reform process do not contradict one another but pull in the same direction. It is for this reason that it is vital for government to articulate its vision of an all-through lifelong learning system and the steps and stages towards its development.

All-through thinking leads to asking different questions about the purposes of education, particularly in the early years of schooling. Currently, the priority is getting young people to attain at normative levels by certain ages, on the premise that this will provide them with the capacity to continue in education and training. This is undoubtedly important. However, the emphasis on testing and benchmarking is highly pressurized and can lead to a dull or mechanical educational experience and a sense of failure at an early age. The current emphasis on attaining examinations should, we feel, be balanced with an equal emphasis on motivating all students to want to continue learning. A lifelong learning perspective would still stress the need for early success, but above all it would emphasize the importance of creating a confidence in learning and the expectation that all learners could progress at their own pace.

A further reason why all-through system vision is important is that it encourages an identification of barriers that make their appearance early on in both compulsory and post-compulsory education. If lifelong learning is seen as simply the domain of adults, then there is not the urgency to tackle some of the barriers that affect younger learners and effectively turn them off learning before the age of 16. This would require, among other things, a 'latticework' of provision and an all-age qualifications and credit system that would ensure that learners and providers could easily identify opportunities for movement and progression at any stage.

A lifelong learning infrastructure

We have stated earlier that while the six current major strands of lifelong learning policy – adult learning opportunities, social exclusion, qualifications, skills and work-based learning, funding and organization, and quality and standards – are to be welcomed, they do not yet constitute the framework for a lifelong learning system. This is partly because some strands are stronger or more developed than others and partly because each strand is largely seen as a separate entity and has not been designed as a constituent part of a holistic system. The strategies being used currently to stimulate learner demand (eg widening participation funding steers, ILAs and the UfI) are a start, but the picture still looks fragmented and is essentially based on a 'deficit model' of lifelong learning. Lifelong learning initiatives are largely being targeted at those who have not traditionally participated, which has led to a piecemeal approach for a minority rather than system building for all.

Moreover, it is arguable that the Government's current overwhelming emphasis on the learner-led nature of lifelong learning runs the risk of being read as 'anti-provider', thus denying that providers are of crucial importance. The rhetoric of 'learner-ledness' effectively underplays what has to be done to improve the capacity of education and training providers. We would argue that a network of strong providers – schools, colleges, employers, universities and adult and community organizations – is an essential prerequisite of a system for lifelong learning. Learners need to see their potential pathways through lifelong learning provision and providers need to have a picture of how the system is put together and how their particular part of the system relates to the whole.

While the elements of an all-through lifelong learning system would need to be debated more extensively than we have space for here, we would suggest that a minimum infrastructure would require the development of:

- an all-age, flexible and inclusive national credit and qualifications system;
- a regulatory framework to underpin the involvement of employers and trade unions in 'local learning systems';
- a statutory right to educational leave for all employees;
- a fair and transparent system of funding for both providers and individual learners; and
- strong, locally based lifelong learning guidance systems.

The latter two features have begun to emerge as a result of current policies on lifelong learning, but the first three are clearly still viewed by government as holding some political risk and are being developed much more slowly within an overall voluntarist policy approach.

Developing the capacity for lifelong learning

Finally, we believe that developing a vision of an all-through lifelong learning system will, as Michael Young points out in Chapter 7, require a broader debate about the nature of learning. This is likely to include a discussion of strategies for building personal and collective learning capacity and ways of creating the optimum contexts for learning. To date, there has been little room for debate about learning for the future due to the Government's preoccupation with addressing past deficits. Hence, its emphasis on numeracy and literacy for learners in compulsory education, on the three key skills for 16–19 year olds and on basic skills acquisition for adults. Again, this can be seen as a necessary emergency response to the Conservative legacy. But, like on so many issues outlined in this chapter, it is time to move on. Developing personal capacity for lifelong learning will mean developing more than basic skills. It will require the development of critical thinking, of wider problem-solving and collaborative skills, underpinned by a pervasive philosophy of wanting to learn, not only for economic gain but also for personal growth. Moreover, this will become an issue for people as members of social groups as well as for individual learners.

In this chapter we have argued that the concept of personal responsibility for learning is important and a necessary ingredient of lifelong learning. However, lifelong learning cannot simply be left to the individual because this would reproduce social divisions between those who are able and motivated to learn and those who are not. On the other hand, the Government cannot legislate to ensure that people learn throughout their lives. The role of government, we would argue, is to articulate a vision for lifelong learning and to put into place an infrastructure of strong frameworks to encourage participation, progression and achievement. This will mean removing some of the deep-seated barriers, both within the education and training system and beyond, which inhibit learning and creativity. We have argued that these are intensified at points of transition and particularly, in this country, in the 14–19 phase. This is one of the areas where there is the most urgent need for reform to motivate more learners to achieve and to want to continue to learn.

Realizing the vision of 'all-throughness', for which we have argued throughout this chapter, will mean an active recognition that the willingness to learn throughout life is instilled and encouraged very early in a child's life and that it is vital to ensure that compulsory education is a positive experience for all children. At the moment we are doubtful whether the Government's strategy of simply boosting literacy, numeracy and basic skills provides a sustainable and long-term approach to this issue. One of the major functions of compulsory education should not only be to provide the basic skills to cope with day-to-day life, but also to build learners' capacity to think creatively and to have the confidence to work with others to address the complex problems that all of us will face in the 21st century and throughout the different stages of our lives. It is a vision and strategies that will develop this kind of capacity in all learners that we believe should underpin all lifelong learning policies in this country. In our view, it is high time to open the debate about what is required to build a lifelong learning system for the future.

References

Callender, C (1999) *The Hardship of Learning: Students' income and expenditure and their impact on participation in further education*, FEFC, Coventry

Department for Education and Employment (DfEE) (1997a) *Excellence in Schools*, DfEE, London

DfEE (1997b) *Qualifying for Success: A consultation paper on the future of post-16 qualifications*, DfEE, London

DfEE (1998a) The Learning Age: A renaissance for a new Britain, Cm 3790, DfEE, London

DfEE (1998b) *Higher Education for the 21st Century: Response to the Dearing Report*, DfEE, London

DfEE (1998c) *Further Education for the New Millennium: Response to the Kennedy Report*, DfEE, London

DfEE (1998d) *Towards a National Skills Agenda*, First Report of the National Skills Task Force, DfEE, London

DfEE (1999a) *Learning to Succeed: A new framework for post-16 learning*, DfEE, London

DfEE (1999b) *Learning and Skills Council Prospectus*, DfEE, London

DfEE (1999c) *Delivering Skills for All*, Second Report of the National Skills Task Force, DfEE, London

DfEE (2000) *Tackling the Adult Skills Gap: Upskilling adults and the role of workplace learning*, Third Report of the National Skills Task Force, DfEE, London

Education and Training Action Group for Wales (ETAG) (1999) *An Education and Training Action Plan for Wales*, ETAG, Cardiff

Gray, J, Jesson, D and Tranmer, M (1993) *Boosting Post-16 Participation in Full-Time Education: A study of some key factors in England and Wales*, Youth Cohort Study No 20, Employment Department, Sheffield

Green, A and Steedman, H (1997) *Into the Twenty First Century: An assessment of British skill profiles and prospects*, Centre for Economic Performance, London School of Economics, University of London

Hodgson, A and Spours, K (1997) *Dearing and Beyond: 14–19 qualifications, frameworks and systems*, Kogan Page, London

Hodgson, A and Spours, K (1999) *New Labour's Educational Agenda: Issues and policies for education and training from 14+*, Kogan Page, London

Hodgson, A and Spours, K (2000) *Qualifying for Success: Towards a framework of understanding*, Institute of Education/Nuffield Foundation Project Working Paper 1, Institute of Education, University of London

Keep, E and Mayhew, K (1996) Evaluating assumptions that underlie training policy, in *Acquiring Skills: Market Failures, their Symptoms and Policy Responses*, ed A Booth and D Snower, Cambridge University Press, Cambridge

Kennedy, H (1997) *Learning Works: Widening participation in further education*, FEFC, Coventry

Macrae, S, Maguire, M and Ball, S (1997) Whose 'learning society'? A tentative deconstruction, *Journal of Education Policy*, **12** (6), pp 499–509

Moser, Sir C (1999) *Improving Literacy and Numeracy: A fresh start*, DfEE, London

National Advisory Group for Continuing Education and Lifelong Learning (NAGCELL) (1999) *Creating Learning Cultures: Next steps in achieving the learning age*, Second report of the NAGCELL, The Stationery Office, London

National Committee of Inquiry into Higher Education (NCIHE) (1997) *Higher Education in the Learning Society. Full Report*, NCIHE, London

Oppenheim, C (1998) *An Inclusive Society: Strategies for tackling poverty*, IPPR, London

Robinson, P (1998) Employment and social inclusion, in *An Inclusive Society: Strategies for tackling poverty*, ed C Oppenheim, IPPR, London

Scottish Office (1998) *Opportunity Scotland: A paper on lifelong learning*, The Stationery Office, London

Senker, P *et al* (1999) Working to learn: an holistic approach to young people's education and training, in *Apprenticeship: Towards a new paradigm of learning*, ed P Ainley and H Rainbird, Kogan Page, London

Social Exclusion Unit (SEU) (1999) *Bridging the Gap: New opportunities for 16–18 year olds not in education, employment or training*, The Stationery Office, London

Welsh Office (1998) *Learning is for Everyone*, The Stationery Office, London

Index

DATE DUE

HIGHSMITH #45230

Printed
In USA